W9-BPQ-810

30 DAYS

TO

UNDERSTANDING

THE BIBLE

UNLOCK THE SCRIPTURES IN
JUST 15 MINUTES A DAY

MAX ANDERS

THOMAS NELSON
Since 1798

30 Days to Understanding the Bible, © 1988, 1994, 2004, 2011, and 2018 by Max Anders. All rights reserved. No part of this publication may be reproduced, stored in a retrieval system, or transmitted in any form or by any means—electronic, mechanical, photocopy, recording, or any other—except for brief quotations in printed reviews, without the prior permission of the publisher.

Published in Nashville, Tennessee, by Thomas Nelson, a division of HarperCollins Christian Publishing, Inc.

Unless otherwise indicated, Scripture quotations are from The New American Standard Bible®, copyright © 1960, 1962, 1963, 1968, 1971, 1972, 1973, 1975, 1977, 1995 by The Lockman Foundation. Used by permission.

Those indicated (NIV) are from The Holy Bible, New International Version®. Copyright © 1973, 1978, 1984, 2011 by Biblica, Inc.® Used by permission. All rights reserved worldwide.

Those indicated (NKJV) are from The Holy Bible, New King James Version. Copyright © 1982 by Thomas Nelson.

Those indicated (KJV) are taken from The Holy Bible, King James Version.

Printed in the United States of America

20 21 22 23 24 25 /LSC/ 12 11 10 9 8 7 6

To good friends!

Ken and Carleen Axt
Joel and Marylee Berger
David and Jane Reeves

CONTENTS

INTRODUCTION

L et's make a bargain.

If you'll give me fifteen minutes a day for thirty days, I'll give you an understanding of the Bible, the most widely distributed publication in history (approximately five billion copies). In one month, you'll learn the story of the entire Bible . . .

all the major men and women,

all the major events, and

all the major points of geography.

You will be able to put these people and facts together in their proper chronological order and trace the geographical movement as you think your way through the entire Bible!

Yet the Bible is more than history. It is a treasure-house of important teachings that have been the foundation of Western civilization from the Roman Empire until today, including important and profound ideas that have been embraced by Christians for the last two thousand years. You will learn about the Ten Great Subjects of the Bible:

Bible	Man
God	Sin
Jesus	Salvation
Holy Spirit	Church
Angels	Future Things

The information is presented at face value as it is found in Scripture. No previous knowledge is assumed. A beginner will not be overwhelmed, and the established student will find much help clarifying, organizing, and expanding what he or she may already know.

You will also learn about some of the more puzzling things about the Bible:

Why there are four Gospels

How to understand the parables of Jesus

The importance of miracles

The relationship between the Passover Feast and the Lord's
    Supper

The importance of the resurrection of Jesus

. . . and much more

The Bible is an enormous book covering much information and many subjects. It is not possible to learn everything about it in thirty days. But you can gain a beginning knowledge, an overview, that you can use to build a more complete understanding in the years ahead. In just fifteen minutes a day for thirty days, you can gain a foundational grasp of the most important book ever written.

THE STORY OF THE
OLD TESTAMENT

CHAPTER 1

THE STRUCTURE OF THE BIBLE

Charles Steinmetz was an electrical engineer of towering intellect. After he retired, he was asked by a major appliance manufacturer to locate a malfunction in their electrical equipment. None of the manufacturer's experts had been able to locate the problem. Steinmetz spent some time walking around and testing the various parts of the machine complex. Finally, he took out of his pocket a piece of chalk and marked an X on a particular part of one machine. The manufacturer's people disassembled the machine, discovering to their amazement that the defect lay precisely where Steinmetz's chalk mark was located.

Some days later, the manufacturer received a bill from Steinmetz for ten thousand dollars. They protested the amount and asked him to itemize it. He sent back an itemized bill:

Making one chalk mark $1
Knowing where to place it $9,999

If you know where the chalk marks go, the most overwhelming tasks are easily solved. If you don't, even simple tasks can be impossible.

Learning about the Bible can be much the same. If you don't know much about it, it can be like trying to cross the Sahara Desert blindfolded. Yet if you learn where a few of the major "chalk marks" go, the Bible will unfold itself to you, allowing you to begin to master it.

My own experience bears this out. Many years ago, I decided I was going to master the Bible. I was going to begin with Genesis and read through Revelation, and I wasn't going to put it down until I understood it. I soon became hopelessly entangled in a jungle of fantastic stories, unpronounceable names, broken plots, unanswered questions, and endless genealogies. I stubbed my toe on Leviticus, sprained my ankle on Job, hit my head on Ecclesiastes, and fell headlong into the mud on Habakkuk.

I was defeated. I threw my Bible down, concluding that the Bible was a series of unrelated stories put together in random order!

Then one day I discovered a key. With this key, the fog that enshrouded my understanding of the Bible began to lift. Not that things came into sharp focus, but at least I began to see shapes on the horizon.

The key: *Learning the structure of the Bible.* If you want to learn architecture, you must first learn how buildings are put together. If you want to learn sailing, you must first learn how ships are put together. And if you want to learn to understand the Bible, you must first learn how the Bible is put together.

THE OLD AND NEW TESTAMENTS

The Bible has two major divisions: the Old Testament and the New Testament. The Old Testament begins with creation and tells the story of the Jewish people up to the time of Christ. It is made up of *thirty-nine* individual "books" (the book of Genesis, the book of Exodus, etc.) written by twenty-eight different authors and spans a period of over two thousand years.

The New Testament is the record of the birth of Jesus, His life and ministry, and the ministry of His disciples, which was carried on after Jesus was crucified. The New Testament is composed of *twenty-seven* books written by nine different authors and covers a time period of less than one hundred years. The total number of books in the entire Bible is *sixty-six.*

SELF-TEST

*What you can learn tomorrow is built
on what you learn today!*

As you work through these chapters, you will be asked to fill in many blanks. This is not by accident or whim. *Repetition is the key to mental ownership.*

Each time you review this information, electrical impulses travel through the brain, creating neurological pathways for memory. As you complete these exercises, you will construct superhighways of memory in your brain and begin to "own" this information on a level that would be impossible any other way.

In addition, what you can learn today is built on what you learned yesterday, and **what you can learn tomorrow is built on what you learn today**. So, by being faithful to complete the review exercises and self-tests, you are not only gaining mastery of important information today, but you are also creating a powerful foundation of knowledge that will enable multiplied learning tomorrow.

So, with a ready mind and expectant heart, carry on!

How many?

_39_ books in the Old Testament   *28 authors over ≥ 2000 yrs*
_27_ books in the New Testament   *9 authors in ≤ 100 yrs*
_66_ books in the whole Bible

OLD TESTAMENT BOOKS

Genesis	2 Chronicles	Daniel
Exodus	Ezra	Hosea
Leviticus	Nehemiah	Joel
Numbers	Esther	Amos
Deuteronomy	Job	Obadiah
Joshua	Psalms	Jonah
Judges	Proverbs	Micah
Ruth	Ecclesiastes	Nahum
1 Samuel	Song of Solomon	Habakkuk
2 Samuel	Isaiah	Zephaniah
1 Kings	Jeremiah	Haggai
2 Kings	Lamentations	Zechariah
1 Chronicles	Ezekiel	Malachi

NEW TESTAMENT BOOKS

Matthew	Ephesians	Hebrews
Mark	Philippians	James
Luke	Colossians	1 Peter
John	1 Thessalonians	2 Peter
Acts	2 Thessalonians	1 John
Romans	1 Timothy	2 John
1 Corinthians	2 Timothy	3 John
2 Corinthians	Titus	Jude
Galatians	Philemon	Revelation

THE OLD TESTAMENT

Here is the key to understanding the Old Testament. Of the thirty-nine books in the Old Testament, *there are three different kinds of books:* Historical Books, Poetical Books, and Prophetical Books.

What kind of information would you expect to find in the Historical Books?. . . . .**history!**

What kind of information would you expect to find in the Poetical Books? . . . . **poetry!**

What kind of information would you expect to find in the Prophetical Books?. . . . .**prophecy!**

If you know what kind of book you are reading, then you will know what kind of information to expect, and you can more easily follow the logical flow of the Old Testament!

In the Old Testament:

. . . the first seventeen books are historical,
. . . the next five books are poetical, and
. . . the next seventeen books are prophetical!

THE THREE KINDS OF BOOKS IN THE OLD TESTAMENT

Historical	Poetical	Prophetical
Genesis	Job	Isaiah
Exodus	Psalms	Jeremiah
Leviticus	Proverbs	Lamentations
Numbers	Ecclesiastes	Ezekiel

Historical	Poetical	Prophetical
Deuteronomy	Song of Solomon	Daniel
Joshua		Hosea
Judges		Joel
Ruth		Amos
1 Samuel		Obadiah
2 Samuel		Jonah
1 Kings		Micah
2 Kings		Nahum
1 Chronicles		Habakkuk
2 Chronicles		Zephaniah
Ezra		Haggai
Nehemiah		Zechariah
Esther		Malachi

If you want to read the story of the Hebrew nation in the Old Testament, you must read the first seventeen books. These books compose a historical timeline for the nation of Israel.

If you want to read the poetry of Israel, you must read the next five books of the Old Testament.

If you want to read about the prophecy of Israel, you must read the final seventeen books.

This is somewhat oversimplified, because there is some poetry in the Historical Books, and some history in the Prophetical Books, and so on. The point is, however, that each of the books fits into a primary category. If you keep this structure in mind, the Old Testament will begin to take shape for you.

My mistake was in assuming that the whole Old Testament was one long, unbroken story and that the history would flow evenly and consistently out of one book into the next until they were all finished. Now I know the storyline is contained in the first seventeen books.

Of the seventeen Historical Books, eleven are *primary* Historical

Books and six are *secondary* Historical Books. The history of Israel is advanced in the eleven primary books and repeated or amplified in the six secondary books. The Poetical and Prophetical Books were written during the time period that is constructed in the first seventeen books.

Let's take a look at the historical timeline of the Old Testament in chart form:

TIMELINE OF THE OLD TESTAMENT

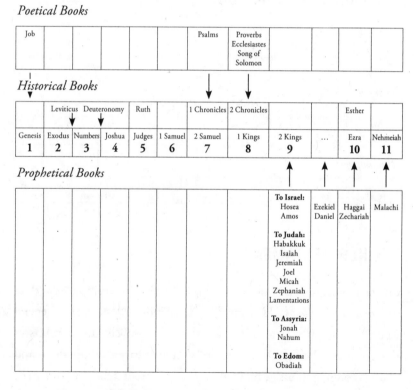

Poetical Books

| Job | | | | | | Psalms | Proverbs Ecclesiastes Song of Solomon | | | | |

Historical Books

	Leviticus	Deuteronomy		Ruth			1 Chronicles	2 Chronicles			Esther	
Genesis	Exodus	Numbers	Joshua	Judges	1 Samuel	2 Samuel	1 Kings	2 Kings	...	Ezra	Nehmeiah
1	**2**	**3**	**4**	**5**	**6**	**7**	**8**	**9**		**10**	**11**

Prophetical Books

| | | | | | | To Israel: Hosea Amos To Judah: Habakkuk Isaiah Jeremiah Joel Micah Zephaniah Lamentations To Assyria: Jonah Nahum To Edom: Obadiah | Ezekiel Daniel | Haggai Zechariah | Malachi |

As you can see, Job was written during the time period of the book of Genesis, and Psalms during the time of 2 Samuel, while Proverbs, Ecclesiastes, and Song of Solomon were written during the time of 1 Kings, and so on.

To use an analogy, we constructed a similar chart for U.S. history. Imagine that you read an American history book for the main storyline. The history book would give you the major periods in U.S. history. Some of these periods might be associated with a major poet or writer and a major philosopher. The poets would correspond to the poets of Israel, and the philosophers would correspond to the biblical prophets.

TIMELINE OF U.S. HISTORY

Poets/Writers

Jonathan Edwards	Thomas Paine	Henry W. Longfellow	Walt Whitman	Emily Dickinson	F. Scott Fitzgerald	Robert Frost

Historical Period

Colonial Period **1**	Revolutionary War **2**	Federal Period **3**	Civil War **4**	Gilded Age **5**	Industrial Expansion **6**	Modern Era **7**

Philosophers

Benjamin Franklin	Thomas Jefferson	Henry David Thoreau	Abraham Lincoln	Mark Twain	William Jennings Bryan	Martin Luther King Jr.

THE NEW TESTAMENT

Of the twenty-seven books of the New Testament, *there are also three different kinds of books:* Historical Books, Pauline Epistles, and General Epistles. The Historical Books are the four Gospels and the Acts of the Apostles. The Epistles are letters written to various individuals and church congregations. The Pauline Epistles are letters written by the apostle Paul. The General Epistles are letters written to individuals and congregations by a number of different people, hence the rather generic name General Epistles. The primary content in all the Epistles is instruction on Christian doctrine and lifestyle.

What kind of information would you expect to find in the Historical Books? .... **history!**

What kind of information would you expect to find in the Pauline Books? .... **instruction!**

What kind of information would you expect to find in the General Epistles? .... **instruction!**

In the New Testament:

. . . the first five books are Historical Books,
. . . the next thirteen books are Pauline Epistles, and
. . . the next nine books are General Epistles!

THE THREE KINDS OF BOOKS IN THE NEW TESTAMENT

Historical	Pauline Epistles	General Epistles
Matthew	*To Churches:*	Hebrews
Mark	Romans	James
Luke	1 Corinthians	1 Peter
John	2 Corinthians	2 Peter
Acts	Galatians	1 John
	Ephesians	2 John
	Philippians	3 John
	Colossians	Jude
	1 Thessalonians	Revelation
	2 Thessalonians	
	To Individuals:	
	1 Timothy	
	2 Timothy	
	Titus	
	Philemon	

If you want to read the story of Jesus and the church He established, you must read the first five books of the New Testament. These five books form the historical framework for understanding the entire New Testament!

If you want to read the apostle Paul's instruction to churches and individuals, you must read the next thirteen books.

If you want to read the instruction to churches and individuals by men like the apostles Peter and John, you must read the final nine books of the New Testament.

REFERENCES

To find something in the Bible, you use a standard reference system. This consists of the name of the book of the Bible, the chapter number followed by a colon, and the verse number (each chapter is divided into numbered verses). For example:

Genesis 1:1 =   Genesis   1:   1

            (book)   (chapter)   (verse)

When you see a reference such as Joshua 1:21, you will either need to memorize the books of the Bible to know where Joshua is, or you can look it up in the table of contents. It is well worth the time to memorize the books, and it is easiest to memorize them according to their categories.

For example, you now know that there are three types of books in both the Old Testament (Historical, Poetical, and Prophetical) and the New Testament (Historical, Pauline Epistles, and General Epistles), and how many books are in each section. Memorize the first seventeen Historical Books. Then, when you have these memorized, learn the five Poetical Books, and so on. This system is much easier than attempting to memorize an unbroken list of sixty-six books.

There is no substitute for reading the whole book for yourself, of course, but it is possible to offer a quick overview. To read "The Story of the Bible," turn to the appendix.

SUMMARY

1. There are 39 books in the Old Testament. There are 27 books in the New Testament. There are 66 books in the whole Bible.

2. The Old Testament is the story of God and the Hebrew people, their poets, and prophets.
   There are 3 kinds of books in the Old Testament:

   17 Historical Books
   5 Poetical Books
   17 Prophetical Books

3. The New Testament is the story of Jesus of Nazareth, the church He founded, and its growth under the leadership of His apostles after His death and resurrection.
   There are 3 kinds of books in the New Testament:

   5 Historical Books
   13 Pauline Epistles
   9 General Epistles

SELF-TEST

What you can learn tomorrow is built on what you learn today!

The Bible:

How many?

___39___ books in the Old Testament

___27___ books in the New Testament

___66___ books in the whole Bible

The Old Testament:

The Old Testament is the story of G__od___ and the H__ebrew__ people, their poets, and prophets.

There are 3 kinds of books in the Old Testament:

H__17___ Books, *historical*

P__5___ Books, and *poetic*

P__17___ Books. *prophetic*

___39___

There are ___17___ Historical Books.

There are ___5___ Poetical Books.

There are ___17___ Prophetical Books.

___39___

The New Testament:

The New Testament is the story of J__esus___ of Nazareth, the c__hurch__ He founded, and its growth under the leadership of His a__postle__s after His death and resurrection.

There are 3 kinds of books in the New Testament:

H _istorical_ Books,
P _auline_ Epistles
G _eneral_ Epistles

There are __5__ Historical Books.
There are __13__ Pauline Epistles.
There are __9__ General Epistles.
__27__

Congratulations! You are off to a fine start. As we move from the general to the specific, you can build your knowledge of the Bible like rows of bricks on a house. In twenty-nine more days, your house will be finished.

THE GEOGRAPHY OF THE OLD TESTAMENT

The size of our solar system is beyond comprehension. To get some perspective, imagine you are in the middle of the Bonneville Salt Flats with nothing but tabletop flat ground around you for miles and miles. There you put down a beach ball two feet in diameter, which you use to represent the sun. To get a feel for the immensity of the solar system, walk about a city block and put down a mustard seed for the first planet, Mercury. Go another block and for Venus put down an ordinary BB. Mark off yet another block and put down a green pea to represent Earth. A final block from there, put down a mustard seed to represent Mars. Then sprinkle some grass seed around for an asteroid belt.

We have now walked about four blocks, and we have a beach ball (sun), mustard seed (Mercury), BB (Venus), pea (Earth), mustard seed (Mars), and grass seed (asteroid belt). Now things begin to stretch out.

Continue for another quarter of a mile. Place an orange on the ground for Jupiter. Walk another third of a mile and put down a golf ball for Saturn.

Now lace up your tennis shoes and check their tread. Then step off another mile and, for Uranus, drop a marble. Go another mile and place a cherry there for Neptune. Finally, walk for another two miles and put down another marble for Pluto.

At last, go up in an airplane and look down. On a smooth surface almost ten miles in diameter we have a beach ball, a mustard seed, a BB, a pea, another mustard seed, some grass seed, an orange, a golf ball, a marble, a cherry, and another marble.

To understand our replica of the solar system even better, use another beach ball to represent Alpha Centauri, the next-nearest star to our sun. You would have to go another 6,720 miles and put it down in Japan!

Understanding the size and location of things and the relationships and distances between them gives us perspective. Just as this example gives us perspective about the solar system, a knowledge of geography can give perspective about the events of the Bible. It is helpful to know the names, locations, and relative positions of important places. Otherwise, we skim over information without comprehension or visualization, and this makes the Bible less interesting and less easily understood.

The one who is ignorant of geography cannot know history. The Bible is largely history. So, to begin our mastery of the history of the Bible, we must start with the geography of the Bible.

BODIES OF WATER

The primary anchor points for mastering the geography of the Bible are the bodies of water. *(As you read each description, go to the Work Map and insert the name of the body of water beside the matching number.)*

1. The Mediterranean Sea

The land of the Old Testament lies east of this beautiful blue body of water.

2. The Sea of Galilee

To call this body a sea seems to be an overstatement. It is a fresh-water lake that is seven miles wide and fourteen miles long. It lies about thirty-six miles inland from the Mediterranean.

3. The Jordan River

Flowing south out of the Sea of Galilee, the Jordan River travels for sixty-five miles, as the crow flies, to empty into the Dead Sea. Many are surprised at how much history has revolved around such a small river.

4. The Dead Sea

Shaped like a giant hot dog with a bite out of the lower third, the Dead Sea lies at the "bottom of the world." It is the lowest point on land, almost three thousand feet below sea level at its lowest point, so that water flows into it, but no water flows out of it. As a result, the water has a very high concentration of mineral deposits and does not support normal plant or animal life. Hence the name Dead Sea.

5. Nile River

Perhaps the most famous river in the world, the Nile flows through the heart of Egypt, spreads out like so many fingers, and empties into the waiting arms of the Mediterranean.

6. Tigris and (7.) Euphrates Rivers

These twin rivers flow for almost a thousand miles each before they join and flow into the Persian Gulf.

8. Persian Gulf

These last three bodies of water—the Tigris, the Euphrates, and the Persian Gulf—form the easternmost boundary for the lands of the Old Testament. The Tigris and Euphrates flow through present-day Iraq, while the Persian Gulf separates Iran from Saudi Arabia.

WORK MAP

BODIES OF WATER OF THE OLD TESTAMENT

1. _Mediterraan See_
2. _Sea of Galilee_
3. _Jordan River_
4. _Dead See_
5. _Nile River_
6. _Tigress River_
7. _Euphrates River_
8. _Persian Gulf_

pg 6 of workbook

LOCATIONS

With the geographical framework offered by the bodies of water, we can establish the locations that are relevant to the Old Testament. _(As you read the description of each location, insert its name beside the appropriate letter on the Location Work Map that follows.)_

A. The Garden of Eden

The exact location of the Garden of Eden, where everything began, is impossible to pinpoint. However, it was near the convergence of four rivers, two of which were the Tigris and Euphrates.

B. Canaan/Israel

This smallish piece of real estate, which lies between the Mediterranean coast and the Sea of Galilee-Jordan River-Dead Sea, changes names throughout the Old Testament. In Genesis it is called *Canaan*. After the Hebrew people establish themselves in the land in the book of Joshua, it becomes known as *Israel*. Thirteen hundred years later, at the beginning of the New Testament, the land is known by its regions (from south to north): Judea, Samaria, and Galilee.

C. Jerusalem

Located just off the northwestern shoulder of the Dead Sea, this city, nestled in the central mountains of Israel, is so central to the story of the Old Testament that it must be singled out and identified. It is the capital of the nation of Israel.

D. Egypt

The *grande dame* of ancient civilization, Egypt plays a central role in the history of the Old Testament.

E. Assyria

Located at the headwaters of the Tigris and Euphrates, this great world power is notable in the Old Testament for conquering the Northern Kingdom of Israel and dispersing her people to the four winds.

F. Babylonia

Another gigantic historical world power, this fabulous, albeit short-lived, nation conquered Assyria. It also conquered the Southern Kingdom of Judah 136 years after Assyria conquered the Northern Kingdom of Israel. It is found in Mesopotamia, between the Tigris and

Euphrates. (*Mesopotamia* means "in the middle of" [*meso*]—"rivers" [*potamus*].)

G. Persia

The final historical superpower of the Old Testament is located at the northern bank of the Persian Gulf. Persia comes into play by conquering Babylonia and by allowing the Hebrews to return from captivity to rebuild the city of Jerusalem and reinstate temple worship.

If these historical notes are foreign to you, don't worry about it now. Instead, content yourself with learning these locations so that, as the story unfolds, the names of these locations will mean something to you.

LOCATION WORK MAP

LOCATIONS OF THE OLD TESTAMENT

Now compare the ancient map you have just filled in with the following contemporary map of the same region. *pg 6 of workbook*

It might also help to get this Old Testament information into perspective by seeing how the map of the Old Testament compares with an overlay of a map of the state of Texas.

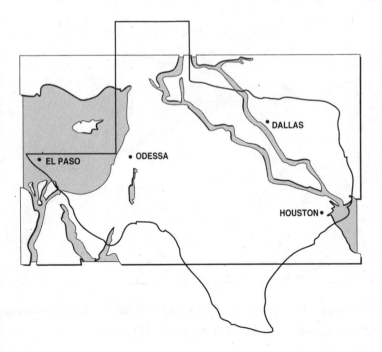

The entire land of the Old Testament is approximately the same size as the state of Texas. Traveling from the Persian Gulf to Israel would be like going the 875 miles from the southern tip at the Gulf of Mexico to the top of the panhandle. Traveling from Israel to Egypt would be like going the 275 miles from Odessa to El Paso. If you keep this in mind as the story of the Bible unfolds, it will help you keep geographical perspective.

REVIEW

Repetition is the key to mental ownership!

THE GEOGRAPHY OF THE OLD TESTAMENT

Review the eight bodies of water and the seven locations by placing the numbers and letters by the appropriate names below.

Bodies of Water

___1___ Mediterranean Sea

___2___ Sea of Galilee

___3___ Jordan River

Locations

___A___ Eden

___B___ Israel

___C___ Jerusalem

_4_ Dead Sea   _D_ Egypt
_5_ Nile River   _E_ Assyria
_6_ Tigris River   _F_ Babylonia
_7_ Euphrates River   _G_ Persia
_8_ Persian Gulf

SELF-TEST

*What you can learn tomorrow is built
on what you learn today!*

THE GEOGRAPHY OF THE OLD TESTAMENT

As the final exercise, fill in the blanks from memory.
(Remember, the blanks with numbers are bodies of water, and
the blanks with letters are locations.)

Excellent! Your knowledge of the geography of the Old Testament will enable you to understand and envision the history
that unfolds from it. You have just mastered an important section.

ANSWERS

THE GEOGRAPHY OF THE OLD TESTAMENT

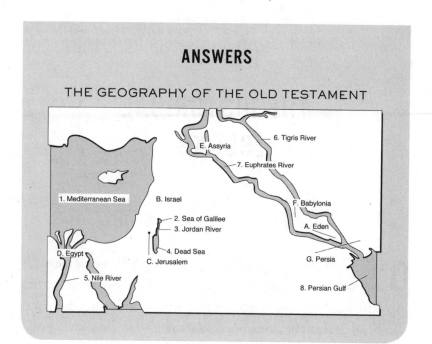

CHAPTER 3

THE HISTORICAL BOOKS

On the flight from Los Angeles to Portland, one flies over the entire length of the Cascade Mountains. From thirty-five thousand feet it is difficult to get the perspective to determine which are the higher mountain peaks. The closer peaks look taller while the distant peaks look shorter, regardless of their actual height.

One day in late October as I was making that flight, the air was crisp and clear after a light snowfall, and the puzzle of how to differentiate the higher from the lower peaks was answered. The snow only fell on elevations of about seven thousand feet and higher. As we flew over them, regardless of how close or far away they were, the highest peaks were easy to determine: they were the ones with snow on them.

As we begin to look into the stories of the Old Testament, we will only look at the highest peaks, the ones with snow on them.

To do so, it will be helpful to continue the analogy with the story of the United States. If you were going to condense just the story of the United States, omitting the poets and philosophers, you would take the main periods of history, link them with the central historic figure of the era, and add the primary location. In chart form, it might look like this:

TIMELINE OF U.S. HISTORY

Key Figure

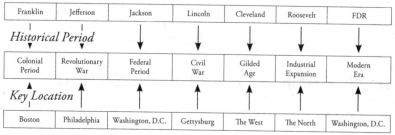

Franklin	Jefferson	Jackson	Lincoln	Cleveland	Roosevelt	FDR

Historical Period

Colonial Period	Revolutionary War	Federal Period	Civil War	Gilded Age	Industrial Expansion	Modern Era

Key Location

Boston	Philadelphia	Washington, D.C.	Gettysburg	The West	The North	Washington, D.C.

Include a brief storyline summary of the era, and the story of the United States could be overviewed in a chart, such as the following:

STORY OF THE UNITED STATES

Key Era	Key Figure	Location	Storyline
Colonial	Franklin	Boston	As the thirteen colonies long for independence, Franklin leads in the formulation of necessary strategy.
Revolution	Jefferson	Philadelphia	Jefferson writes the Declaration of Independence
Etc.	Etc.	Etc.	Etc.

This same approach can be used in condensing the story of the Bible, charting the main periods (or eras), the central figures, the main locations, and a summary storyline. The storyline of the Bible can be divided into twelve main eras, with a central figure and main location for each era. Nine of the eras are found in the Old Testament, and three are found in the New Testament.

In this chapter, we will deal with only the Old Testament and will complete only the first three aspects of the chart: the main eras, the central figures, and the main locations. The summary storyline and the New Testament events will be added in the following chapters.

THE NINE MAIN ERAS OF THE OLD TESTAMENT

1. Creation

The *creation* of the world and man, and early events.

2. Patriarch

The birth of the Hebrew people through a family of *patriarchs*, covering a period of two hundred years.

3. Exodus

The *exodus* of the Hebrew people as they are delivered out of four hundred years of slavery in Egypt, to return to their Promised Land.

4. Conquest

The *conquest* of the Promised Land by the Hebrew people upon their return from Egypt.

5. Judges

A four-hundred-year period during which Israel is governed by rulers called *judges*.

6. Kingdom

An additional four-hundred-year period during which Israel is a full-fledged nation ruled by a *monarchy*.

7. Exile

A seventy-year period during which Israel's leaders live in *exile*, having been conquered by foreign powers.

8. Return

The *return* of exiled Jews to Jerusalem to rebuild the city and the temple.

9. Silence

A final four-hundred-year period between the close of the Old Testament (when the last book of the Old Testament was written) and the opening of the New Testament (when the first book of the New Testament was written).

Following the pattern of the chart for the Story of the United States, let's begin to chart the Story of the Old Testament.

STORY OF THE OLD TESTAMENT

Era	Figure	Location	Storyline
Creation *Patriarch* *Exodus* *Conquest* *Judges* *Kingdom* *Exile* *Return* *Silence*	To be supplied later	To be supplied later	To be supplied later

Another way to help us remember the historical storyline of the Bible is to visualize the main eras with symbols, such as in the Arc of Bible History.

ARC OF BIBLE HISTORY

1. Creation	5. Judges	9. Silence
2. Patriarch	6. Kingdom	*To be*
3. Exodus	7. Exile	*supplied*
4. Conquest	8. Return	*later*

REVIEW

Repetition is the key to mental ownership!
(Write in the correct number from the descriptions on the left.)

Era:	Number:	Description:
Exile	_____	1. The *creation* of the world and man, and early events
Judges	_____	2. The birth of the Hebrew people through a family of *patriarchs*, covering a period of two hundred years
Creation	_____	3. The *exodus* of the Hebrew people as they are delivered out of four hundred years of slavery in Egypt, to return to the Promised Land

Era:	Number:	Description:
Kingdom	_____	4. The *conquest* of the Promised Land by the Hebrew people upon their return from Egypt
Patriarch	_____	5. A four-hundred-year period during which Israel is governed by rulers called *judges*
Conquest	_____	6. An additional four-hundred-year period during which Israel becomes a full-fledged nation ruled by a *monarchy*
Return	_____	7. A seventy-year period during which Israel's leaders live in *exile*, having been conquered by foreign powers
Silence	_____	8. The *return* of the exiled Jews to Jerusalem to rebuild the city and the temple
Exodus	_____	9. A final four-hundred-year period between the close of the Old Testament and the opening of the New Testament

THE NINE CENTRAL FIGURES OF THE OLD TESTAMENT

Era:	Figure:	Description:
Creation	Adam	The first *man*
Patriarch	Abraham	The first *patriarch*
Exodus	Moses	The leader of the *exodus*
Conquest	Joshua	The leader of Israel's *army*
Judges	Samson	The most famous *judge*
Kingdom	David	The most well-known Israelite *king*
Exile	Daniel	The major *prophet* during the Exile
Return	Ezra	The main leader of the *return*
Silence	Pharisees	The *religious* leaders of the Jews

REVIEW

Repetition is the key to mental ownership!
(Fill in the blank.)

Era:	Figure:	Description:
Creation	Adam	The first _____
Patriarch	Abraham	The first _____
Exodus	Moses	The leader of the _____
Conquest	Joshua	The leader of Israel's _____
Judges	Samson	The most famous _____
Kingdom	David	The most well-known Israelite _____
Exile	Daniel	The major _____ during the Exile
Return	Ezra	The main leader of the _____
Silence	Pharisees	The _____ leaders of the Jews

(Match the era with the key figure.)

Era:	Figure:	Options:
Creation	_____	*Moses*
Patriarch	_____	*Daniel*
Exodus	_____	*Abraham*
Conquest	_____	*Joshua*
Judges	_____	*Pharisees*
Kingdom	_____	*Ezra*
Exile	_____	*David*
Return	_____	*Samson*
Silence	_____	*Adam*

Now we will add the central figure to our storyline chart.

STORY OF THE OLD TESTAMENT

Era	Figure	Location	Storyline
Creation	Adam	To be supplied later	To be supplied later
Patriarch	Abraham		
Exodus	Moses		
Conquest	Joshua		
Judges	Samson		
Kingdom	David		
Exile	Daniel		
Return	Ezra		
Silence	Pharisees		

Our final task is to identify the general or primary geographic location of the events of the main eras of the Old Testament. Beginning with Creation and Adam, as an exercise in memory, write in the name of each main era and its central historical figure as you read the description of the location of each of the eras.

THE NINE MAIN LOCATIONS OF THE OLD TESTAMENT

Era:	Figure:	Location:	Description:
1. _____	_____	Eden	The Garden of Eden, where Adam is created. Near the convergence of the Tigris and Euphrates Rivers.
2. _____	_____	Canaan	Abraham migrates from Ur, near Eden, to Canaan, where he and the other patriarchs live until the time of slavery in Egypt.

Era:	Figure:	Location:	Description:
3. _____ _____		Egypt	During a severe famine, the Israelites migrate to Egypt and are enslaved four hundred years before their exodus to freedom.
4. _____ _____		Canaan	Joshua leads the conquest of the Promised Land in Canaan.
5. _____ _____		Canaan	The Israelites live in Canaan under a loose tribal system ruled by judges for the next four hundred years.
6. _____ _____		Israel	With the formation of a formal monarchy, the land is now referred to by the national name of *Israel*.
7. _____ _____		Babylonia	Because of judgment for national moral corruption, Israel is conquered by foreign nations, finally forcing her leaders into seventy years of exile in Babylonia.
8. _____ _____		Jerusalem	The exiled Israelites are allowed to return to Jerusalem to rebuild the city and temple, though they remain under the dominion of Persia.
9. _____ _____		Jerusalem	Though dominion of the land changes from Persia to Greece to Rome, Israel is allowed to worship in Jerusalem without disruption for the next four hundred years of "silence."

Along with the main era and the central figure, we are now able to add the main location to our chart.

STORY OF THE OLD TESTAMENT

Era	Figure	Location	Storyline
Creation	Adam	Eden	To be supplied later
Patriarch	Abraham	Canaan	
Exodus	Moses	Egypt	
Conquest	Joshua	Canaan	
Judges	Samson	Canaan	
Kingdom	David	Israel	
Exile	Daniel	Babylonia	
Return	Ezra	Jerusalem	
Silence	Pharisees	Jerusalem	

ARC OF BIBLE HISTORY

(Fill in the names of the eras. To check your answers, see the appendix.)

1. C_____	5. J_____	9. S_____
2. P_____	6. K_____	10.
3. E_____	7. E_____	11.
4. C_____	8. R_____	12.

REVIEW

Repetition is the key to mental ownership!

On the following map draw arrows to show the movement during the major eras of the Old Testament that we have just learned. Begin at Eden and draw an arrow to the next location as it changes: Eden to Canaan, to Egypt, to Canaan, to Babylonia, to Jerusalem.

In its most basic form, your map should look something like this:

From the options given, fill in the blanks in the following chart, matching the location to the era and central figure. *(A location may be used more than once.)*

Babylonia   Eden   Israel   Canaan   Egypt   Jerusalem

STORY OF THE OLD TESTAMENT

Era	Figure	Location	Storyline
Creation	Adam	_____	To be supplied later
Patriarch	Abraham	_____	
Exodus	Moses	_____	
Conquest	Joshua	_____	
Judges	Samson	_____	
Kingdom	David	_____	
Exile	Daniel	_____	
Return	Ezra	_____	
Silence	Pharisees	_____	

You are now ready to begin final mastery of a very critical chart. Once you master this chart, you have come a long way in understanding the overview of the Old Testament. Fill in the blanks.

STORY OF THE OLD TESTAMENT

Era	Figure	Location	Storyline
Creation	Adam	_____	To be supplied later
Patriarch	_____	Canaan	
	Moses	Egypt	
Conquest	Joshua	_____	
Judges	_____	Canaan	
	David	Israel	
Exile	Daniel	_____	
Return	_____	Jerusalem	
_____	Pharisees	Jerusalem	

SELF-TEST

*What you can learn tomorrow is built
on what you learn today!*

Finally, fill in the following chart from memory. It might be easiest to fill in the eras, then go back and fill in the central figures and main locations. *(To check your answers, see the appendix for a completed Story of the Bible chart.)*

STORY OF THE OLD TESTAMENT

Era	Figure	Location	Storyline
_____	_____	_____	To be supplied later
_____	_____	_____	
_____	_____	_____	
_____	_____	_____	
_____	_____	_____	
_____	_____	_____	
_____	_____	_____	
_____	_____	_____	

Congratulations! You have just taken a major step toward mastering an overview of the Old Testament. From now on, we will become more and more specific, but you have laid a good foundation that can be built upon in successive chapters.

CHAPTER 4

THE CREATION ERA
(Genesis 1–11)

Far from the land of everyday, out in the distant curves of the universe, lay strange and fantastic realms, unlike anything in our wildest dreams. Hidden by the barriers of time and space, they have lived forever beyond the reach of man, unknown and unexplored.

But now, just now, the cosmic veils have begun to lift a little. Man has had his first glimpses of these once-secret domains, and their bizarre ways have left him stunned. They challenge his very notions of matter and energy. Along with Alice in Wonderland, he says, "One can't believe impossible things."

And impossible, indeed, they seem to be. In those far reaches of the universe, in those bewildering worlds, are far places . . .

> where a teaspoon of matter weighs as much as two hundred
> million elephants . . .
> where a tiny whirling star winks on and off thirty times a
> second . . .
> where a small, mysterious object shines with the brilliance
> of ten trillion suns . . .
> where matter and light are continually sucked up by
> devouring black holes, never to be seen again.

Small wonder that the late British scientist J. B. S. Haldane could say, "The universe is not only [stranger] than we suppose, but [stranger] than we can suppose."

We used to think that the universe was simply our Milky Way Galaxy. Today we know that galaxies are as common as blades of grass in a meadow. They number perhaps a hundred billion.

How does one comprehend the incredible size of this galaxy-filled universe? For such awesome distances, scientists and astronomers think in terms of time, and they use the telescope as a time machine. They measure space by a unit called the light-year, the distance light travels in one year at the rate of 186,282 miles per second—about six trillion miles. (From *National Geographic*, May 1974.)

If you could shoot a gun whose bullet would travel around the world at the speed of light, the bullet would go around the world and pass through you seven times in one second!

Perhaps more than anything else, the mystery and the immensity of our universe capture our imagination and incite in us a fascination about the subject of Creation. There are countless unknowns and just as many "unbelievables." As we begin to explore the Creation Era, we will adopt a pattern that will be followed throughout the remainder of this section:

I. You will review the main era, central figure, and main location you learned in the last chapter.

II. You will read a brief storyline summary of the events of that era, built around the central figure, with a three-word theme of each summary appearing in italics. Then you will be asked to review those three words to fill in the blanks.

III. You will read an expansion of the summary of the events of that era.

I. REVIEW

Repetition is the key to mental ownership!
Fill in the blanks for this era:

STORY OF THE OLD TESTAMENT

Era	Figure	Location	Storyline Summary
_____	_____	_____	To be completed in this chapter.

II. STORYLINE SUMMARY

Adam is created by God, but he *sins* and *destroys* God's original *plan* for man.

Era	Summary
Creation	Adam is created by God, but he _____ and _____ God's original _____ for man.

III. EXPANSION

There are four major events within the Creation Era. They are the accounts of:

1. Creation
2. Fall
3. Flood
4. Tower of Babel

1. Creation: Man created in the image of God (Genesis 1–2)

After a dramatic display of power in creating the heavens and the earth, God creates man. When Genesis chapter 1 uses the word *man*, it includes both man and woman. *Man*, in this context, has the sense of "mankind" or "humankind." Adam and Eve are created in the image of God, in perfect fellowship and harmony with Him. Living in an idyllic setting in the Garden of Eden, they are individuals of beauty and high intelligence. The "image" is not a physical likeness, but a spiritual and personal likeness. Man is a spirit and will live forever. He has intellect, emotion, and will. He has an understanding of a divine being (God), with a moral sense of right and wrong. He is a creative being. These are some characteristics of God that are shared by man, and in this sense, *man is created in the image of God.*

2. Fall: Sin entered the world (Genesis 3)

Satan, appearing in the form of a serpent, lures Adam and Eve into rebelling against God and violating the one prohibition God had given them: not to eat from the Tree of the Knowledge of Good and Evil. As a consequence, they are driven out of the Garden of Eden, and a curse falls on all creation. When Adam and Eve rebel, *sin enters the world.* All the pain, all the evil, all the suffering endured by mankind for all time can be traced to that one act, which is, therefore, appropriately called the "Fall" of man.

3. Flood: Judgment for sin (Genesis 6–10)

Over the next several hundred years, as man multiplies in numbers, so his tendency to sin multiplies, until a time comes when God can find only eight people who are willing to live in a righteous relationship with Him: Noah, his wife, his three sons, and their wives. So, in *judgment for sin*, God performs surgery on the human race, cutting out the cancerous tissue, as it were, and leaving behind the healthy tissue to restore itself. He does this by sending a worldwide flood, which destroys mankind, except for Noah and his family, who are saved in Noah's ark.

4. Tower: Beginning of the nations (Genesis 11)

God's post-flood mandate to man was to spread out, populate, and subdue the whole earth. In direct disobedience to that command, man stays in one place and begins building a monument to himself, the Tower of Babel. God causes this large congregation of people to begin speaking different languages. Lack of communication prevents them from further progress on the tower, and the people of each tongue disperse to the four corners of the earth and form the *beginning of the nations* of the world as we know them today.

SELF-TEST

*What you can learn tomorrow is built
on what you learn today!*

A. The Four Main Events of the Creation Era

(Write the correct number in the blank from the options on the right.)

Event:	Number:	Description:
Creation	_____	1. Judgment for sin
Fall	_____	2. Beginning of the nations
Flood	_____	3. Sin entered the world
Tower	_____	4. Man in the image of God

B. Storyline Summary

(Fill in the blanks from memory.)

Era	Summary
Creation	Adam is created by God, but he _____ and _____ God's original _____ for man.

C. Arc of Bible History

(Fill in the name of the era. To check your answer, see the appendix.)

1. C_____	5.	9.
2.	6.	10.
3.	7.	11.
4.	8.	12.

D. The Geography of the Creation Era

(Circle the dot indicating the possible location of Eden.)

E. Story of the Old Testament

(Fill in the blanks. To check your answers, see the appendix.)

Era	Summary
Creation	Adam is created by God, but he _____ and _____ God's original _____ for man.

CHAPTER 5

THE PATRIARCH ERA

(Genesis 12–50)

Any parent will admit that rearing children is a challenging task. In *I Want to Enjoy My Children*, psychologist Henry Brandt tells the story of the time he and his wife invited the president of the college he was attending to their house for dinner. They were nervous and had spent considerable time preparing the house and meal for a good impression. When the president arrived, they stumbled over themselves to make him comfortable. They sat him next to their two-year-old daughter for the meal. That was a mistake. During the meal, this little tot said to the president in her bird-like voice: "Please pass the salt." No one paid attention; they were listening to the president. So she tried again: "Will you please pass the salt?" Her small voice was easy to ignore as the adults strained for the president's every word. Finally, she hammered the distinguished guest on the arm and yelled, "Pass the salt, or I'll knock your block off!"

Even a president of the United States was perplexed by the antics of his child. Alice Roosevelt, daughter of Theodore Roosevelt, was an unruly girl whose antics scandalized the staid Washington "society" during her father's tenure at the White House. When a visitor objected to the girl's wandering in and out of the president's office while he was conducting important business with her father, Roosevelt said, "I can be president of the United States, or I can control Alice. I cannot possibly do both."

The Patriarch Era was a time of godly men (patriarchs) presiding over their growing family. Abraham, Isaac, Jacob, and Joseph, successive generations of the same family, ruled over the Hebrew people in the earliest days of their existence.

On more than one occasion, Abraham must have felt a little like Brandt and Roosevelt. His descendants did not always behave the way he wanted them to. Passion for God and what He wanted to do in and through the Hebrew people burned like a flame in Abraham's heart. But the flame dimmed in successive generations. However, the time of slavery in Egypt sharpened the spiritual hunger of the Hebrew people, and a great family, which became a great nation, emerged.

I. REVIEW

Repetition is the key to mental ownership!
Fill in the blanks to bring the chart up to date with this era. (To check your answers, see the appendix.)

STORY OF THE OLD TESTAMENT

Era	Figure	Location	Storyline Summary
_____	_____	_____	Adam is created by God, but he _____ and _____ God's original _____ for man.
_____	_____	_____	To be completed in this chapter.

II. STORYLINE SUMMARY

Abraham is *chosen* by God to "father" a *people* to *represent* God to the world.

Era	Summary
Patriarch	Abraham is _____ by God to "father" a _____ to _____ God to the world.

III. EXPANSION

There are four major men in the Patriarch Era:

1. Abraham
2. Isaac Ishmael
3. Jacob Esau
4. Joseph All 12 sons

1. Abraham: Father of the Hebrew people (Genesis 12–23)

Because of Adam's sin and the Fall of man, God's attention is now focused on a plan of redemption for mankind. God wants a people through whom He can work to produce a reflection of Himself, and through whom He can spread the message of redemption to the world. He chooses Abraham, who becomes the *father of the Hebrew people*, and promises him a country (land), countless descendants (seed), and a worldwide and timeless impact (blessing). Abraham is living in Ur, near the convergence of the Tigris and Euphrates Rivers, at the time. God leads him to the land of Canaan, where Abraham settles and has two sons, Ishmael and Isaac.

2. Isaac: Second father of promise (Genesis 24–26)

Isaac becomes the *second father of promise* as the fulfillment of Abraham's promises is passed down to him. He witnesses several major miracles during his life. He lives in the land of Abraham, becomes prosperous, and dies at an old age after having fathered two sons, Esau and Jacob.

3. Jacob: Father of the nation of Israel (Genesis 27–35)

The promises given to Abraham are passed through Isaac to Jacob, Isaac's younger son. Jacob begins life as a conniving scoundrel. However, through a series of miracles and other encounters with God, he mends his ways. Jacob has twelve sons, and the promises of Abraham are passed down to them all as a family. While Abraham is the father of the Hebrew people, Jacob is the *father of the nation of Israel*, as from his twelve sons emerge the twelve tribes of the nation of Israel.

4. Joseph: Leader in Egypt (Genesis 37–50)

Jacob's sons, for the most part, have very little commitment to God's call on them as a nation. They sell their brother Joseph as a slave, and he is taken to Egypt. Because of his righteousness and God's faithfulness, Joseph rises to become a great *leader in Egypt*. During a severe famine, his family comes to Egypt for food, is reunited with Joseph, and as a result, enjoys peace and comfort. After Joseph dies, however, his people are enslaved for the next four hundred years. This time of trial sharpens the spiritual hunger of the Hebrew people, and they cry out to God for deliverance.

SELF-TEST

What you can learn tomorrow is built
on what you learn today!

A. Major Figures of the Patriarch Era

(Write the correct number in the blank from the options on the right.)

Figure:	Number:	Description:
Abraham	_____	1. Father of the nation of Israel
Isaac	_____	2. Leader in Egypt
Jacob	_____	3. Father of the Hebrew people
Joseph	_____	4. Second father of promise

B. Storyline Summary

(Fill in the blanks from memory.)

Era	Summary
Patriarch	Abraham is _____ by God to "father" a _____ to _____ God to the world.

C. Arc of Bible History

(Fill in the names of the eras. To check your answers, see the appendix.)

1. C_____	5.	9.
2. P_____	6.	10.
3.	7.	11.
4.	8.	12.

D. The Geography of the Patriarch Era

(Draw an arrow from Ur, where Abraham lived, to Canaan, and from Canaan to Egypt, to represent the geographical movements of the Patriarch Era.)

E. Story of the Old Testament

(Fill in the blanks.)

Era	Figure	Location	Storyline Summary
_____	_____	_____	Adam is created by God, but he _____ and _____ God's original _____ for man.
_____	_____	_____	Abraham is _____ by God to "father" a _____ to _____ God to the world.

CHAPTER 6

THE EXODUS ERA

(Exodus–Deuteronomy)

The Exodus was the mass movement of the Israelites out of slavery in Egypt back to the Promised Land in Canaan. It was not an easy movement. The Pharaoh of Egypt did not want them to go, and he threatened them with military retaliation. The miracles God performed during this time are among the most spectacular recorded in the Bible—the Nile River turned to blood, shepherds' rods turned into snakes, the firstborn of every Egyptian household died, and the Red Sea parted to allow the Israelites to cross over on dry land, escaping the Egyptian army.

Vintage movies sometimes portrayed this event as a little band of nomads roaming about the desert, camping under palm trees and singing Hebrew folk songs around a campfire. This picture could hardly be further from the truth. With the advances in computer-generated imaging, movies now reflect more accurately the almost unimaginable magnitude of the exodus. The book of Numbers tells us that when the Israelites left Egypt, there were six hundred thousand fighting men. It is reasonable to assume that if there were six hundred thousand fighting men, there were also six hundred thousand women. That's 1,200,000. Each of those families may have had at least two children. That's another 1,200,000. In addition, there were the men who were too old to fight, and their wives. There was the priestly tribe, the Levites, who didn't fight, and their wives and their children. There were, perhaps, between two and a half to three million people who left Egypt during this "exodus."

This was not a little tribe of nomads roaming about the desert. This was a nation on the move. Look at the state of Texas on a map and imagine the city of Dallas beginning to move across the map, and you get an idea of the magnitude of the exodus. When you add all the animals they took with them for food and milk, as well as for sacrifices, this qualified as a horde! Instead of looking for a flat spot under a palm tree to camp, they had to look for a valley ten miles square. When they lined up to cross the Red Sea, it was more than a little aisle that was required. If they crossed the Red Sea one hundred abreast, counting the animals, the column would have stretched perhaps as far as fifty miles back into the desert.

Personal beliefs aside, this ranks as one of the greatest historical events of the ancient world, and this was an event over which Moses presided. To get a better look at the specifics of the exodus, we will now review our previous chapters and then look at the four main events of the Exodus Era.

I. REVIEW

Repetition is the key to mental ownership!
Fill in the blanks to bring the chart up-to-date with this era.
(To check your answers, see the appendix.)

STORY OF THE OLD TESTAMENT

Era	Figure	Location	Storyline Summary
			Adam is created by God, but he _____ and _____ God's original _____ for man.
_____	_____	_____	

Era	Figure	Location	Storyline Summary
_____	_____	_____	Abraham is _____ by God to "father" a _____ to _____ God to the world.
_____	_____	_____	To be completed in this chapter.

II. STORYLINE SUMMARY

Through Moses God *delivers* the Hebrew people from *slavery* in Egypt and then gives them the *Law.*

Era	Summary
Exodus	Through Moses God _____ the Hebrew people from _____ in Egypt and then gives them the _____.

III. EXPANSION

There are four major events in the Exodus Era:

1. Deliverance
2. The Law
3. Kadesh Barnea
4. Forty Years of Wandering

1. Deliverance: Freedom from slavery in Egypt (Exodus 1–18)

The Hebrews have languished under slavery in Egypt for four hundred years when their cry to God for deliverance is answered. God raises up Moses as His spokesman to Pharaoh, the ruler of Egypt, asking for spiritual freedom for the Hebrew people. Pharaoh refuses, and a series of ten plagues is levied on Egypt to prompt Pharaoh to let the people go. The plagues start out bad and they get worse—from frogs, to gnats, to water turned to blood, to the death of the firstborn in every household of Egypt. Finally, Pharaoh consents to let the Hebrews leave Egypt. After they have gone, he changes his mind and attempts to recapture them. They make it as far as the Red Sea when God parts the Red Sea and the Hebrew people cross over to the other side. The waters come together again, protecting them from the Egyptian army and *freeing them from slavery in Egypt*. God, of course, has only one destination for them: the Promised Land of Canaan, the land "flowing with milk and honey." The land in which their father Abraham had first settled is again to be their home.

2. The Law: God's commandments at Mount Sinai (Exodus 19–40)

The Hebrew people now begin to take on a national identity as Israel. From the Red Sea, the Israelites travel south to the bottom of the Sinai Peninsula and camp at Mount Sinai. They receive *God's commandments at Mount Sinai*. Moses meets with God alone at the top of Mount Sinai, where he receives the Ten Commandments written on tablets of stone by the finger of God. Moses also receives a full revelation of the Law that is to govern Israel's national life as well as her relationship to God. God promises to bless her abundantly for obedience and curse her soundly for disobedience.

3. Kadesh Barnea: Place of rebellion against God (Numbers 10–14)

Israel leaves Mount Sinai and migrates north to an oasis, Kadesh Barnea, which is the southern gateway into the Promised Land. From this vantage point, twelve spies are sent into the Promised Land, one spy from each of the twelve tribes of Israel. The land is inhabited by the Canaanites, who would not take kindly to an Israelite horde invading their land. When the spies return, they have some good news and some bad news. The good news is that the land is beautiful and bountiful, "flowing with milk and honey." The bad news is that there are giants and hostile armies throughout the land. Ten spies report that the land is indomitable (in spite of the fact that God has promised to give them victory over any opposing forces). Two spies, Joshua and Caleb, exhort the people to believe God and go into the land. However, the people believe the majority report and refuse to follow Moses into the land. Thus, this becomes known as *a place of rebellion against God.*

4. Forty Years of Wandering: Consequences of rebelling against God (Numbers 20–36)

As a *consequence of rebelling against God* at Kadesh Barnea, the "exodus" generation is condemned to wander in the wilderness until everyone twenty years old or older at the time dies. In the ensuing forty years, a new generation rises to leadership, and the people are willing to follow the leaders into the land. Moses leads them to the north of the Dead Sea near Jericho, the eastern gateway to the Promised Land. Moses encourages the people, gives them additional instruction found in the book of Deuteronomy, and then dies.

SELF-TEST

*What you can learn tomorrow is built
on what you learn today!*

A. Four Major Events in the Exodus Era

*(Write the correct number in the blank from the options on
the right.)*

Event:	Number:	Description:
Deliverance	_____	1. God's commandments at Mount Sinai
The Law	_____	2. Place of rebellion against God
Kadesh Barnea	_____	3. Consequences of rebelling against God
Forty Years of Wandering	_____	4. Freedom from slavery in Egypt

B. Storyline Summary

(Fill in the blanks from memory.)

Era	Summary
Exodus	Through Moses God _____ the Hebrew people from _____ in Egypt and then gives them the _____.

C. Arc of Bible History

*(Fill in the names of the eras. To check your answers, see the
appendix.)*

1. C_____	5.	9.
2. P_____	6.	10.
3. E_____	7.	11.
4.	8.	12.

D. The Geography of the Exodus Era

(Draw an arrow from Egypt through the Red Sea to Mount Sinai to Kadesh Barnea, and then to the top of the Dead Sea on the east side of the Jordan River. This represents the geographical movement of the Exodus Era.)

E. Story of the Old Testament

(Fill in the blanks. To check your answers, see the appendix.)

Era	Figure	Location	Storyline Summary
_____	_____	_____	Adam is created by God, but he _____ and _____ God's original _____ for man.
_____	_____	_____	Abraham is _____ by God to "father" a _____ to _____ God to the world.
_____	_____	_____	Through Moses God _____ the Hebrew people from _____ in Egypt and then gives them the _____.

CHAPTER 7

THE CONQUEST ERA

(Joshua)

The days were dark indeed for Great Britain in 1940. The British people were at war with Germany and were being pressed hard on every side by the Nazi military machine. Supplies and morale were low. Their national destiny hung in the balance. Then a new prime minister came on the scene: Winston Churchill, whom history judges to be one of the greatest leaders of modern times. He was a man of intense conviction, deep resolve, and unquenchable optimism. His speeches, which historians consider to be among the finest ever given, burst upon the world with sudden and magnificent power. From them we read:

> To form an administration of this scale and complexity is a serious undertaking in itself, but it must be remembered that we are in the preliminary stage of one of the greatest battles in history, that we are in action at many points in Norway and in Holland, that we have to be prepared in the Mediterranean, that the air battle is continuous, and that many preparations have to be made here at home. I would say to the House, as I said to those who have joined this Government: I have nothing to offer but blood, toil, tears, and sweat.
>
> You ask what is our policy? I will say: It is to wage war by sea, land, and air with all our might and with all the strength

that God can give us: to wage war against a monstrous tyranny, never surpassed in the dark, lamentable catalogue of human crime. That is our policy. You ask, what is our aim? I can answer in a word: Victory—victory at all costs, victory in spite of all the terror, victory however long and hard the road may be; for without victory, there is no survival.

I have, myself, full confidence that if all do their duty, if nothing is neglected, and if the best arrangements are made, as they are being made, we shall prove ourselves once again able to defend our island home . . . to ride out the storm of war, and to outlive the menace of tyranny. Even though large tracts of Europe and many old and famous states have fallen or may fall into the grip of the Gestapo and all the odious apparatus of Nazi rule, we shall not flag or fail. We shall go on to the end, we shall fight in France, we shall fight on the seas and oceans, we shall fight with growing confidence and growing strength in the air, we shall defend our island, whatever the cost may be, we shall fight on the beaches, we shall fight on the landing grounds, we shall fight in the fields and in the streets, we shall fight in the hills; we shall never surrender.

While the circumstances were different for Churchill and England than for the Israelites after the exodus, in both situations, the situation was perilous for the respective nations. The Israelites had wandered in the wilderness for forty years because of rebellion and unbelief at Kadesh Barnea. Now they were at Jericho, and the test was the same as it was at Kadesh Barnea: would they resolve to forge ahead, or would they shrink from the circumstances as their fathers had done?

The task of rallying and leading the people fell to Joshua. Moses, the great leader of the last forty years, was dead. Would the people galvanize behind Joshua? Or would they refuse his leadership? Just as

England faced a crossroads when Churchill became its leader, so also the Israelites faced a critical junction in the road.

I. REVIEW

Repetition is the key to mental ownership!
Fill in the blanks to bring the chart up-to-date with this era.
(To check your answers, see the appendix.)

STORY OF THE OLD TESTAMENT

Era	Figure	Location	Storyline Summary
_____	_____	_____	Adam is created by God, but he _____ and _____ God's original _____ for man.
_____	_____	_____	Abraham is _____ by God to "father" a _____ to _____ God to the world.
_____	_____	_____	Through Moses God _____ the Hebrew people from _____ in Egypt and then gives them the _____.
_____	_____	_____	To be completed in this chapter.

II. STORYLINE SUMMARY

Joshua leads the *conquest* of the *Promised Land*.

Era	Summary
Conquest	Joshua leads the _____ of the _____ _____.

III. EXPANSION: THERE ARE FOUR MAIN EVENTS IN THE CONQUEST ERA

1. Jordan
2. Jericho
3. Conquest
4. Dominion

1. Jordan: A miraculous parting of water (Joshua 1–5)

Moses dies, and God handpicks Joshua to succeed him. Joshua's first challenge is to cross the Jordan River at flood stage. God commands him to prepare the nation for a ceremonial procession and to begin walking, priests first, toward the Jordan River. When the priests touched water, God would part the water for them. (This is the second *miraculous "parting of water"* that God performed for Israel. The first was the parting of the Red Sea.) The people respond, and God parts the Jordan River for a distance of about twenty miles. They cross without incident, and the water begins flowing again.

2. Jericho: A miraculous conquest of a city (Joshua 6)

The city of Jericho, a small oasis on the west side of the Jordan River near the Dead Sea, is not only the eastern gateway to the Promised Land, but it is also a fortified city and poses a threat to the welfare of Israel. As Joshua stands overlooking the city, contemplating how to conquer it, the angel of the Lord appears to him and instructs him to march around the city once a day for seven days. On the seventh day, he is to march around it seven times and the people are to shout. The city wall will fall down. They do, and it does . . . *a miraculous conquest of a city!*

3. Conquest: The defeat of Canaan (Joshua 7–12)

The Canaanites are united in their fear and hatred of the Israelites, but not in their military opposition to them. Primarily, the region is characterized by individual kings, each with his own city and surrounding country. Joshua cuts through the midsection toward the Mediterranean Sea. Having divided the land, he then begins to conquer, from south to north. In about seven years the initial *defeat of Canaan* is complete.

4. Dominion: Finalizing dominion (Joshua 13–20)

Each of the twelve tribes of Israel is given a land area by lottery and is responsible for *finalizing dominion* over that area. All twelve tribes inhabit their areas and form a loose federation with the other tribes.

SELF-TEST

*What you can learn tomorrow is built
on what you learn today!*

A. Four Major Events in the Conquest Era

*(Write the correct number in the blank from the options on
the right.)*

Event:	Number:	Description:
Jordan	_____	1. The defeat of Canaan
Jericho	_____	2. A miraculous parting of water
Conquest	_____	3. Finalizing dominion
Dominion	_____	4. A miraculous conquest of a city

B. Storyline Summary

(Fill in the blanks from memory.)

Era	Summary
Conquest	Joshua leads the _____ of the _____ _____.

C. Arc of Bible History

(Fill in the names of the eras. To check your answers, see the appendix.)

1. C_____	5.	9.	
2. P_____	6.	10.	
3. E_____	7.	11.	
4. C_____	8.	12.	

D. The Geography of the Conquest Era

(Draw an arrow from Jericho across to the Mediterranean Sea. Then draw an arrow into the southern half of the land. Now draw an arrow into the northern half of the land. This represents the geographical movement of the Conquest Era.)

E. Story of the Old Testament

(Fill in the blanks.)

Era	Figure	Location	Storyline Summary
_____	_____	_____	Adam is created by God, but he _____ and _____ God's original _____ for man.
_____	_____	_____	Abraham is _____ by God to "father" a _____ to _____ God to the world.
_____	_____	_____	Through Moses God _____ the Hebrew people from _____ in Egypt and then gives them the _____.
_____	_____	_____	Joshua leads the _____ of the _____ _____.

CHAPTER 8

THE JUDGES ERA
(Judges–Ruth)

WOMAN IN RAGS, GARBAGE, REVEALED AS HEIRESS

So read the headline in the San Francisco Chronicle concerning a lady known as "Garbage Mary" who was picked up in a shopping mall in Delray Beach, Florida. She gave the impression of being just another destitute soul whose mind had deserted her. She was often seen rummaging through dumpsters and garbage cans looking for food and other valuables, which she would stash in her car and apartment. There were mounds of garbage in the small apartment, stuffed in the refrigerator, the stove, the sink, the cabinets, and the bathtub. There were paths through the garbage. Other than in the kitchen, there were no chairs to sit in because they were piled with trash.

Police finally identified her as the daughter of a well-to-do lawyer and bank director from Illinois who had died several years earlier. In addition to the garbage, police found Mobil Oil stock worth more than four hundred thousand dollars, documents indicating ownership of oil fields in Kansas, stock certificates from some of the most valuable *Fortune* 500 companies, and passbooks for eight large bank accounts.

Garbage Mary was a millionaire who was living like a derelict.

Untold wealth was at her disposal, and yet she scrounged through garbage rather than claim the resources that were rightly hers.

The parallel between Garbage Mary and Israel during the time of the judges is striking. This was a dark period indeed in the history of the Jewish people. They had lost their spiritual moorings, and, as is recorded in the final verse of the Book of Judges, "everyone did what was right in his own eyes." The result was a morally degraded, socially perverted, and spiritually bankrupt time of almost four hundred years. The people of Israel had all the wealth of the promises of God at their disposal. Yet they scavenged through the garbage of life, eking out a pitiful existence. They could have been kings but lived like paupers.

I. REVIEW

Repetition is the key to mental ownership!
Fill in the blanks to bring the chart up-to-date with this era.
(To check your answers, see the appendix.)

STORY OF THE OLD TESTAMENT

Era	Figure	Location	Storyline Summary
_____	_____	_____	Adam is created by God, but he _____ and _____ God's original _____ for man.
_____	_____	_____	Abraham is _____ by God to "father" a _____ to _____ God to the world.
_____	_____	_____	Through Moses God _____ the Hebrew people from _____ in Egypt and then gives them the _____.

Era	Figure	Location	Storyline Summary
_____	_____	_____	Joshua leads the _____ of the _____ _____.
_____	_____	_____	To be completed in this chapter.

II. STORYLINE SUMMARY

Samson and others were chosen as *judges* to *govern* the people for *four hundred* rebellious years.

Era	Summary
Judges	Samson and others were chosen as _____ to _____ the people for _____ _____ rebellious years.

III. EXPANSION

There are four main subjects in the Judges Era:

1. Judges
2. Rebellion
3. Cycles
4. Ruth

1. Judges: The leaders of Israel (Judges)

As seen in the Book of Judges, these judges are not men who wear long, flowing black robes, sit on high benches, and make legal decisions. Rather, they are political-military *leaders of Israel* who exercise nearly absolute power because of their office and abilities. The four major judges are:

- Deborah, a female judge early in the Judges Era
- Gideon, who defeats an army of thousands with only three hundred men
- Samson, the most famous judge, whose fabulous strength has captured our collective imagination for thousands of years
- Samuel, a transitional character held in very high regard in Scripture, who is both the last judge and the first prophet

2. Rebellion: The breaking of God's Law (Judges)

The Book of Judges records the darkest period in Israel's history, following one of the brightest eras: the Conquest Era under Joshua. Just before Moses dies, he instructs Israel (in Deuteronomy 7:1–5) to do three things in order to keep the future nation of Israel from being corrupted by the moral cancer of the Canaanites:

1. Destroy all the inhabitants of Canaan.
2. Avoid intermarriage with the Canaanites.
3. Shun worship of the Canaanite gods.

Israel fails on all three accounts. *The breaking of God's Law* and the record of Israel's subsequent moral degradation are sad indeed.

3. Cycles: Repetition of Israel's misfortunes (Judges)

Much of the era of Judges involves a series of seven cycles that are recorded in the Book of Judges. Each cycle has five component parts: (1) Israel "sins," (2) God disciplines them through military "conquest" by a neighboring country, (3) Israel "repents" and cries out to God for deliverance, (4) God raises up a judge, who "delivers" them from bondage, and (5) God "frees" the land from military oppression for the remainder of that judge's life. That is one cycle: sin, conquest, repentance, deliverance, and freedom. Then, when a judge dies, the *repetition of Israel's misfortunes* begins again. The Israelites fall into sin again, followed by conquest, followed by repentance, and so on. Seven such cycles are recorded in the Book of Judges.

4. Ruth: A model woman (Ruth)

Standing out in refreshing contrast to the general background of the Judges Era is Ruth, described in the book that bears her name. This *model woman* who lives during the era of Judges is an example of moral and spiritual strength. Her story is one of love, purity, and commitment. She is a living illustration of the blessings that God showers on those who live in faithful obedience to Him. One example of God's blessings toward Ruth is that she, a non-Hebrew, is listed in the lineage from Abraham to Jesus.

SELF-TEST

What you can learn tomorrow is built on what you learn today!

A. Four Major Subjects in the Judges Era

(Write the correct number in the blank from the options on the right.)

Subject:	Number:	Description:
Judges	_____	1. A model woman
Rebellion	_____	2. The leaders of Israel
Cycles	_____	3. The breaking of God's Law
Ruth	_____	4. Repetition of Israel's misfortunes

B. Storyline Summary

(Fill in the blanks from memory.)

Era	Summary
Judges	Samson and others were chosen as _____ to _____ the people for _____ _____ rebellious years.

C. Arc of Bible History

(Fill in the names of the eras. To check your answers, see the appendix.)

1. C_____	5. J_____	9.
2. P_____	6.	10.
3. E_____	7.	11.
4. C_____	8.	12.

D. The Geography of the Judges Era

(Match the numbers below with the blanks on the map to see the countries conquering Israel in the Judges Era.)

1. Philistia   3. Mesopotamia   5. Ammon
2. Moab   4. Canaan   6. Midian

E. Story of the Old Testament

(Fill in the blanks.)

Era	Figure	Location	Storyline Summary
_____	_____	_____	Adam is created by God, but he _____ and _____ God's original _____ for man.
_____	_____	_____	Abraham is _____ by God to "father" a _____ to _____ God to the world.

Era	Figure	Location	Storyline Summary
_____	_____	_____	Through Moses God _____ the Hebrew people from _____ in Egypt and then gives them the _____.
_____	_____	_____	Joshua leads the _____ of the _____ _____.
_____	_____	_____	Samson and others were chosen as _____ to _____ the people for _____ _____ rebellious years.

CHAPTER 9

THE KINGDOM ERA
(1 Samuel–2 Chronicles)

By nature, man desires something he cannot have: total freedom. There are certain freedoms we can have, but they have corresponding bondages. And there are certain bondages we can have that afford us corresponding freedoms. For example, you can be free from the toothbrush and in bondage to cavities, or you can make yourself a slave to the toothbrush and be free from cavities. You cannot be free from the toothbrush *and* free from cavities. That kind of freedom—total freedom—does not exist.

Throughout life, we are constantly making choices, and for those choices, we pay certain inescapable consequences. Freedom comes with a price.

The kings of Israel wanted total freedom. They wanted the freedom to ignore the directives God had given them on how to rule and wage war. But at the same time, they wanted the freedom to have economic and military prosperity. This was not possible. As a result, the Kingdom Era was a very turbulent time with many ups and downs. When a righteous king ruled, the nation would prosper. When an unrighteous king gained the throne, the nation would falter.

The barnacles of unrighteousness began to affix themselves to the Israeli ship of state, and before the books of history were completed, the nation had collapsed and suffered at the hands of warring neighbors.

I. REVIEW

Repetition is the key to mental ownership!
Fill in the blanks to bring the chart up-to-date with this era.
(To check your answers, see the appendix.)

STORY OF THE OLD TESTAMENT

Era	Figure	Location	Storyline Summary
_____	_____	_____	Adam is created by God, but he _____ and _____ God's original _____ for man.
_____	_____	_____	Abraham is _____ by God to "father" a _____ to _____ God to the world.
_____	_____	_____	Through Moses God _____ the Hebrew people from _____ in Egypt and then gives them the _____.
_____	_____	_____	Joshua leads the _____ of the _____ _____.
_____	_____	_____	Samson and others were chosen as _____ to _____ the people for _____ _____ rebellious years.
_____	_____	_____	To be completed in this chapter.

II. STORYLINE SUMMARY

David, the greatest king in the new *monarchy*, is followed by a succession of mostly *unrighteous* kings, and God eventually *judges* Israel for her sin, sending her into exile.

Era	Summary
Kingdom	David, the greatest king in the new _____, is followed by a succession of mostly _____ kings, and God eventually _____ Israel for her sin, sending her into exile.

III. EXPANSION

There are four main periods in the Kingdom Era:

1. United Kingdom
2. Divided Kingdom
3. Northern Kingdom
4. Southern Kingdom

1. United Kingdom: A new monarchy (1 and 2 Samuel)

The twelve tribes of Israel, jealous of other nations around them, are united in their demand to God for a king. God allows Samuel, the last judge, to anoint Saul to be the first king, beginning *a new monarchy*. Because Saul is not a righteous king, God does not honor his reign or establish his family on the throne of Israel. His successor, David, though having shortcomings, is a righteous king, and Israel prospers under him. David's son Solomon becomes king upon David's death. Solomon rules righteously at first, then drifts from the Lord.

2. Divided Kingdom: A civil war (1 Kings)

As a result of Solomon's spiritual drifting, *a civil war* erupts upon his death, and the kingdom is divided. There is now a Northern Kingdom, consisting of ten tribes, and a Southern Kingdom, consisting of the tribes of Judah and Benjamin. The northern ten tribes retain the name "Israel," and the southern two tribes adopt the name "Judah," after the name of the larger tribe.

3. Northern Kingdom: The unrighteous kingdom (2 Kings)

In the civil war that splits the kingdom, Jeroboam commands the Northern Kingdom of Israel. He is unrighteous, and every other king (nineteen total) who succeeds him during the two-hundred-fifty-year life of the Northern Kingdom is also unrighteous. Because of this unrighteousness, God raises up Assyria to conquer the Northern Kingdom and scatter His people to the four winds. *The unrighteous kingdom* is never restored.

4. Southern Kingdom: The inconsistent kingdom (2 Kings)

Rehoboam, Solomon's son, commands the Southern Kingdom of Judah. He is also unrighteous, but the Southern Kingdom fares somewhat better than the northern. Lasting for four hundred years, its life is prolonged by eight righteous kings out of a total of twenty. Judah's sins finally catch up to her, however, and God brings judgment on *the inconsistent kingdom* by raising up Babylonia (which had conquered Assyria) to conquer Judah. Babylonia gathers all the leaders, artisans, musicians, and promising children, and takes them away to captivity in Babylonia.

SELF-TEST

*What you can learn tomorrow is built
on what you learn today!*

A. Four Major Subjects in the Kingdom Era

*(Write the correct number in the blank from the options on
the right.)*

Subject:	Number:	Description:
United Kingdom	_____	1. The unrighteous kingdom
Divided Kingdom	_____	2. A new monarchy
Northern Kingdom	_____	3. The inconsistent kingdom
Southern Kingdom	_____	4. A civil war

B. Storyline Summary

(Fill in the blanks from memory.)

Era	Summary
Kingdom	David, the greatest king in the new _____, is followed by a succession of mostly _____ kings, and God eventually _____ Israel for her sin, sending her into exile.

C. Arc of Bible History

*(Fill in the names of the eras. To check your answers, see the
appendix.)*

1. C_____	5. J_____	9.
2. P_____	6. K_____	10.
3. E_____	7.	11.
4. C_____	8.	12.

D. The Geography of the Kingdom Era

(Draw an arrow from Israel to Assyria. Draw another arrow from Judah to Babylonia. This represents the geographical movement of the Kingdom Era.)

E. Story of the Old Testament

(Fill in the blanks.)

Era	Figure	Location	Storyline Summary
_____	_____	_____	Adam is created by God, but he _____ and _____ God's original _____ for man.
_____	_____	_____	Abraham is _____ by God to "father" a _____ to _____ God to the world.
_____	_____	_____	Through Moses God _____ the Hebrew people from _____ in Egypt and then gives them the _____.
_____	_____	_____	Joshua leads the _____ of the _____ _____.
_____	_____	_____	Samson and others were chosen as _____ to _____ the people for _____ _____ rebellious years.
_____	_____	_____	David, the greatest king in the new _____, is followed by a succession of mostly _____ kings, and God eventually _____ Israel for her sin, sending her into exile.

CHAPTER 10

THE EXILE ERA

(Ezekiel–Daniel)

A troubled man was standing at the top of the Empire State Building in New York, and finally he decided to jump off, ending his own life. After he had fallen awhile and was only one hundred stories off the ground, he realized he had made a mistake. It was wrong to commit suicide, and he knew it. He said, "O God, if you hear me . . . I'm sorry for the foolish mistake I made in jumping off this building. I repent, and I would like to know if you would forgive me." A voice came back. "Of course I forgive you. Don't think a thing about it. I will never bring it up again. And by the way, I'll see you in just a minute."

Sin is a fact of human existence. And God will forgive whoever comes to Him in repentance. But that doesn't change the fact that sin has consequences. God forgives the man for jumping off the building, but the man will still fall to the ground.

Israel tasted this bitter reality. Their relationship with the Lord deteriorated. They lived in roller-coaster rebellion against Him for four hundred years during the Kingdom Era, continually paying the price. Finally, the debt became so great that judgment came in the form of military conquest. During the time of the Exile, there were some great spiritual leaders, and there was repentance on the part of a segment of the Jewish people. However, this did not remove the penalty for the years of rebellion, and the full price of the Exile was exacted.

I. REVIEW

Repetition is the key to mental ownership!
Fill in the blanks to bring the chart up-to-date with this era.
(To check your answers, see the appendix.)

STORY OF THE OLD TESTAMENT

Era	Figure	Location	Storyline Summary
_____	_____	_____	Adam is created by God, but he _____ and _____ God's original _____ for man.
_____	_____	_____	Abraham is _____ by God to "father" a _____ to _____ God to the world.
_____	_____	_____	Through Moses God _____ the Hebrew people from _____ in Egypt and then gives them the _____.
_____	_____	_____	Joshua leads the _____ of the _____ _____.
_____	_____	_____	Samson and others were chosen as _____ to _____ the people for _____ _____ rebellious years.

Era	Figure	Location	Storyline Summary
			David, the greatest king in the new _____, is followed by a succession of mostly _____ kings, and God eventually _____ Israel for her sin, sending her into exile.
_____	_____	_____	To be completed in this chapter.

II. STORYLINE SUMMARY

Daniel gives *leadership* and encourages *faithfulness* among the *exiles* for the next seventy years.

Era	Summary
Exile	Daniel gives _____ and encourages _____ among the _____ for the next seventy years.

III. EXPANSION

As mentioned before in Chapter 1 of this book, some history is contained in books that are primarily Prophetical Books, and that is the case in the Exile Era. You will note that the biblical references for the four main divisions of this era will include some Prophetical Books. There are four main divisions in the Exile Era:

1. Prophecy
2. Prophets
3. Exiles
4. Power Change

1. Prophecy: Warning of impending captivity (Jeremiah)

The Northern Kingdom, Israel, has been conquered by Assyria and is dispersed in 722 B.C. During the time of the events described in 2 Kings, the Southern Kingdom, Judah, receives a *warning of impending captivity* through Jeremiah (called the "Weeping Prophet"), who prophesies that the nation will be taken into captivity at the hands of the Babylonians. This happens in 586 B.C. He also accurately prophesies that the captivity will last seventy years.

2. Prophets: Encouraging faithfulness of exiles (Ezekiel and Daniel)

There are two prophets who write books of the Bible during the Exile: Ezekiel and Daniel. Not a great deal is known about the prophet Ezekiel since his book is mostly prophetic and not autobiographical. He foretells of national restoration and *encourages faithfulness among the exiles*. Daniel's book, while also a book of prophecy, is more biographical. He is a prominent governmental leader, much like Joseph in Egypt. While Daniel's personal life is an example to his people, his prophecies tend to concern the future destruction of the world.

3. Exiles: Assimilated into the culture (Daniel)

The Book of Daniel also gives us a glimpse of life among the exiles. Apparently, the Jews are *assimilated into the culture* in which they are exiled. They experience discrimination, which has always been true of displaced Jews. Yet, in spite of this, they seem fairly well integrated into society, and some of them achieve positions of prominence.

4. Power Change: Persian Empire expands (Daniel)

While the Jews are in exile in Babylonia, Persia rises to become the dominant military power of that region. Persia conquers Babylonia (which had conquered Assyria), so now Persia rules not only her own land, but the land once dominated by Assyria and Babylonia. The *Persian Empire expands* from the Tigris River to the Mediterranean Sea.

SELF-TEST

*What you can learn tomorrow is built
on what you learn today!*

A. Four Major Subjects in the Exile Era

(Write the correct number in the blank from the options on the right.)

Subject:	Number:	Description:
Prophecy	_____	1. Persian Empire expands
Prophets	_____	2. Assimilated into the culture
Exiles	_____	3. Warning of impending captivity
Power Change	_____	4. Encouraging faithfulness among the exiles

B. Storyline Summary

(Fill in the blanks from memory.)

Era	Summary
Exile	Daniel gives _____ and encourages _____ among the _____ for the next seventy years.

C. Arc of Bible History

(Fill in the names of the eras. To check your answers, see the appendix.)

1. C_____	5. J_____	9.
2. P_____	6. K_____	10.
3. E_____	7. E_____	11.
4. C_____	8.	12.

D. The Geography of the Exile Era

(Draw a line from Babylonia toward Assyria and circle Assyria. Draw another line from Persia toward Babylonia, encircling both Babylonia and Assyria. This represents the shift in power during the Exile Era. Assyria had conquered Israel. Then Babylonia conquered Assyria and Judah. Finally, Persia conquered Babylonia and ended up ruling everyone.)

E. Story of the Old Testament

(Fill in the blanks. To check your answer, see the appendix.)

Era	Figure	Location	Storyline Summary
_____	_____	_____	Adam is created by God, but he _____ and _____ God's original _____ for man.
_____	_____	_____	Abraham is _____ by God to "father" a _____ to _____ God to the world.
_____	_____	_____	Through Moses God _____ the Hebrew people from _____ in Egypt and then gives them the _____.

Era	Figure	Location	Storyline Summary
_____	_____	_____	Joshua leads the _____ of the _____ _____.
_____	_____	_____	Samson and others were chosen as _____ to _____ the people for _____ _____ rebellious years.
_____	_____	_____	David, the greatest king in the new _____, is followed by a succession of mostly _____ kings, and God eventually _____ Israel for her sin, sending her into exile.
_____	_____	_____	Daniel gives _____ and encourages _____ among the _____ for the next seventy years.

THE RETURN ERA

(Ezra–Esther)

A s a young man, Peter Jenkins walked across America. He had grown up in the 1960s and was consumed by the disillusionment of his generation, so he set out to find his country and himself.

His amazing story is one of long hours, days, and weeks of solitude and drudgery punctuated by occasional life-threatening surprises. He faced danger from weather, accidents, wild animals, and people. He almost died in a snowstorm, was attacked by animals, and hunted by cruel men who might have killed him if they had caught him.

Many times he wanted to quit his search. Each time, he was befriended by people who restored his body, his soul, and his faith in America. He lost his dog but gained a wife, a new worldview, and a deep appreciation for the grandeur of his country and its people.

Finally, after more than five long and grueling years of walking, he stepped into the Pacific Ocean. His journey was done. When Peter Jenkins walked into the Oregon waters, he was quite a different person from the one who left his home in Alfred, New York. The trials, the time, the solitude, the people, and the physical and mental challenges had transformed him. On his departure, he was little more than a confused boy. On his return, he was a man.

The return of the nation of Israel from seventy years of captivity in Babylonia parallels in many ways the story of Peter Jenkins. The Israelites went into exile a drifting and confused people. They spent agonizing years in solitude, and in physical and mental torment. They were ministered to unexpectedly by people sent from God. They returned to Israel a sobered people. They were home, refocused in their purpose as a nation, ready to begin again the worship of Jehovah: the God of creation and the God of Israel.

I. REVIEW

Repetition is the key to mental ownership!
Fill in the blanks to bring the chart up-to-date with this era. (To check your answers, see the appendix.)

STORY OF THE OLD TESTAMENT

Era	Figure	Location	Storyline Summary
____	____	____	Adam is created by God, but he _____ and _____ God's original _____ for man.
____	____	____	Abraham is _____ by God to "father" a _____ to _____ God to the world.
____	____	____	Through Moses God _____ the Hebrew people from _____ in Egypt and then gives them the _____.
____	____	____	Joshua leads the _____ of the _____ _____.

Era	Figure	Location	Storyline Summary
_____	_____	_____	Samson and others were chosen as _____ to _____ the people for _____ _____ rebellious years.
_____	_____	_____	David, the greatest king in the new _____, is followed by a succession of mostly _____ kings, and God eventually _____ Israel for her sin, sending her into exile.
_____	_____	_____	Daniel gives _____ and encourages _____ among the _____ for the next seventy years.
_____	_____	_____	To be completed in this chapter.

II. STORYLINE SUMMARY

Ezra *leads* the people back from *exile* to rebuild *Jerusalem*.

Era	Summary
Return	Ezra _____ the people back from _____ to rebuild _____.

III. EXPANSION

There are four major subjects in the Return Era:

1. Disrepair
2. Temple
3. People
4. Walls

1. Disrepair: Destruction from war and neglect (Nehemiah 1:1–3)

During the seventy years of captivity, the leadership of Judah has been taken into exile, and the city of Jerusalem falls into disrepair. Not only has the city suffered the ravages of the military campaign during the initial conquest, but it has also fallen victim to the erosion of neglect. The *destruction from war and neglect* leaves Jerusalem in a state of abject ruin.

2. Temple: Rebuilding the temple (Ezra 1–6)

God prompts Cyrus, king of Persia, to initiate the financing and rebuilding of the Jewish temple in Jerusalem. Under the direction of Zerubbabel, a notable Jewish figure in Persia, the *rebuilding of the temple* is begun. Considerable opposition from Gentiles around Jerusalem is encountered. At the urging of Haggai and Zechariah, two Jewish prophets living in Jerusalem, the restoration of the temple is completed.

3. People: Spiritual rebuilding (Ezra 7–10)

Rebuilding the temple is a direct parallel to the *spiritual rebuilding* of the Jewish people. Temple worship has been discontinued for seventy years. Most of the Jews have never seen or heard the Law of Moses. They have to be instructed in a national reeducation program. Ezra sets his heart to study the Law of the Lord, to practice it, and to teach God's statutes and ordinances in Israel to rebuild the people as they return from exile.

4. Walls: Restoration complete (Nehemiah)

Even though not all Jews returned when they could have (see the Book of Esther, whose events take place during this era) many Jews are now back home in Jerusalem. The temple stands restored as the dominant structure in the city, but the walls of the city are still broken down. This is a security threat as well as a source of national humiliation. Nehemiah—another Jewish notable serving Artaxerxes, king of Persia—is burdened to rebuild the walls. He is given permission and financing by the king of Persia to do so. A short time later, the walls frame the noble city of Jerusalem, home of the temple of God. *Restoration is complete* as the temple is rebuilt, the people are rebuilt, and the walls are rebuilt.

SELF-TEST

*What you can learn tomorrow is built
on what you learn today!*

A. Four Major Subjects in the Return Era

(Write the correct number in the blank from the options on the right.)

Subject:	Number:	Description:
Disrepair	_____	1. Spiritual rebuilding
Temple	_____	2. Rebuilding the temple
People	_____	3. Destruction from war and neglect
Walls	_____	4. Restoration complete

B. Storyline Summary

(Fill in the blanks from memory.)

Era	Summary
Return	Ezra _____ the people back from _____ to rebuild _____.

C. Arc of Bible History

(Fill in the names of the eras. To check your answers, see the appendix.)

1. C_____	5. J_____	9.
2. P_____	6. K_____	10.
3. E_____	7. E_____	11.
4. C_____	8. R_____	12.

D. The Geography of the Return Era

(Draw an arrow from Persia to Jerusalem on the map at the top of the next page to represent geographical movements during the Return Era.)

E. Story of the Old Testament

(Fill in the blanks. To check your answers, see the appendix.)

Era	Figure	Location	Storyline Summary
_____	_____	_____	Adam is created by God, but he _____ and _____ God's original _____ for man.
_____	_____	_____	Abraham is _____ by God to "father" a _____ to _____ God to the world.
_____	_____	_____	Through Moses God _____ the Hebrew people from _____ in Egypt and then gives them the _____.

Era	Figure	Location	Storyline Summary
_____	_____	_____	Joshua leads the _____ of the _____ _____.
_____	_____	_____	Samson and others were chosen as _____ to _____ the people for _____ _____ rebellious years.
_____	_____	_____	David, the greatest king in the new _____, is followed by a succession of mostly _____ kings, and God eventually _____ Israel for her sin, sending her into exile.
_____	_____	_____	Daniel gives _____ and encourages _____ among the _____ for the next seventy years.
_____	_____	_____	Ezra _____ the people back from _____ to rebuild _____.

CHAPTER 12

THE SILENCE ERA
(Between the Old and New Testaments)

A lion who was caught up with his mastery of the jungle decided to make sure all the other animals knew he was king of the jungle. He was so confident that he bypassed the smaller animals and went straight to the bear. "Who is king of the jungle?" the lion demanded. The bear replied, "Why, you are, of course." The lion gave a mighty roar of approval.

Next, he went to the tiger. "Who is the king of the jungle?" he roared. The tiger quickly responded, "Everyone knows that you are, O mighty lion." The lion swelled with pride.

Next on the list was the elephant. The lion faced the elephant and leveled his question. "Who is king of the jungle?" he challenged. The elephant grabbed the lion with his trunk, whirled him around in the air five or six times, and slammed him against a tree. Then he pounded him on the ground several times, sat on him once, dipped him in the lake, and dumped him out on the shore.

The lion, battered and bruised, struggled to his feet, peered at the elephant through his good eye, and said, "Look, just because you don't know the answer is no reason to get mean about it."

The religious leaders of the Silence Era were very much like the lion. They pretended to have power, and they became self-absorbed.

It has been said that some people drink at the fountain of knowledge while others only gargle. All this pride caused a pattern of religious hypocrisy that was leading to self-destruction and made this period one of the more disappointing eras in the nation's history.

I. REVIEW

Repetition is the key to mental ownership!
Fill in the blanks to bring the chart up-to-date with this era.
(To check your answers, see the appendix.)

STORY OF THE OLD TESTAMENT

Era	Figure	Location	Storyline Summary
_____	_____	_____	Adam is created by God, but he _____ and _____ God's original _____ for man.
_____	_____	_____	Abraham is _____ by God to "father" a _____ to _____ God to the world.
_____	_____	_____	Through Moses God _____ the Hebrew people from _____ in Egypt and then gives them the _____.
_____	_____	_____	Joshua leads the _____ of the _____ _____.
_____	_____	_____	Samson and others were chosen as _____ to _____ the people for _____ _____ rebellious years.

Era	Figure	Location	Storyline Summary
_____	_____	_____	David, the greatest king in the new _____, is followed by a succession of mostly _____ kings, and God eventually _____ Israel for her sin, sending her into exile.
_____	_____	_____	Daniel gives _____ and encourages _____ among the _____ for the next seventy years.
_____	_____	_____	Ezra _____ the people back from _____ to rebuild _____.
_____	_____	_____	To be completed in this chapter.

II. STORYLINE SUMMARY

Pharisees and others *entomb* the *Israelites* in *legalism* for the next *four hundred* years.

Era	Summary
Silence	Pharisees and others _____ the _____ in _____ for the next _____ _____ years.

III. EXPANSION

There are four major subjects in the Silence Era:

1. The Changing Guard
2. Political Sects
3. Religious Sects
4. Messianic Hope

1. The Changing Guard: The march of nations

At the close of the Old Testament, Jerusalem is ruled by Persia. Alexander the Great defeats the Persians in 333 B.C. and establishes Greek culture and the Greek language as a unifying force for that part of the world. When Alexander dies, his kingdom is quartered, but Hellenistic (Greek) culture is still advanced and remains the dominant influence. When Rome conquers that part of the world, Roman influences are introduced, but for now the Greek influence is still strong. *The march of nations* passes from Persia to Greece to Rome.

2. Political Sects: The Maccabeans and Zealots

Throughout the four hundred silent years, there are militant Jews who attempt to revolt against foreign rule and make Jerusalem and the surrounding area of Judea an independent country. These include the *Maccabeans* and the *Zealots*.

3. Religious Sects: Pharisees and Sadducees

There are two primary religious "parties" in Jerusalem during this time. Unfortunately, neither offers much guidance in true spirituality, as they are caught up in promoting a religious "legalism" of external adherence to rules while overlooking inner motivations and attitudes. The Pharisees are orthodox and conservative, and they foster separation between themselves and "secular" society. The Sadducees are more liberal. They are the party of the Jerusalem aristocracy, and they use their wealth and influence to keep the political waters calm. A ruling board, called the Sanhedrin, is made up of representatives from both the *Pharisees* and *Sadducees*, but the two groups have little in common except their desire for religious freedom and, later, their antagonism for Jesus of Nazareth.

4. Messianic Hope: Expectation of a savior

The "Messiah," or "Savior," is one who is prophesied throughout the Old Testament to come save the Jews. Some feel they need spiritual salvation, and others are looking only for political salvation. For both reasons, the expectation and hope for the coming of the Messiah is strong during the four hundred silent years. Events of the Silence Era seem to especially prepare the world for the coming of the Messiah: (1) This part of the world has a common language and a common culture, which facilitates the spread of a Messianic message. (2) The Roman Empire has brought this region military peace, an extensive system of roads and sea travel, and a common government so that people can travel extensively without interference. (3) The Jews are suffering such religious persecution and political humiliation that widespread hope and *expectation of a savior* exists. These facts make the coming of Jesus of Nazareth, claiming to be the Messiah, an event that captures the attention of the entire Jewish world.

SELF-TEST

*What you can learn tomorrow is built
on what you learn today!*

A. Four Major Subjects in the Silence Era

*(Write the correct number in the blank from the options on
the right.)*

Subject:	Number:	Description:
The Changing Guard	_____	1. Pharisees and Sadducees
Political Sects	_____	2. The march of nations
Religious Sects	_____	3. Expectations of a savior
Messianic Hope	_____	4. Maccabeans and Zealots

B. Storyline Summary

(Fill in the blanks from memory.)

Era	Summary
Silence	Pharisees and others _____ the _____ in _____ for the next _____ _____ years.

C. Arc of Bible History

*(Fill in the names of the eras. To check your answers, see the
appendix.)*

1. C_____	5. J_____	9. S_____
2. P_____	6. K_____	10.
3. E_____	7. E_____	11.
4. C_____	8. R_____	12.

D. The Geography of the Silence Era

(Put a 1 next to Persia, a 2 next to Greece, and a 3 next to Rome. Then draw an arrow from Persia to Greece to Rome, to represent the geographical movement of the Silence Era.)

E. Story of the Old Testament

(Fill in the blanks.)

Era	Figure	Location	Storyline Summary
_____	_____	_____	Adam is created by God, but he _____ and _____ God's original _____ for man.
_____	_____	_____	Abraham is _____ by God to "father" a _____ to _____ God to the world.
_____	_____	_____	Through Moses God _____ the Hebrew people from _____ in Egypt and then gives them the _____.
_____	_____	_____	Joshua leads the _____ of the _____ _____.
_____	_____	_____	Samson and others were chosen as _____ to _____ the people for _____ _____ rebellious years.

Era	Figure	Location	Storyline Summary
_____	_____	_____	David, the greatest king in the new _____, is followed by a succession of mostly _____ kings, and God eventually _____ Israel for her sin, sending her into exile.
_____	_____	_____	Daniel gives _____ and encourages _____ among the _____ for the next seventy years.
_____	_____	_____	Ezra _____ the people back from _____ to rebuild _____.
_____	_____	_____	Pharisees and others _____ the _____ in _____ for the next _____ _____ years.

Congratulations! You have just passed another milestone! You have completed the overview of the Historical Books of the Old Testament, the ones that tell the story of the Old Testament. Now we will take a look at the Poetical Books and the Prophetical Books in the next two chapters.

CHAPTER 13

THE POETICAL BOOKS

(Job–Song of Solomon)

It is no secret that, historically speaking, poets have "marched to the beat of a different drummer," and not everyone has appreciated their poetry. Charles Babbage, a British mathematician, objected to Alfred Lord Tennyson's line from "The Vision of Sin": "Every moment dies a man, / Every moment one is born," saying that if that were true, "the population of the world would be at a standstill." In the interest of accuracy, he wrote to Tennyson, the lines should be amended to read, "Every moment dies a man, / Every moment one and one-sixteenth is born."

Those who like poetry either think they can write it or wish they could. It is much more difficult to write enduring poetry than one imagines, however, and amateur attempts are rarely widely appreciated. Euripides once confessed that it had taken him three days to write three verses. His astonished friend, a poet of lesser abilities, exclaimed, "I could have written a hundred in that time!" "I believe it," replied Euripides, "but they would have lived only three days."

King Louis XIV showed Nicolas Beaulieu, a French poet of the day, some poems he had written and asked his opinion of them. The great poet was also an accomplished diplomat: "Sire, nothing is impossible for Your Majesty. Your Majesty has set out to write bad verses and has succeeded."

Poetry is a song of the soul. Wherever great civilizations have existed, poetry has been written, and the poetry of Israel is among the finest. The psalms of David and the proverbs of Solomon stand up well when compared with any other body of poetry ever written.

I. REVIEW

Repetition is the key to mental ownership!

We remind ourselves that there are three kinds of books in the Old Testament: Historical, Poetical, and Prophetical. There are five Poetical Books that follow the first seventeen Historical Books, as seen below.

THE THREE KINDS OF BOOKS
IN THE OLD TESTAMENT

Historical	Poetical	Prophetical
Genesis	Job	Isaiah
Exodus	Psalms	Jeremiah
Leviticus	Proverbs	Lamentations
Numbers	Ecclesiastes	Ezekiel
Deuteronomy	Song of Solomon	Daniel
Joshua		Hosea
Judges		Joel
Ruth		Amos
1 Samuel		Obadiah
2 Samuel		Jonah
1 Kings		Micah
2 Kings		Nahum
1 Chronicles		Habakkuk
2 Chronicles		Zephaniah
Ezra		Haggai
Nehemiah		Zechariah
Esther		Malachi

To review, history has now come to an end. The Historical Books are completed, and the books of poetry of the people of Israel begin. The Poetical Books, the middle five books of the Old Testament, can be located in the timeline constructed by the Historical Books. Job was written during the time of the events of the Book of Genesis; Psalms, during the life of David in 2 Samuel; and Proverbs, Ecclesiastes, and Song of Solomon were written during the lifetime of Solomon in the time covered in 1 Kings. See the following figure for a visual representation.

Poetical Books

Job					Psalms	Proverbs Ecclesiastes Song of Solomon				

Historical Books

	Leviticus	Deuteronomy		Ruth		1 Chronicles	2 Chronicles			Esther	
Genesis	Exodus	Numbers	Joshua	Judges	1 Samuel	2 Samuel	1 Kings	2 Kings	...	Ezra	Nehemiah
1	**2**	**3**	**4**	**5**	**6**	**7**	**8**	**9**		**10**	**11**

II. OVERVIEW SUMMARY:

The Poetical Books fall into three major *types* of poetry within which the poets used a number of different literary *techniques* to communicate God's message.

REVIEW

The Poetical Books fall into three major _____ of poetry within which the poets used a number of different literary _____ to communicate God's message.

The three major types of Hebrew poetry are:

1. *Lyric poetry*—to be *accompanied by music*, like a song.
2. *Instructional poetry*—to *teach principles of living* through pithy maxims.
3. *Dramatic poetry*—a narrative that *tells a story* in poetic form.

REVIEW

The three major types of Hebrew poetry are:

1. *Lyric poetry*—to be _____ _____ _____, like a song.
2. *Instructional poetry*—to _____ _____ _____ _____ through pithy maxims.
3. *Dramatic poetry*—a narrative that _____ _____ _____ in poetic form.

The two main literary techniques are

1. *Parallelism*
2. *Figures of speech*

1. Parallelism: The matching of ideas

Summary Definition: Rather than matching sounds, a Hebrew poet was more concerned with *matching ideas*, a technique called *parallelism*.

REVIEW

Rather than matching sounds, a Hebrew poet was more concerned with _____ _____, a technique called _____.

Six of the most common forms of parallelism are:

1. *Synonymous parallelism:* The ideas presented are similar.
    Make me know Your ways, O LORD;
    Teach me Your paths. (Psalm 25:4)
2. *Synthetic parallelism:* The second thought completes the first thought.
    The LORD is my shepherd,
    I shall not want. (Psalm 23:1)
3. *Antithetic parallelism:* The second thought contrasts with the first.
    For the LORD knows the way of the righteous,
    But the way of the wicked will perish. (Psalm 1:6)
4. *Emblematic parallelism:* The first line uses a figure of speech to illustrate the idea stated in the second line.
    As the deer pants for the water brooks,
    So my soul pants for You, O God. (Psalm 42:1)
5. *Climactic parallelism:* The second line repeats the first with the exception of the last word or words.
    It is not for kings, O Lemuel,
    It is not for kings to drink wine. (Proverbs 31:4)
6. *Formal parallelism:* Both lines of poetry must exist for a complete thought.

"But as for Me, I have installed My King
Upon Zion, My holy mountain." (Psalm 2:6)

REVIEW

(Fill in the blanks from the options listed.)

1. In synonymous parallelism, the ideas are _____.
   a) ridiculous
   b) similar
   c) spelled the same

2. In synthetic parallelism, _____.
   a) the second thought is made of nylon
   b) the second thought completes the first
   c) the second thought doesn't exist

3. In antithetic parallelism, _____.
   a) the second thought is written backward
   b) the second thought contrasts with the first
   c) the first thought has no counterpart in the universe

4. In emblematic parallelism, _____.
   a) a small metallic emblem is affixed to the first line
   b) a figure of speech in the first line illustrates the idea
      in the second line
   c) the ideas are drawn in primitive art form

5. In climactic parallelism, _____.
   a) the second thought is very cold
   b) the second line repeats the first with the exception
      of the last word or words
   c) the thought is completed in the third act

6. In formal parallelism, _____.
   a) the first line appears in a black tie
   b) both lines of poetry must exist for a complete thought
   c) the second line doesn't slurp its soup

(The answer to all the above questions is the first letter in the word basketball.)

2. Figures of Speech: Creating visual images

Summary Definition: Since the Hebrew poets wanted mental pictures to pop into the reader's mind, a prime consideration was *creating visual images*, which they accomplished with vivid "figures of speech."

REVIEW

Since the Hebrew poets wanted mental pictures to pop into the reader's mind, a prime consideration was _____ _____ _____, which they accomplished with vivid "figures of speech."

Five of the most common figures of speech are:

1. *Simile:* a comparison between two unlike things.
   Keep me as the apple of the eye. (Psalm 17:8)
2. *Metaphor:* a comparison in which one thing is said to be another.
   The LORD is my shepherd. (Psalm 23:1)

3. *Hyperbole:* a deliberate overstatement for the sake of emphasis.

> Every night I make my bed swim,
> I dissolve my couch with my tears. (Psalm 6:6)

4. *Rhetorical question:* asking a question for the purpose of making a statement.

> Who can speak of the mighty deeds of the LORD,
> Or can show forth all His praise? (Psalm 106:2)

5. *Personification:* assigning the characteristics of a human to lifeless objects.

> The sun knows the place of its setting. (Psalm 104:19)

While there are other figures of speech, these are the most notable. The ones listed here, in particular, express the visual imagery to which the Hebrew poets were committed.

If you can get away from the need to hear rhyme and rhythm, you can gain an appreciation for Hebrew poetry. These men were "wordsmiths" and "thoughtsmiths" who played with words and ideas, contrasting them, comparing them, completing them in ways that lifted them above mere prose.

III. EXPANSION: THE FIVE POETICAL BOOKS

1. Job
2. Psalms
3. Proverbs
4. Ecclesiastes
5. Song of Solomon

1. Job: Suffering and God's sovereignty

Job is a very wealthy, godly man whose fortunes are suddenly and dramatically reversed. He loses his health, his wealth, and his family and is plunged into profound suffering. The book presents, in "dramatic poetry," the internal struggles of Job, and a series of debates with three friends trying to gain a proper perspective on *suffering and God's sovereignty*. In the end, God reveals His majesty and power. Though Job's questions are never fully answered, he willingly submits to the sovereignty of God, and his fortunes are restored and doubled.

2. Psalms: Praise in public worship

Psalm originally meant "to strike the strings of an instrument." Therefore, the word became synonymous with "praise." The Book of Psalms is a collection of 150 psalms that are divided into five smaller "books." The Psalms are used as a book of prayer and *praise in public worship* in the tabernacle, temple, and synagogues. There are three primary types of psalms: praise, thanksgiving, and lament. King David writes almost half of them, while several different authors complete the rest.

3. Proverbs: Wisdom, skill for living

The purpose of proverbs is to impart *wisdom*, or *skill for living*. More specifically, they highlight practical wisdom, discernment, self-discipline, and moral courage. This "instructional poetry" is written in short, pithy maxims focusing on one's relationship to God and others—money, morals, speech, industry, honesty, etc. The message is that a life of wisdom and righteousness should preempt a life of foolishness and unrighteousness.

4. Ecclesiastes: Futility of temporal pursuits

Solomon, with his unlimited resources and opportunity, tries to find meaning in life through industry, pleasure, wealth, wisdom, and power, and finds them all unsatisfying. After he reviews these efforts and the *futility of temporal pursuits*, he concludes in this "instructional poetry" that there is only one thing that can satisfy man: to "fear God and keep His commandments" (12:13).

5. Song of Solomon: God's marriage manual

The Song of Solomon is *God's marriage manual.* This "dramatic poetry" pictures the intimate love relationship between Solomon and his Shulammite bride. In doing so, it presents God's perspective on married love.

SELF-TEST

What you can learn tomorrow is built on what you learn today!

The Five Poetical Books

(Write the correct number in the blank from the options on the right.)

Book:	Number:	Description:
Job	_____	1. Futility of temporal pursuits
Psalms	_____	2. Suffering and God's sovereignty
Proverbs	_____	3. God's marriage manual
Ecclesiastes	_____	4. Praise in public worship
Song of Solomon	_____	5. Wisdom; skill for living

CHAPTER 14

THE PROPHETICAL BOOKS
(Isaiah–Malachi)

Prophecy gets a grip on us like nothing else. We are mesmerized and spellbound by it. What does the future hold? Some look into crystal balls, read tea leaves, study astrological charts, and consult prophets for a glimpse into the unknown. From "When will the world end?" to "What should I wear tomorrow?" they hunger to probe into the depths of that which has not yet happened.

There is an intuitive sense that a veil hangs between the human and the divine, and that prophets will help us peer beyond the veil. Outside of the Bible, however, prophets have had an uneven track record. Croesus lived in the sixth century B.C. and was king of Lydia in Asia Minor. Deliberating whether to attack the Persian Empire, he asked the oracle at Delphi if the undertaking would prosper. The oracle replied that if he went to war, he would destroy a great empire. Encouraged, Croesus invaded the Persian realms. He was decisively beaten, and the Persians then invaded Lydia, captured its capital, and threw Croesus himself into chains. Croesus again sent an emissary to Delphi, this time with the question, "Why did you deceive me?" The priestess of the oracle replied that she had not deceived him—Croesus had indeed destroyed a great empire.

Girolamo Cardano, an Italian mathematician of the sixteenth century, was known throughout Europe as an astrologer, even visiting England to cast the horoscope of the young king, Edward VI. A steadfast believer in the accuracy of his so-called science, Cardano constructed a horoscope predicting the hour of his own death. When the day dawned, it found him in good health and safe from harm. Rather than have his prediction fail, Cardano killed himself.

Biblical prophets find themselves in a different league, however. If a man was a true prophet from God, no prediction of his would ever fail. If a prophet ever voiced a prophecy that failed, he was to be stoned to death. This discouraged the impostors and made the biblical prophets highly reliable. There were many true prophets in the Old Testament, but not all of them committed their messages to writings that were preserved. In the Bible, we have sixteen men who wrote down their messages. These writings are called the Prophetical Books, and they comprise the final seventeen books of the Old Testament, as seen in the review below.

I. REVIEW

Repetition is the key to mental ownership!

STRUCTURE OF THE OLD TESTAMENT

Historical	Poetical	Prophetical
Genesis	Job	Isaiah
Exodus	Psalms	Jeremiah
Leviticus	Proverbs	Lamentations
Numbers	Ecclesiastes	Ezekiel
Deuteronomy	Song of Solomon	Daniel
Joshua		Hosea
Judges		Joel

Historical	Poetical	Prophetical
Ruth		Amos
1 Samuel		Obadiah
2 Samuel		Jonah
1 Kings		Micah
2 Kings		Nahum
1 Chronicles		Habakkuk
2 Chronicles		Zephaniah
Ezra		Haggai
Nehemiah		Zechariah
Esther		Malachi

Our history is completed. From Genesis, the first Historical Book, to Nehemiah, the last Historical Book, we stretched out a timeline that told the story of ancient Israel. Then we dropped the Poetical Books in their proper place. Now we do the same with the Prophetical Books, as seen below.

Historical Books

	Leviticus	Deuteronomy		Ruth		1 Chronicles	2 Chronicles			Esther	
	↓	↓									
Genesis	Exodus	Numbers	Joshua	Judges	1 Samuel	2 Samuel	1 Kings	2 Kings	…	Ezra	Nehmeiah
1	**2**	**3**	**4**	**5**	**6**	**7**	**8**	**9**		**10**	**11**

Prophetical Books

									To Israel: Hosea Amos To Judah: Habakkuk Isaiah Jeremiah Joel Micah Zephaniah Lamentations To Assyria: Jonah Nahum To Edom: Obadiah	Ezekiel Daniel	Haggai Zechariah	Malachi

Twelve of the Prophetical Books were written during the time covered in the Book of 2 Kings, which records the decline of the nations of Israel and Judah. This is because the primary message of the prophets was to the nations to stop sinning and return to the Lord. The prophets predicted what would happen to the nations if the people did not heed the warning. Of the remaining books, two prophets (Ezekiel and Daniel) ministered during the Exile, and three (Haggai, Zechariah, and Malachi) during the return.

II. OVERVIEW SUMMARY:

Prophecy is *proclaiming* the Word of God, both for the *future* and in the *present*.

REVIEW

Prophecy is _____ the Word of God, both for the _____ and in the _____.

III. EXPANSION

There are four main features of the Prophetical writings:

1. Designation
2. Time Period
3. Foretelling
4. Forthtelling

1. Designation: Major and Minor Prophets

In recent history, the Prophetical Books have had two designations: *Major Prophets* and *Minor Prophets*. The Major Prophets are the first five Prophetical Books: Isaiah, Jeremiah, Lamentations, Ezekiel, and Daniel. The Minor Prophets are the remaining twelve. The Major Prophets are called "major" because they are longer books, while the others are called "minor" because they are shorter.

2. Time Period: Pre-Exile, Exile, or Post-Exile

The Prophetical Books are divided into three chronological periods: *Pre-Exile, Exile,* and *Post-Exile*. Most of the prophetical ministries and books occur before the Exile. Three prophets—Haggai, Zechariah, and Malachi—prophesy during the return. Of those who prophesy before the Exile, two prophesy primarily to Israel (the Northern Kingdom), seven primarily to Judah (the Southern Kingdom), and three to other countries, as seen in the following lists.

STRUCTURE OF THE PROPHETICAL BOOK

Pre-Exile			
To Israel:	*To Judah:*	*To Assyria:*	*To Edom:*
Hosea	Habakkuk	Jonah	Obadiah
Amos	Isaiah	Nahum	
	Jeremiah		
	Joel		
	Micah		
	Zephaniah		
	Lamentations		

Exile	Post-Exile		
From Babylonia:	*To Jerusalem:*		
Ezekiel	Haggai		
Daniel	Zechariah		
	Malachi		

3. Foretelling: Predicting the future

The most famous characteristic of an Old Testament prophet was that he could occasionally *predict the future*. This was not an ability inherent within himself. Rather, this information was given to him by God. In Israel, the test of a true prophet was that he must be 100 percent accurate. If a prophet ever said something that did not come true, he was not a prophet of God. And the penalty for giving a prophecy that did not come true was death by stoning. This kept the ranks of the true prophets pure (although under the auspices of unrighteous kings, false prophets did occasionally arise).

4. Forthtelling: Proclaiming the teachings of God

While the ministry of "foretelling" (telling the future) is more dramatic, the ministry of "forthtelling" is vastly more common in the life of a prophet. Forthtelling means simply *proclaiming the teachings of God* to the people. Primarily it relates to righteous living. There are three characteristics of this part of a prophet's ministry:

1. Exposing sin and calling people to a higher moral lifestyle
2. Warning of judgment if the people don't reform
3. Proclaiming the coming Messiah

The prophets usually warned about judgments related to the nation of Israel or Judah being militarily conquered and taken out of the land.

SELF-TEST

*What you can learn tomorrow is built
on what you learn today!*

A. Four Main Features of the Prophetical Books

*(Write the correct number in the blank from the options on
the right.)*

Feature:	Number:	Description:
Designation	_____	1. Predicting the future
Time Period	_____	2. Proclaiming the teachings of God
Foretelling	_____	3. Pre-Exile, Exile, Post-Exile
Forthtelling	_____	4. Major and Minor Prophets

B. The Geography of the Prophetical Books

The primary locations in which prophets ministered are
found on the map below. Match the country with the location
by filling in the blanks according to the numbers.

1. Israel
2. Judah
3. Edom
4. Assyria
5. Babylonia
6. Jerusalem

Wonderful! You have now completed Section 1, The Story of the Old Testament. This is a major milestone in understanding the Bible. The remaining sections have been structured so that they are challenging, but not overwhelming. If you completed the Old Testament, you can complete the entire book, and you're almost halfway through!

Now, having just overviewed the Poetical and Prophetical Books of the Old Testament and having seen where they fit into the story of the Bible, we are ready to continue that story as we begin Section 2, The Story of the New Testament.

THE STORY OF THE
NEW TESTAMENT

CHAPTER 15

THE GEOGRAPHY AND STRUCTURE OF THE NEW TESTAMENT

Hiding among the giant Andes Mountains in the South American country of Peru lies a flat valley about forty miles long, isolated from the rest of the world. Roads and paths lie all over the floor of this vast valley, strewn like long, thin trees that have fallen at random. For years, archaeologists have guessed that they were a forgotten network of roads, left by an ancient civilization.

Perspective was changed radically, however, when someone chanced to study the valley from the air. From this vantage point, what seemed to be haphazard and random now became quite clear. They were not roads and paths at all, but a monumental desert mural picturing objects that were many miles in height. What the murals are, what they mean, how they were built, for whom they were built, and by whom they were built are all lost to the mist of time.

The monumental mural has a symbolic message for us all, however. Often, the whole picture of something cannot be seen if we are too close to it. We must get back, away from the details of what we are studying, to see the overview.

This is certainly true of the geography of the New Testament.

When in the Gospels you read of going from the cities of Jericho to Jerusalem to Cana, those are just words on a page with no meaning until you have overviewed the geography. You have no realization that someone has just walked seventy-five miles (the distance from Baltimore to Philadelphia) or that the trip also included walking up thirteen hundred feet in altitude and then down another one thousand.

In fact, gaining perspective on the geography of the New Testament is in itself a fascinating study. Israel is a tiny country compared to the United States. Draw a line fifty miles wide from New York to Boston, or stand Massachusetts on end, or shrink New Hampshire by 10 percent, and you have the approximate land area of Israel.

Yet it is a remarkably varied land. From low desert to high mountain, with lush valleys and rolling hills in between, the gamut is run in topography. Any body of water that you cannot swim across is a "sea," and every hill higher than your head is a "mountain." The Sea of Galilee is seven miles by fourteen miles, almost a mud puddle compared to the Great Lakes. The Dead Sea is ten miles by fifty miles, smaller than some virtually nameless reservoirs in the U.S. The "mighty" Jordan is little more than a strong-running creek compared to the truly mighty rivers of the world like the Amazon or Mississippi. Perhaps because it is such a small country, everything is exaggerated.

To be able to create mental pictures as you read through the events of the New Testament is to help the narrative come alive. So, as we begin looking at the New Testament, we begin with the geography.

THE GEOGRAPHY OF THE GOSPELS AND ACTS

The difference between the geography of the Gospels and the geography of the Book of Acts is significant enough to warrant separate treatment.

BODIES OF WATER IN THE GOSPELS

Once you have mastered the geography of the Old Testament, the geography of the New Testament is fairly simple. The bodies of water are among those of the Old Testament studied in Chapter 2. (To review, go to the map that follows and write in the name of the bodies of water by matching the numbers.)

1. Mediterranean Sea
2. Sea of Galilee
3. Jordan River
4. Dead Sea

BODIES OF WATER IN THE GOSPELS

(Fill in the appropriate blanks on the following map. The names and numbers should match those on the preceding list.)

PROVINCES AND CITIES IN THE GOSPELS

The primary geographical area in the Gospels is the same as that which was ruled by the nation of Israel in the Old Testament. However, the land is ruled by Rome and has been divided into sections, or provinces.

(As you read these descriptions, write the location on the map that follows by matching the letters.)

A. The Province of Galilee

Located between the Mediterranean Sea and the sea that shares its name, Galilee, is the province Jesus considered His home. Both Nazareth, His early home, and Capernaum, His later home, are in Galilee. Hence the phrase, "the man from Galilee."

B. The Province of Samaria

Located between the Mediterranean Sea and the Jordan River, Samaria is home to Samaritans. A people of mixed race—part Jewish, part Gentile—they live in constant animosity with the Jews.

C. The Province of Judea

Located between the Mediterranean Sea and the Dead Sea, Judea is approximately the same area as the southern tribe of Judah in the Old Testament. Encompassing the city of Jerusalem, it is home to most of the Jews in the New Testament.

D. The Province of Perea

A long, narrow province on the east bank of the Jordan River, Jesus spent some concentrated time there with His disciples toward the end of His ministry.

E. The City of Nazareth

Located in Galilee just west of the Sea of Galilee, it is the town where Mary and Joseph lived, and in which Jesus grew up.

F. The City of Capernaum

Located on the very top of the Sea of Galilee, it is the town Jesus called home during His ministry years.

G. The City of Jerusalem

Located in Judea, just off the top of the Dead Sea, it is the home of the temple, the holy city, and the center of activity for Jews.

H. The City of Bethlehem

The birthplace of Jesus, it is five miles southwest of Jerusalem.

PROVINCES AND CITIES IN THE GOSPELS
(Fill in the appropriate blanks below. The letters and names should match those from the list above.)

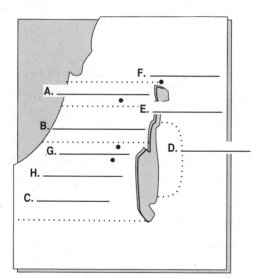

BODIES OF WATER IN ACTS

The bodies of water are the same as for the Gospels, only more of the Mediterranean is involved. Therefore, you already know them.

COUNTRIES AND CITIES IN ACTS

As we move out of the Gospels and into Acts, our geography expands from the Holy Land further into the Roman Empire.

(As you read the descriptions, write the location on the map that follows.)

1. Galatia

Located in modern-day Turkey, it was the destination of the apostle Paul's first missionary journey to take the gospel message to Gentiles.

2. Greece

Located in modern Greece, it was the destination for Paul's second missionary journey.

3. Asia

Located on the western coast of modern Turkey, it was the destination of Paul's third missionary journey.

4. Italy

Located in modern Italy, it was the country of Paul's final imprisonment and death.

5. The City of Jerusalem

Located in modern Jerusalem, it is the location of the beginning of the early Christian church.

6. The City of Damascus

Located in modern Damascus, in the modern country of Syria, it was Paul's destination when he was temporarily blinded by Jesus and converted to Christianity.

7. The City of Caesarea

Located on the Mediterranean coast just south of the Sea of Galilee, it was the site of Paul's trials in the Book of Acts.

8. The City of Antioch

On the Mediterranean coast north of Israel, near modern Turkey, it was the beginning point for all three of Paul's missionary journeys.

9. The City of Rome

Located in modern Rome, it was the political and cultural heart of the Roman Empire.

THE GEOGRAPHY OF ACTS

SELF-TEST

What you can learn tomorrow is built on what you learn today!

The Geography of the Gospels

(From the options listed, fill in the bodies of water, provinces, and cities on the map that follows.)

Numbers = bodies of water	Letters = cities and provinces
Dead Sea	Bethlehem
Jordan River	Capernaum
Mediterranean Sea	Galilee
Sea of Galilee	Jerusalem
	Judea
	Nazareth
	Perea
	Samaria

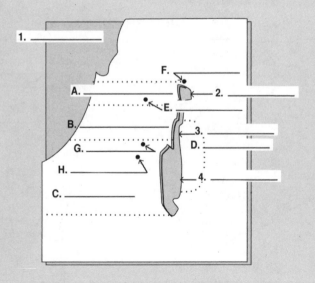

THE GEOGRAPHY OF ACTS

(From the options listed, fill in the countries and cities on the following map.)

Countries:

Asia

Galatia

Greece

Italy

Cities:

Antioch

Caesarea

Damascus

Jerusalem

Rome

THE HISTORICAL BOOKS OF THE NEW TESTAMENT

Having mastered the geography of the New Testament, we are now ready to continue the story of the Bible with the three main eras that remain. You will recall that the twenty-seven books of the New Testament can be divided into three different kinds of books: five Historical Books, thirteen Pauline Epistles, and nine General Epistles.

As we did with the Historical Books in the Old Testament, first we will overview the events of the Historical Books of the New Testament, the Gospels and Acts. Then, in the following chapters, we will expand the storyline.

THE THREE MAIN ERAS OF THE NEW TESTAMENT

1. Gospel

The life of Jesus of Nazareth as told in the *Gospels*.

2. Church

The formation of the Christian *church*.

3. Missions

The expansion of the church into the Roman empire through *missions*.

REVIEW

(Write the correct number in the blank from the options on the right.)

Subject:	Number:	Description:
Missions	_____	1. The life of Jesus of Nazareth, as told in the *Gospels*
Gospel	_____	2. The formation of the Christian *church*
Church	_____	3. The expansion of the church into the Roman Empire through *missions*

We are now able to add this new information to our storyline chart from the Old Testament.

STORY OF THE BIBLE

Era	Figure	Location	Storyline Summary
Creation	Adam	Eden	Adam is created by God, but he *sins* and *destroys* God's original *plan* for man.
Patriarch	Abraham	Canaan	Abraham is *chosen* by God to "father" a *people* to *represent* God to the world.
Exodus	Moses	Egypt	Through Moses God *delivers* the Hebrew people from *slavery* in Egypt and then gives them the *Law*.
Conquest	Joshua	Canaan	Joshua leads the *conquest* of the *Promised Land*.
Judges	Samson	Canaan	Samson and others were chosen as *judges* to *govern* the people for *four hundred* rebellious years.
Kingdom	David	Israel	David, the greatest king in the new *monarchy*, is followed by a succession of mostly *unrighteous* kings, and God eventually *judges* Israel for her sin, sending her into exile.
Exile	Daniel	Babylonia	Daniel gives *leadership* and encourages *faithfulness* among the *exiles* for the next seventy years.
Return	Ezra	Jerusalem	Ezra *leads* the people back from *exile* to rebuild *Jerusalem*.
Silence	Pharisees	Jerusalem	Pharisees and others *entomb* the *Israelites* in *legalism* for the next *four hundred* years.
Gospel	To be supplied later.	To be supplied later.	To be supplied later.
Church	To be supplied later.	To be supplied later.	To be supplied later.
Missions	To be supplied later.	To be supplied later.	To be supplied later.

THE THREE CENTRAL FIGURES OF THE NEW TESTAMENT

Era:	Figure:	Description:
Gospel	Jesus	The predicted *Messiah*
Church	Peter	The *leader* of the early Church
Missions	Paul	The first Christian *missionary*

REVIEW

(Fill in the blanks.)

Era:	Figure:	Description:
Gospel	Jesus	The predicted _____
Church	Peter	The _____ of the early church
Missions	Paul	The first Christian _____

We are now able to add the central figures from the New Testament to our storyline chart, which shows just the New Testament eras.

Era:	Figure:	Location:	Storyline Summary:
Gospel	Jesus	To be supplied later.	To be supplied later.
Church	Peter	To be supplied later.	To be supplied later.
Missions	Paul	To be supplied later.	To be supplied later.

Our final task is to identify the general or primary geographic location of the events of the three main eras of the New Testament. As an exercise in memory, write in each main era and central historical figure as you read the description of the geographical location.

THE THREE MAIN LOCATIONS OF THE NEW TESTAMENT

Era:	Figure:	Location:	Description:
G_____	J_____	Galilee, Samaria, and Judea	The general land area that was known as Canaan and Israel in the Old Testament is commonly known as the Roman provinces of Galilee, Samaria, and Judea.
C_____	P_____	Jerusalem	The ancient city of Jerusalem has been in the same location throughout most of biblical history after the Kingdom Era. It is the city that gave birth to the early church.
M_____	P_____	Roman Empire	As Paul spread the message of Christianity he took it to the heart of the Roman Empire: from Judea, north into what is modern Turkey, and west through modern Greece, to Italy.

REVIEW

(Write the correct number in the blank from the options on the right.)

Era:	Figure:	Number:	Location:
Gospel	Jesus	_____	Roman Empire
Church	Peter	_____	Galilee, Samaria, and Judea
Missions	Paul	_____	Jerusalem

We are now able to add the main locations from the New Testament to our storyline chart, as seen in the following.

Era:	Figure:	Location:	Storyline Summary:
Gospel	Jesus	Galilee, Samaria, and Judea	To be supplied later.
Church	Peter	Jerusalem	To be supplied later.
Missions	Paul	Roman Empire	To be supplied later.

ARC OF BIBLE HISTORY

(Fill in the names of the eras. To check your answers, see the appendix.)

1. C_____	5. J_____	9. S_____
2. P_____	6. K_____	10. G_____
3. E_____	7. E_____	11. C_____
4. C_____	8. R_____	12. M_____

From memory fill in the New Testament storyline chart.

Era:	Figure:	Location:	Storyline Summary:
_____	_____	_____	To be supplied later.
_____	_____	_____	To be supplied later.
_____	_____	_____	To be supplied later.

Congratulations! You have just taken a big step toward mastering an overview of the New Testament. From now on, we will get more specific, but you have the basic structure well in hand.

CHAPTER 16

THE GOSPEL ERA
(Matthew–John)

Dr. Richard Selzer is a brilliant surgeon who wrote a penetrating book entitled *Mortal Lessons: Notes on the Art of Surgery*. In it he writes:

> I stand by the bed where a young woman lies, her face postoperative, her mouth twisted in a palsy, clownish. A tiny twig of a facial nerve, the one to the muscles of her mouth, has been severed. She will be thus from now on. The surgeon had followed with religious fervor the curve of her flesh; I promise you that. Nevertheless, to remove the tumor in her cheek, I had to cut the little nerve.
>
> Her husband is in the room. He stands on the opposite side of the bed, and together, they seem to dwell in the evening lamplight. Isolated from me, private. Who are they, I ask myself, he and this wry-mouth I have made, who gaze at each other, and touch each other generously, greedily?
>
> The young woman speaks. "Will I always be like this?" she asks. "Yes," I say. "It is because the nerve was cut." She nods and is silent. But the young man smiles. "I like it," he says. "It's kind of cute."

All at once I know who he is. I understand, and I lower my gaze. One is not bold in an encounter with a god. Unmindful, he bends to kiss her crooked mouth, and I am so close I can see how he twists his own lips to accommodate hers, to show that their kiss still works. I remember that the gods appeared in ancient Greece as mortals, and I hold my breath and let the wonder in.

That is the spirit of Jesus. Man's link with God had been severed through sin. He twisted Himself to accommodate us, and gave us the kiss of eternal life. But to do so He gave His own life on our behalf. Jesus. At the same time, so tender and powerful. The most remarkable figure ever to have lived. And why not? He is God incarnate.

The birth of Jesus split history like a thunderbolt on a hot July evening. Everything before His birth we call B.C., before Christ. Everything after, we call A.D., *anno Domini*, in the year of our Lord. His story, predicted throughout the Old Testament, is told in the four Gospels: Matthew, Mark, Luke, and John. While the Gospels are biographical, they are actually thematic portraits of Christ's life that place very little emphasis on His early life and great emphasis on the last week of His life. The Gospels tend to follow the chronology of His life, but not slavishly. Not all the Gospels cover the same events in His life. When all four Gospels are put together and "harmonized," only about fifty days of Jesus' active ministry are covered.

I. REVIEW

Repetition is the key to mental ownership!
Fill in the blanks to bring the chart up-to-date with this era.
(To check your answers, see the appendix.)

STORY OF THE NEW TESTAMENT

Era	Figure	Location	Storyline Summary
_____	_____	_____	To be supplied in this chapter.

II. STORYLINE SUMMARY

Jesus comes in fulfillment of the Old Testament *prophecies* of a savior and offers *salvation* and the true kingdom of God. While some accept Him, most *reject* Him, and He is crucified, buried, and resurrected.

Era	Summary
Gospel	Jesus comes in fulfillment of the Old Testament _____ of a savior and offers _____ and the true kingdom of God. While some accept Him, most _____ Him, and He is crucified, buried, and resurrected.

III. EXPANSION

There are four main divisions in the Gospel Era:

1. Early Life
2. Early Ministry
3. Later Ministry
4. Death and Resurrection

1. Early Life: Childhood to baptism

Through a miraculous conception by the Holy Spirit, Jesus is born of the Virgin Mary in Bethlehem of Judea. After a brief excursion into Egypt to save Him from Herod's attempt on His life, Jesus travels with Mary and her husband Joseph to live in Nazareth. There He learns the trade of a carpenter and apparently lives a fairly normal life from *childhood to the time of His baptism*, when He is thirty years old. His cousin, John the Baptist, is ministering and baptizing people in the Jordan River near the Dead Sea. After Jesus is baptized by John, a remarkable event takes place. God the Father is heard speaking from heaven, saying, "This is My beloved Son, in whom I am well pleased," and the Holy Spirit, in the visible form of a dove, descends on Him. Then He is led by the Holy Spirit into the wilderness of Judea, where He is tempted by Satan for forty days. Satan makes every attempt to get Jesus to follow him rather than God. The evil one offers Jesus everything God the Father offers Him, but on a different timetable and with different requirements. Jesus remains sinless and validates His readiness to begin making Himself known as the Messiah.

2. Early Ministry: Initial acceptance

It is not until after Jesus' baptism and temptation that He begins His public ministry. His message has a twofold focus. First, He is the predicted Messiah or, as the word is translated in the New Testament, the Christ, and people should believe in Him. Second, He challenges people to live a life of genuine righteousness, not the external hypocrisy of the religious leaders. He validates His message by performing astounding miracles, and the signs of *initial acceptance* by the crowds are encouraging. Much of this early activity takes place around Jerusalem.

3. Later Ministry: Growing rejection

Jesus' initial popularity does not last. The religious leaders are profoundly jealous of Him and begin stirring up animosity toward Him. This *growing rejection* results in a progression in Jesus' ministry pattern. He begins to focus more attention on the mounting opposition from the religious leaders, warning them of the seriousness of their attitude. At the same time, He begins setting aside more and more time for the twelve disciples whom He has chosen, preparing them to carry on without Him. Also, He begins challenging the multitude to count the cost of following Him. Though Jesus travels quite a bit during this time, His home base is Capernaum, on the north bank of the Sea of Galilee.

4. Death and Resurrection: Final rejection

The Jews become more and more polarized about Jesus, either following Him enthusiastically or resenting Him deeply. In the volatile atmosphere of the festival time of the Passover when Jesus and many other Jews are in Jerusalem, the religious leaders are able to stir up enthusiasm for Jesus' crucifixion, the *final rejection*. They subject Him to a series of mock trials on false charges. Then Jesus is crucified on Friday, buried that night, and resurrected on Sunday.

SELF-TEST

*What you can learn tomorrow is built
on what you learn today!*

A. Four Main Divisions in the Gospel Era

(Write the correct number in the blank from the options on the right.)

Division:	Number:	Description:
Early Life	_____	1. Initial acceptance
Early Ministry	_____	2. Final rejection
Later Ministry	_____	3. Childhood to baptism
Death and Resurrection	_____	4. Growing rejection

B. Storyline Summary

(Fill in the blanks from memory.)

Era	Summary
Gospel	Jesus comes in fulfillment of the Old Testament _____ of a savior and offers _____ and the true kingdom of God. While some accept Him, most _____ Him, and He is crucified, buried, and resurrected.

C. Arc of Bible History

(Fill in the names of the eras. To check your answers, see the appendix.)

1. C_____	5. J_____	9. S_____
2. P_____	6. K_____	10. G_____
3. E_____	7. E_____	11.
4. C_____	8. R_____	12.

D. The Geography of the Gospel Era

(Draw an arrow from Bethlehem to Egypt to Nazareth to represent the geographical movement in Jesus' early life, and label

it 1. Draw an arrow from Nazareth to Jerusalem to represent His initial acceptance, and label it 2. Draw an arrow from Jerusalem to Capernaum to represent the growing rejection, and label it 3. Draw an arrow from Capernaum to Jerusalem to represent His final rejection, and label it 4.)

E. Story of the Bible

(Fill in the blanks. To check your answers, see the appendix.)

Era	Figure	Location	Storyline Summary
			Adam is created by God, but he _____ and _____ God's original _____ for man.
_____	_____	_____	

Era	Figure	Location	Storyline Summary
_____	_____	_____	Abraham is _____ by God to "father" a _____ to _____ God to the world.
_____	_____	_____	Through Moses God _____ the Hebrew people from _____ in Egypt and then gives them the _____.
_____	_____	_____	Joshua leads the _____ of the _____ _____.
_____	_____	_____	Samson and others were chosen as _____ to _____ the people for _____ _____ rebellious years.
_____	_____	_____	David, the greatest king in the new _____, is followed by a succession of mostly _____ kings, and God eventually _____ Israel for her sin, sending her into exile.

Era	Figure	Location	Storyline Summary
_____	_____	_____	Daniel gives _____ and encourages _____ among the _____ for the next seventy years.
_____	_____	_____	Ezra _____ the people back from _____ to rebuild _____.
_____	_____	_____	Pharisees and others _____ the _____ in _____ for the next _____ _____ years.
_____	_____	_____	Jesus comes in fulfillment of the Old Testament _____ of a savior and offers _____ and the true kingdom of God. While some accept Him, most _____ Him, and He is crucified, buried, and resurrected.

CHAPTER 17

THE CHURCH ERA
(Acts 1–12)

The story is told of a man who had been shipwrecked on a desert island for six years. For the entire 2,190 days, he never saw another human being. So, when a cruise ship happened to anchor nearby and send a party ashore, he was beside himself with joy. At last, he was with people again. All he wanted to do was talk, talk, talk.

The captain of the ship looked down the beach and saw three straw huts. He asked the castaway what the three huts were.

The castaway beamed. "Well, the first one is my church," he said with pride. "That's where I worship. And the middle one is my house. That's where I live."

The captain asked, "Well, what's that third hut over there?"

A dark cloud crossed the castaway's face momentarily as he replied, "Oh, that's the church I used to go to."

We smile, and yet it is only funny because it contains a seed of truth. Getting along with other Christians can be so hard that sometimes, if we had to get along with ourselves, we couldn't do it.

In spite of its obvious imperfections, however, the church is the instrument that God has chosen to carry the message of the gospel to the world. One wonders why a better system could not have been devised. Then one realizes that any system that has people in it is going to be imperfect.

Aleksandr Solzhenitsyn wrote in the *Gulag Archipelago* that it was in prison where he learned that the line separating good and evil passes not through states, not through classes, and not through political parties either, but right through every human heart.

However, God is at work in the lives of all willing people, changing and transforming them into something more than they were.

"Imagine yourself a living house," wrote C. S. Lewis. "God comes in to rebuild that house. At first, perhaps, you can understand what He is doing. He is getting the drains right and stopping the leaks in the roof and so on. But presently He starts knocking the house about in a way that hurts abominably and does not seem to make any sense. What on earth is He up to? The explanation is that He is building quite a different house from the one you thought of—throwing out a new wing here, putting on an extra floor there, running up towers, making courtyards. You thought you were going to be made into a decent little cottage; but He is building a palace."

And thus is the message of the church. The gospel is carried *to* imperfect people *by* imperfect people. Then those imperfect people are to band together to help one another grow to spiritual maturity.

I. REVIEW

Repetition is the key to mental ownership!
Fill in the blanks to bring the chart up-to-date with this era.
(To check your answers, see the appendix.)

STORY OF THE NEW TESTAMENT

Era	Figure	Location	Storyline Summary
_____	_____	_____	Jesus comes in fulfillment of the Old Testament _____ of a savior and offers _____ and the true kingdom of God. While some accept Him, most _____ Him, and He is crucified, buried, and resurrected.
_____	_____	_____	To be supplied in this chapter.

II. STORYLINE SUMMARY

Peter, shortly after the *ascension* of Jesus, is used by God to *establish* the *church*, God's next major plan for man.

Era	Summary
Church	Peter, shortly after the _____ of Jesus, is used by God to _____ the _____, God's next major plan for man.

III. EXPANSION

There are four major subjects in the Church Era:

1. Creation
2. Growth
3. Persecution
4. Transition

1. Creation: Birth of the church (Acts 1–5)

The birthplace of the church is Jerusalem. After His death, burial, and resurrection, Jesus instructs His disciples to wait in Jerusalem until they receive the power of the Holy Spirit and then to be witnesses to Him in Jerusalem (their city), Judea and Samaria (the surrounding provinces), and the remotest part of the earth (the rest of the world). Then Jesus ascends into heaven right before their eyes. Shortly after that, on the Jewish feast day of Pentecost, the Holy Spirit comes upon Jesus' disciples. While they are gathered in a house, a sound like a violent, rushing wind fills the place. Tongues of fire rest on each disciple, and they are filled with the Holy Spirit. They begin speaking in different foreign languages, with the result that many of the Jews from different parts of the world hear them speak in their own language. This and other notable miracles associated with the *birth of the church* take place as the number of converts to Christianity increases rapidly in Jerusalem.

2. Growth: Organization of the church (Acts 6)

As the number of converts increases, some measures are taken for the *organization of the church*, giving structure to their activities and responsibilities. Peter organizes a relief effort for needy Christians. Those who have possessions can sell them and give money to the apostles, who distribute it according to the needs. Then deacons are chosen to look after the material needs of the church while the apostles attend to the spiritual needs.

3. Persecution: The first Christian martyr (Acts 7)

Stephen, one of the early preachers, is arrested by the Jewish leaders for preaching about Jesus. When he does not recant his message but presses it further, the Jews stone him to death on the spot, making Stephen *the first Christian martyr*. This incident kicks off a round of persecution against new Christians that is so severe many of them flee Jerusalem for their very lives. As they do, they take the message of the gospel with them to the surrounding provinces of Judea and Samaria.

4. Transition: A missionary to the Gentiles (Acts 8–12)

A zealous Pharisee, Saul of Tarsus, looks after the cloaks of those who stone Stephen. Shortly afterward, he is journeying to Damascus to find and persecute other Christians when Jesus appears to him from heaven, and Saul is converted to Christianity. Jesus changes Saul's name to Paul, and he becomes known as the apostle Paul. Jesus expressly tells Paul that he will become *a missionary to the Gentiles.* Shortly after that, the apostle Peter has a vision in which the Lord tells him that the message of the gospel is to be taken to the Gentiles also. This marks a transition in the nature of the church because, up to this time, the message has been circulated exclusively to Jews.

SELF-TEST

*What you can learn tomorrow is built
on what you learn today!*

A. Four Major Subjects of the Church Era

(Write the correct number in the blank from the options on the right.)

Subject:	Number:	Description:
Creation	_____	1. Organization of the church
Growth	_____	2. A missionary to the Gentiles
Persecution	_____	3. Birth of the church
Transition	_____	4. The first Christian martyr

B. Storyline Summary

(Fill in the blanks from memory.)

Era	Summary
Church	Peter, shortly after the _____ of Jesus, is used by God to _____ the _____, God's next major plan for man.

C. Arc of Bible History

(Fill in the names of the eras. To check your answers, see the appendix.)

1. C_____	5. J_____	9. S_____
2. P_____	6. K_____	10. G_____
3. E_____	7. E_____	11. C_____
4. C_____	8. R_____	12.

D. The Geography of the Church Era

(Draw an arrow from Jerusalem into Samaria, and one from Jerusalem into Judea to represent the geographical movement of the Church Era.)

E. Story of the Bible

(Fill in the blanks. To check your answers, see the appendix.)

Era	Figure	Location	Storyline Summary
____	____	____	Adam is created by God, but he ____, ____ and ____ God's original ____ for man.
____	____	____	Abraham is ____ by God to "father" a ____ to ____ God to the world.
____	____	____	Through Moses God ____ the Hebrew people from ____ in Egypt and then gives them the ____.

Era	Figure	Location	Storyline Summary
_____	_____	_____	Joshua leads the _____ of the _____ _____.
_____	_____	_____	Samson and others were chosen as _____ to _____ the people for _____ _____ rebellious years.
_____	_____	_____	David, the greatest king in the new _____, is followed by a succession of mostly _____ kings, and God eventually _____ Israel for her sin, sending her into exile.
_____	_____	_____	Daniel gives _____ and encourages _____ among the _____ for the next seventy years.
_____	_____	_____	Ezra _____ the people back from _____ to rebuild _____.
_____	_____	_____	Pharisees and others _____ the _____ in _____ for the next _____ _____ years.

Era	Figure	Location	Storyline Summary
_____	_____	_____	Jesus comes in fulfillment of the Old Testament _____ of a savior and offers _____ and the true kingdom of God. While some accept Him, most _____ Him, and He is crucified, buried, and resurrected.
_____	_____	_____	Peter, shortly after the _____ of Jesus, is used by God to _____ the _____, God's next major plan for man.

CHAPTER 18

THE MISSIONS ERA

(Acts 13–28)

A missionary ministering in the South Sea Islands was teaching his people about Christmas. "The giving of gifts is a spontaneous act of celebration over an extremely joyous event. And that," he explained, "is why many people give gifts to others at Christmastime. It is an act of celebration over the joyous occasion of the birth of Christ."

Following this teaching, one of the young men wanted to give the missionary a gift for Christmas, but since it was a very poor island, presents were not readily available.

On Christmas morning, a knock came at the hut of the missionary. At the door, he found the young man, who then gave him an extremely rare and particularly beautiful seashell that was found only at the distant end of the island.

The missionary thanked the young man for giving him such a rare and beautiful gift from such a distance, to which the young man replied, "Long walk part of gift."

What a beautiful sentiment. "Long walk part of gift." Such was also true of the apostle Paul, who gave up a life of comfort and safety and took upon himself the arduous life of a missionary to take the message of the gospel to the Gentile people in the surrounding nations.

I. REVIEW

Repetition is the key to mental ownership!
Fill in the blanks to bring the chart up-to-date with this era.
(To check your answers, see the appendix.)

STORY OF THE NEW TESTAMENT

Era	Figure	Location	Storyline Summary
_____	_____	_____	Jesus comes in fulfillment of the Old Testament _____ of a savior and offers _____ and the true kingdom of God. While some accept Him, most _____ Him, and He is crucified, buried, and resurrected.
_____	_____	_____	Peter, shortly after the _____ of Jesus, is used by God to _____ the _____, God's next major plan for man.
_____	_____	_____	To be supplied in this chapter.

II. STORYLINE SUMMARY

Paul *expands* the church into the *Roman* Empire during the next two *decades*.

Era	Summary
Missions	Paul _____ the church into the _____ Empire during the next two _____.

III. EXPANSION

There are four major subjects in the Missions Era:

1. First Missionary Journey
2. Second Missionary Journey
3. Third Missionary Journey
4. Trials and Imprisonment

1. First Missionary Journey: Galatia for two years (Acts 13–14)

In Paul's first missionary journey, he and Barnabas are selected by the Holy Spirit to travel to Galatia and take the gospel to Gentiles living there. They depart from Antioch, the point of departure for all three missionary journeys, and are in *Galatia for two years*, experiencing encouraging results. After they return to Jerusalem, a council is held amid much controversy, which determines that the Gentiles do not have to become Jewish in order to become Christians.

2. Second Missionary Journey: Greece for three years (Acts 15–17)

Paul leaves from Antioch to visit the believers from his first journey. However, he receives a vision of a man in Macedonia (Greece) and changes his plans, going to Greece with the gospel message for the Gentiles there. He travels in *Greece for three years*.

3. Third Missionary Journey: Asia for four years (Acts 18–21)

Again, Paul leaves to encourage the believers from his first two trips and to spread the message of the gospel into Asia. He has great success but is also met with great opposition. In Ephesus, the whole city breaks out in riot over his visit. Though Paul is warned that he will be imprisoned upon his return to Jerusalem, he returns anyway, after being in *Asia for four years*, and is immediately arrested.

4. Trials and Imprisonment: Roman prison for two years (Acts 22–28)

Jewish leaders in Jerusalem have Paul arrested on false charges. Since his life is threatened there, even under guard, he is moved to Caesarea, the Roman capital in the area. There, he is tried under three men: Felix, Festus, and Agrippa. In order to thwart a miscarriage of justice in the process, Paul exercises his right as a Roman citizen to take his case before Caesar in Rome. He is taken to Rome, but, as far as we know, his case never comes to trial. After being in a *Roman prison for two years*, it is said he was beheaded (the established means of execution for a Roman citizen).

SELF-TEST

*What you can learn tomorrow is built
on what you learn today!*

A. Four Major Subjects of the Missions Era

*(Write the correct number in the blank from the options on
the right.)*

Subject:	Number:	Description:
First Missionary Journey	_____	1. Roman prison for two years
Second Missionary Journey	_____	2. Galatia for two years
Third Missionary Journey	_____	3. Asia for four years
Trials and Imprisonment	_____	4. Greece for three years

B. Storyline Summary

(Fill in the blanks from memory.)

Era	Summary
Missions	Paul _____ the church into the _____ Empire during the next two _____.

C. Arc of Bible History

(Fill in the names of the eras. To check your answers, see the appendix.)

1. C_____	5. J_____	9. S_____
2. P_____	6. K_____	10. G_____
3. E_____	7. E_____	11. C_____
4. C_____	8. R_____	12. M_____

D. The Geography of the Missions Era

(Draw an arrow from Antioch to Galatia and put a 1 next to it. Draw an arrow from Antioch to Greece and put a 2 next to it. Draw an arrow from Antioch to Asia and put a 3 next to it. This represents the geographical movement of Paul's missionary journeys. Now, draw

an arrow from Caesarea to Rome and put a 4 next to it to represent Paul's trials and imprisonment during the Missions Era.)

E. Story of the Bible

(Fill in the blanks. To check your answers, see the appendix.)

Era	Figure	Location	Storyline Summary
_____	_____	_____	Adam is created by God, but he _____ and _____ God's original _____ for man.
_____	_____	_____	Abraham is _____ by God to "father" a _____ to _____ God to the world.

Era	Figure	Location	Storyline Summary
_____	_____	_____	Through Moses God _____ the Hebrew people from _____ in Egypt and then gives them the _____.
_____	_____	_____	Joshua leads the _____ of the _____ _____.
_____	_____	_____	Samson and others were chosen as _____ to _____ the people for _____ _____ rebellious years.
_____	_____	_____	David, the greatest king in the new _____, is followed by a succession of mostly _____ kings, and God eventually _____ Israel for her sin, sending her into exile.
_____	_____	_____	Daniel gives _____ and encourages _____ among the _____ for the next seventy years.

Era	Figure	Location	Storyline Summary
_____	_____	_____	Ezra _____ the people back from _____ to rebuild _____.
_____	_____	_____	Pharisees and others _____ the _____ in _____ for the next _____ _____ years.
_____	_____	_____	Jesus comes in fulfillment of the Old Testament _____ of a savior and offers _____ and the true kingdom of God. While some accept Him, most _____ Him, and He is crucified, buried, and resurrected.
_____	_____	_____	Peter, shortly after the _____ of Jesus, is used by God to _____ the _____, God's next major plan for man.
_____	_____	_____	Paul _____ the church into the _____ Empire during the next two _____.

CHAPTER 19

THE EPISTLES

(Romans–Revelation)

In a *Reader's Digest* article entitled "Send Someone a Smile," a captivating story is told:

> One day shortly after my third child was born I received a note from another young mother, a friend of mine who lived just three blocks from me. We hadn't seen each other all winter.
>
> "Hi, friend," she wrote. "I think of you often. Someday we'll have time to spend together like in the old days. Keep plugging. I know you're a super mother. See you soon, I hope." It was signed: "Your friend on hold, Sue Ann."
>
> The few words lifted my spirits and added a soothing ointment of love to a hectic day. I remember thinking, *Thanks, Sue Ann. I needed that.*
>
> When I went out to mail a note, I noticed a neighbor checking his mailbox. Mr. Williams' head drooped and his pace seemed slower as he shuffled back to his house empty-handed. I hurried back into my own house because I could hear my baby crying, but I couldn't get Mr. Williams off my mind. It wasn't a check he was waiting for; he was quite well-to-do. He was probably looking for some love in his mailbox. While Meagan

drew a picture of a mailbox with a smile in it and Tami drew a rainbow, I wrote a little note. "We are your secret admirers," it began. We added a favorite story and a poem. "Expect to hear from us often," I wrote on the envelope.

The next day my children and I watched Mr. Williams take out his mail and open the envelope right in the driveway. Even at a distance, we could see he was smiling.

My mind began reeling when I thought of all the people who could use smiles in their mailboxes. What about the 15-year-old Down's-syndrome girl near my parents whose birthday was coming up? The people in the rest home near our house? The invalid woman in our old neighborhood? The endless people I didn't even know who still believed in courtesy and in doing a good job in stores and offices and restaurants? Even on busy days I could find the time to write at least one note.

Notes can be short, and should be anonymous. At first, I wanted credit for the notes. But now, writing them in secret adds a sense of adventure. It's more fun. I once overheard talk of the Phantom Note Lady. They were discussing me, but they didn't know, and I wasn't telling.

While letter-writing was the only means of long-distance communication for centuries, in today's world, it has become almost a thing of the past. Internet-based social media have eliminated pen and paper from most people's experience. Even so, the spirit of the Phantom Note Lady can live on. Whether it is the Internet, phone calls, or something as "ancient" as writing a letter, we can still be a positive force in other people's lives. We can still take whatever means of communication we choose, and find ways to instruct, encourage, and uplift others.

Paul and other writers of the Bible had concerns for people they loved, similar to those of the Phantom Note Lady. They wrote letters both to church congregations and to individuals to encourage them and to instruct them. In the providence of God, some of these letters were saved and eventually compiled in the "Epistles" section of the Bible. The Epistles were simply letters.

You will recall that thirteen of the Epistles were written by the apostle Paul while the remaining nine had a number of different authors. The chart in the review section below shows the distinction between the Pauline Epistles and the General Epistles.

I. REVIEW

Repetition is the key to mental ownership!

STRUCTURE OF THE NEW TESTAMENT

Historical	Pauline Epistles	General Epistles
Matthew	*To Churches:*	Hebrews
Mark	Romans	James
Luke	1 Corinthians	1 Peter
John	2 Corinthians	2 Peter
Acts	Galatians	1 John
	Ephesians	2 John
	Philippians	3 John
	Colossians	Jude
	1 Thessalonians	Revelation
	2 Thessalonians	
	To Individuals:	
	1 Timothy	
	2 Timothy	
	Titus	
	Philemon	

Our history study is now completed. From Matthew through Acts, we stretched out a timeline for the history of the New Testament. Some of the Epistles were written during this timeline, and some of them were written after the timeline ends at the close of the Book of Acts. This makes it a little confusing, and somewhat frustrating, because we wish that the Historical Books told all the history during the time the Epistles were being written. They don't, however, and we are left to piece together what history we can from references in the Epistles.

The following chart shows when the Epistles were written in relationship to the time recorded in the Historical Books. The numbers are the years after Christ's birth. The Gospels cover the time from Christ's birth to His death at approximately age thirty. Acts starts almost immediately after, and records events until about A.D. 60. We see then that Galatians was written during the time of the Book of Acts, A.D. 48 specifically. First and Second Thessalonians were written about A.D. 50. Books in the second section are Pauline Epistles, and the books in the last section are the General Epistles.

TIMELINE OF THE NEW TESTAMENT

Historical Books

Gospel-Acts						Post-Acts		
A.D. **0**	A.D. **30**	A.D. **48**	A.D. **50**	A.D. **53**	A.D. **60**	A.D. **62**	A.D. **67**	A.D. **95**

Pauline Epistles

| | | Galatians | 1 Thessalonians 2 Thessalonians | 1 Corinthians 2 Corinthians Romans | Ephesians Colossians Philemon Philippians | 1 Timothy Titus | 2 Timothy | |

General Epistles

| | | James | | | | 1 Peter 2 Peter | Hebrews Jude | 1 John 2 John 3 John Revelation |

II. OVERVIEW SUMMARY:

The Epistles are letters to churches and to individuals to *encourage* them and *instruct* them in the Christian faith.

REVIEW

The Epistles are letters to churches and to individuals to _____ them and _____ them in the Christian faith.

III. EXPANSION

There are four main topics to be dealt with in studying the Epistles:

1. The Nature of the Epistles
2. Pauline Epistles to Churches
3. Pauline Epistles to Individuals
4. General Epistles

1. The Nature of the Epistles: Doctrine, then duty

Epistles are letters written to churches, individuals, or, in some cases, to the Christian public at large. They deal with specific problems and issues of the day but do so in a way that the information is universal and timeless. The typical pattern is to write a section of doctrinal truth and follow up with the practical implications of that truth. *Doctrine, then duty*. Principle, then practice.

2. Pauline Epistles to Churches: Letters to local churches

Thirteen of the twenty-two Epistles of the New Testament are written by the apostle Paul. Nine of these are *letters to local churches* and are named according to which church they are written.

(As you read the description of the book, notice the words in italics. Immediately following the description of each book, the description is repeated with a blank space in place of the italicized word. Fill in the blank space.)

Romans: heavily doctrinal, with the most complete doctrine of *salvation* by grace through faith in all the Bible.

Romans: heavily doctrinal, with the most complete doctrine of _____ by grace through faith in all the Bible.

1 and 2 Corinthians: heavily practical, dealing with a series of specific *problems* in the Corinthian church.

1 and 2 Corinthians: heavily practical, dealing with a series of specific _____ in the Corinthian church.

Galatians: written to some of Paul's first converts, refuting *legalism*.

Galatians: written to some of Paul's first converts, refuting

_____.

Ephesians: deals with the believer's *position* in Christ and its practical implications.

Ephesians: deals with the believer's _____ in Christ and its practical implications.

Philippians: a warm letter of *joy* despite trials.

Philippians: a warm letter of _____ despite trials.

Colossians: the *preeminence* of Christ is its major theme.

Colossians: the _____ of Christ is its major theme.

1 and 2 Thessalonians: very personal letters dealing with specific issues in the Thessalonian church, including *prophecy* and *practical* living.

1 and 2 Thessalonians: very personal letters dealing with specific issues in the Thessalonian church, including _____ and _____ living.

3. Pauline Epistles to Individuals: Letters to individuals and pastors.

Four of Paul's letters are written *to individuals and pastors* and are named according to whom they were written.

1 and 2 Timothy: two letters to a young pastor in Ephesus. The first letter *counsels* him on local church issues, and the second *encourages* him to remain strong in the faith in the midst of trials.

1 and 2 Timothy: two letters to a young pastor in Ephesus. The first letter _____ him on local church issues, and the second _____ him to remain strong in the faith in the midst of trials.

Titus: written to the pastor of the church on the island of Crete, it deals largely with local church issues, including the *qualifications* for church leaders.

Titus: written to the pastor of the church on the island of Crete, it deals largely with local church issues, including the _____ for church leaders.

Philemon: written to a slave owner, it urges lenient treatment of a runaway *slave* who has become a Christian and is returning to his Christian master.

Philemon: written to a slave owner, it urges lenient treatment of a runaway _____ who has become a Christian and is returning to his Christian master.

4. General Epistles: Letters to the Christian public

Written by various authors, the nine General Epistles are *letters to the Christian public* at large (with the exception of 2 and 3 John). They are usually named according to their authorship.

Hebrews: heavily *doctrinal*, this book draws largely on Old
   Testament truth in teaching New Testament truth to a
   Jewish audience.
Hebrews: heavily _____ , this book draws largely on
   Old Testament truth in teaching New Testament truth to a
   Jewish audience.
James: an incisive and practical treatment of the proper out-
   working of Christian *faith* in everyday life.
James: an incisive and practical treatment of the proper outworking of Christian _____ in everyday life.
1 and 2 Peter: written to believers scattered throughout Asia and
   Galatia, it deals with the proper response to *suffering* and
   opposition.
1 and 2 Peter: written to believers scattered throughout Asia and
   Galatia, it deals with the proper response to _____
   and opposition.
1, 2, and 3 John: letters from the apostle John dealing with the
   love of God and its outworking in Christians' lives.
1, 2, and 3 John: letters from the apostle John dealing with the
   _____ of God and its outworking in Christians' lives.
Jude: a brief but powerful book *warning* against ungodly living.
Jude: a brief but powerful book _____ against ungodly living.
Revelation: a giant of a book, heavily prophetical, dealing with
   the nature and chronology of the *end times*.
Revelation: a giant of a book, heavily prophetical, dealing with
   the nature and chronology of the _____ _____ .

REVIEW

(Match the correct book with its description.)

I. PAULINE EPISTLES TO CHURCHES:

a. Colossians

_____ Heavily doctrinal, this book contains the most complete doctrine of *salvation* by grace through faith in all the Bible.

b. Ephesians

_____ Heavily practical, this letter deals with a series of specific *problems* in the Corinthian church.

c. Galatians

_____ Written to some of Paul's first converts, this epistle refutes *legalism*.

d. 1, 2 Corinthians

_____ This letter deals with the believer's *position* in Christ and the practical implications.

e. Romans

_____ This is a warm letter of *joy* despite trials

f. 1, 2 Thessalonians

_____ The *preeminence* of Christ is its major theme

g. Philippians

_____ These are very personal letters dealing with specific issues in the Thessalonian church, including *prophecy* and *practical* living.

2. PAULINE EPISTLES TO INDIVIDUALS:

a. Philemon

_____ These are two letters to a young pastor in Ephesus. The first letter *counsels* him on local church issues, and the second *encourages* him to remain strong in the faith in the midst of trials.

b. 1, 2 Timothy   _____ Written to the pastor of the church on the island of Crete, it deals largely with local church issues, including the *qualifications* for church leaders.

c. Titus   _____ Written to a slave owner, it urges lenient treatment of a runaway *slave* who has become a Christian and is returning to his Christian master.

3. GENERAL EPISTLES:

a. Revelation   _____ Heavily *doctrinal,* this book draws largely on Old Testament truth in teaching New Testament truth to a Jewish audience.

b. 1, 2, 3 John   _____ This book is an incisive and practical treatment of the proper outworking of Christian *faith* in everyday life.

c. Hebrews   _____ Written to believers scattered throughout Asia and Galatia, it deals with the proper response to *suffering* and opposition.

d. 1, 2 Peter   _____ These are letters from the apostle John dealing with the *love* of God and its outworking in Christians' lives.

e. James   _____ This is a brief but powerful book *warning* against ungodly living.

f. Jude   _____ A giant of a book, it's heavily prophetical, dealing with the nature and chronology of the *end times.*

SELF-TEST

*What you can learn tomorrow is built
on what you learn today!*

Four Main Distinctions to Consider in Studying the Epistles

*(Write the correct number in the blank from the options on
the right.)*

Distinction:	Number:	Description:
The Nature of the Epistles	_____	1. Letters to individuals and pastors
Pauline Epistles to Churches	_____	2. Letters to local churches
Pauline Epistles to Individuals	_____	3. Letters to the Christian public
General Epistles	_____	4. Doctrine, then duty

Congratulations! You have just completed a basic overview of the story of the Bible, all sixty-six books! From the Historical Books of the Old and New Testaments, you have learned: all the main eras, all the central figures, and the main locations of geography, all tied together with a Storyline Summary of the chronological Story of the Bible. You have also learned where the other books—the Poetical and Prophetical books of the Old Testament and the Epistles of the New Testament—fit into that chronological Story of the Bible.

You are now ready for the next section, which will give you a general overview of the Ten Great Doctrines of the Bible.

TEN GREAT DOCTRINES OF
THE BIBLE

CHAPTER 20

OVERVIEW OF BIBLE DOCTRINE

The Bible is more than history. If you would know the Bible, you must go beyond the historical study of people, places, and events, and learn about its teachings; and taking that plunge is not easy. One day, many years ago, Harry Cohen, then the head of Columbia Studios in Hollywood, was in a conversation with his brother Jack, who suggested to Harry that they produce a biblical epic. "What do you know about the Bible?" cried Harry. "I'll lay you fifty dollars you don't even know the Lord's Prayer." After a moment's thought, Jack began, "Now I lay me down to sleep . . ." and recited the well-known child's bedtime prayer. Harry pulled fifty dollars out of his pocket. "Well, I'll be!" he said as he handed the money to his brother. "I didn't think you knew it."

Well, most of us may know the Bible better than Harry did, but most of us would also say that we'd like to know the Bible better than we do.

When you add all the authors and all the books of the Bible together, and then boil them down to their irreducible minimum, what does the Bible teach? What subjects does it cover, and what does it say about each subject? When you add Moses, David, Jesus, and Paul together, what did they teach about God, Christ, angels, the future? As you begin to answer these questions, you are entering the world of "Bible doctrine."

It is difficult to get two people to agree on all points of doctrine. There is an old Irish prayer that says:

O Lord, turn the hearts of our enemies.

And if You can't turn their hearts,

Then turn their ankles,

So we can know them by their limp.

There are many people limping, in the eyes of others, over certain doctrinal distinctions. However, there is a basic body of doctrine that nearly all Christians have historically agreed upon. We will turn our focus to that body in this section.

Depending on how finely you split the hairs, different Bible scholars have come up with different numbers of minimum subjects. For the purpose of our study, we will use ten. The ten great doctrines of the Bible are listed below. Every teaching of the Bible is in a subdivision of one of these doctrines, or subjects.

TEN GREAT DOCTRINES OF THE BIBLE

1. The Bible
2. God
3. Christ
4. Holy Spirit
5. Angels
6. Man
7. Sin
8. Salvation
9. Church
10. Future Things

As you read the following descriptions, note that, to help you remember the doctrine, a symbol has been assigned to each one.

1. **The Bible**, symbolized by a book, deals with the origin and nature of the Scriptures. How did we get them? Are they reliable? Are they the Word of God?

2. **God**, symbolized by the crown of a king, deals with the first person of the Trinity. Who is He? What is He like? And what is our relationship to Him?

3. **Christ**, symbolized by the Lamb of God, deals with Jesus of Nazareth, the second person of the Trinity. Was He a man? Was He God? Is He alive today? Is He coming to earth again?

4. **Holy Spirit**, the third person of the Trinity, is symbolized by a dove. Is He a personal being or the religious equivalent of "school spirit"?

5. **Angels**, symbolized by angel wings, investigates the reality of the spirit world. What about guardian angels? What about demon possession and Satan worship?

6. **Man**, symbolized by an individual, investigates the origin, nature, and destiny of humanity. Were humans created, or did we evolve? Do we have souls? Does the soul live forever?

7. **Sin**, symbolized by a bite taken out of an apple, deals with the nature of mankind's offense against God.

8. **Salvation**, symbolized by a life preserver, deals with the afterlife, heaven, hell, and whether or not it is safe to die.

9. **Church**, a body of organized believers, is symbolized by a church building and investigates what the church is in the eyes of God and what its responsibilities are.

10. **Future Things**, symbolized by an hourglass, looks into biblical prophecy and what the Bible says about future events, the end of the world, and eternity.

REVIEW

(Write the correct number in the blank from the options on the right.)

Doctrine:	Number:	Description:
Salvation	_____	1. The origin and nature of the Scriptures
Christ	_____	2. The first person of the Trinity
Future Things	_____	3. The second person of the Trinity
God	_____	4. The third person of the Trinity
The Bible	_____	5. The spirit world
Sin	_____	6. Organized believers
Angels	_____	7. The origin, nature, and destiny of humanity
Man	_____	8. The afterlife, heaven, hell
Church	_____	9. Man's offense against God
Holy Spirit	_____	10. Biblical prophecy

To further help you remember these ten great doctrines, notice that the order suggests a logical progression. As you read the descriptions below, write the name of the doctrine next to the corresponding number and symbol on the following chart. By following the numbers and arrows on the chart, you can see the logical progression from one doctrine to the next. This will help you remember the ten great doctrines.

1. The Bible

The Bible is the foundation for what we learn about the other nine subjects, so it is first.

2. God

God is the first member of the Trinity.

3. Christ

Christ is the second member of the Trinity.

4. Holy Spirit

The *Holy Spirit* is the third member of the Trinity.

5. Angels

Angels are lower than God, but higher than man, so are placed between God and man.

6. Man

Man is made in the image of God.

7. Sin

Sin is man's shortcomings in God's eyes.

8. Salvation

Salvation is offered by God to man through faith.

9. Church

The *Church* proclaims the message of salvation.

10. Future Things

Future Things are a prophetic record of things that will happen in the future.

2. _____

4. _____

3. _____

5. _____

1. _____

10. _____

6. _____

9. _____

7. _____

8. _____

SELF-TEST

What you can learn tomorrow is built
on what you learn today!

Ten Great Doctrines of the Bible

As a final review, fill in the names of the ten doctrines from memory. See pages 184–185 to check your answers.

1. _____   6. _____

2. _____   7. _____

3. _____   8. _____

4. _____   9. _____

5. _____   10. _____

Now, having established a base of the ten great doctrines of the Bible, we are ready to overview each doctrine separately in the chapters that follow.

CHAPTER 21

THE DOCTRINE OF THE BIBLE

"It is not the things I don't understand about the Bible that bother me. It's the things I do understand."

—Mark Twain

In the Star Wars film *A New Hope*, the future of the galaxy is riding on the success of a single mission to destroy the Death Star. The empire's new battle station is powerful enough to destroy whole planets, but it's not without a weakness. The rebellion, loyal to the ideas of the old republic, have learned that a perfect shot into an exhaust port from a skilled fighter pilot will start a chain reaction that should result in the Death Star's destruction.

After a fierce battle, only one attack ship remains, and it's piloted by the movie's hero, Luke Skywalker. But as Luke makes his final approach toward the Death Star's exhaust port, his departed mentor, Obi-Wan Kenobi, speaks to him from beyond the grave and tells him to turn off his computer and trust "the Force." So, Luke disables his targeting computer, places all his trust in the Force, and makes the near-impossible shot. The Death Star explodes, and peace is restored to the galaxy (until *The Empire Strikes Back*, of course).

A generation has grown up thinking of this memorable scene as a way of life. There may be no such thing as the Force, but the message remains: *Listen to your heart.* At first, that sounds like great advice, but the problem is, the heart is not always right. As the Bible tells us, "A wise man's heart *directs him* toward the right, but the foolish man's heart *directs him* toward the left." (Ecclesiastes 10:2, emphasis added).

Jesus said, "You will know the truth, and the truth will make you free" (John 8:32). To the degree that we do not know the truth, we are vulnerable to ignorance and deception. That is why God has given us His Word—so we might have a final authority on all matters, a source of truth more reliable than every competing voice, even our own hearts.

The Bible gives us ultimate reality, telling us where we came from, where we are now, and where we are going. It is up to us to decide whether we accept the truth it offers.

The Bible does not defend itself. It was written to people who accepted its message and therefore spends little time convincing its readers of its authenticity. The fundamental assertion that the Bible makes concerning itself is that, in spite of the human collaboration involved in its writing, the Bible is a revelation of God to man, was written without error, and can be trusted to reveal truth to us regarding God, man, life, and death.

As we begin our study of the doctrine of the Bible, we will adopt a pattern that will be followed throughout this section:

I. You will be asked to review the previous chapter.

II. You will then be given an overview of the doctrine, focusing on three things:
   A. The four major subdivisions of each doctrine, assigning a visual symbol to each.
   B. A brief definition for each subdivision, followed by an expansion.
   C. A central Scripture passage for each subdivision.

III. Three of the doctrines will require some additional attention, which will be dealt with under the heading "Further Considerations."

I. REVIEW

Repetition is the key to mental ownership!
Fill in the blanks. For answers, see page 184.

Ten Great Doctrines of the Bible

1. B_____
2. G_____
3. C_____
4. H_____ S_____
5. A_____
6. M_____
7. S_____
8. S_____
9. C_____
10. F_____ T_____

II. THE FOUR MAJOR SUBDIVISIONS OF THE DOCTRINE OF THE BIBLE

The four major subdivisions of the doctrine of the Bible are:

1. Revelation

2. Inspiration

3. Illumination

4. Interpretation

(As you read the definitions of the doctrine subdivisions, notice the words in italics. Immediately following the definitions, they are repeated with blank spaces in place of the italicized words. Fill in the blank spaces.)

Symbol:	Subdivision:	Definition:

1. Revelation: The Bible was *revealed* to man by God.

   Revelation: The Bible was _____ to man by God.

God made known to man that which He wanted man to know. Some of the information related to present-day instruction on how to live and be rightly related to God and one's fellow man. Other information related to prophetic statements about the future. Hebrews 3:7 says, "Therefore, just as the Holy Spirit says. . . ." Then it quotes a passage from Psalms, which was written by King David, indicating that the human writing was *revealed* by God.

Central Passage:

Therefore, just as the Holy Spirit says, "Today if you hear His voice. . . ." (Hebrews 3:7)

Symbol:	Subdivision:	Definition:

2. Inspiration: God saw to it that when men wrote down His revelation, they did so *without error.*

   Inspiration: God saw to it that when men wrote down His revelation, they did so _____ _____.

Not all of God's revelation to man was recorded in the Bible. Some of it was very personal, between God and one individual. But for that part of God's revelation to man that was written down, God became involved in the recording process to such a degree that, while He did not dictate or override each individual author's personality, He saw to it that what the writer did record was what He wanted recorded and that it was *without error.*

Central Passage:

Men moved by the Holy Spirit spoke from God. (2 Peter 1:21)

Symbol:	Subdivision:	Definition:

3. Illumination: The Holy Spirit must enable people to *understand* and *embrace* the truth of Scripture.

Illumination: The Holy Spirit must enable people to
_____ and _____ the truth
of Scripture.

Man's natural ability to grasp and embrace the information in the Bible is limited. Much of it is spiritual information that man does not readily understand or accept. To overcome this fact, the Holy Spirit gradually illumines the receptive mind to *understand* and *embrace* more and more of the Bible, as the Christian matures in his or her spiritual walk.

Central Passage:

Now we have received, not the spirit of the world, but the Spirit who is from God, that we may know the things freely given to us by God. (1 Corinthians 2:12)

Symbol:	Subdivision:	Definition:

4. Interpretation: We must be diligent *students* of Scripture to understand its deeper teachings.

Interpretation: We must be diligent _____ of Scripture to understand its deeper teachings.

Gaining a deeper grasp of the Bible is a two-way street. It is true that it will not happen unless the Holy Spirit illumines the mind of the Christian, but neither will it happen unless the Christian is diligent in pursuing biblical knowledge. The more the Christian reads and studies the Bible, the more the Holy Spirit will illumine his or her mind, which encourages the *student* to read and study further.

Central Passage:

Be diligent to present yourself approved to God as a workman who does not need to be ashamed, accurately handling the word of truth. (2 Timothy 2:15)

THE DOCTRINE OF THE BIBLE

(Write the titles of the four subdivisions on the lines below.)

Symbol:	Subdivision:	Definition:

1. R_____ The Bible was *revealed* to man by God.

Central Passage: Hebrews 3:7

Symbol:	Subdivision:	Definition:

2. I_____ God saw to it that when men wrote down His revelation, they did so *without error.*

Central Passage: 2 Peter 1:21

Symbol:	Subdivision:	Definition:

3. I_____ The Holy Spirit must enable people to *understand* and *embrace* the truth of Scripture.

Central Passage: 1 Corinthians 2:12

Symbol:	Subdivision:	Definition:

4. I_____ We must be diligent *students* of Scripture to understand its deeper teachings.

Central Passage: 2 Timothy 2:15

THE DOCTRINE OF THE BIBLE

(Name the four subdivisions of the doctrine of the Bible, and fill in the key words in the definitions.)

Symbol:	Subdivision:	Definition:

1. R_____ The Bible was _____ to man by God.

Central Passage: Hebrews 3:7

Symbol:	Subdivision:	Definition:

2. I_____   God saw to it that when men wrote down His revelation, they did so _____ _____.

Central Passage: 2 Peter 1:21

Symbol:	Subdivision:	Definition:

3. I_____   The Holy Spirit must enable people to _____ and _____ the truth of Scripture.

Central Passage: 1 Corinthians 2:12

Symbol:	Subdivision:	Definition:

4. I_____   We must be diligent _____ of Scripture to understand its deeper teachings.

Central Passage: 2 Timothy 2:15

SELF-TEST

*What you can learn tomorrow is built
on what you learn today!*

THE DOCTRINE OF THE BIBLE

(Fill in the blanks.)

1. R_____   The Bible was _____ to man by God.

2. I_____   God saw to it that when men wrote down His revelation, they did so _____ _____.

3. I_____   The Holy Spirit must enable people to
                  _____ and _____ the
                  truth of Scripture.
4. I_____   We must be diligent _____ of
                  Scripture to understand its deeper teachings.

TEN GREAT DOCTRINES OF THE BIBLE
(From memory, fill in the name of doctrine number one.
See the appendix for the answer.)

1. _____

CHAPTER 22

THE DOCTRINE OF GOD

God cannot be proved or disproved. The existence of God lies outside the reach of scientific confirmation. Therefore, we cannot go to the laboratory and look for proof of God. Rather, we must go to the courtroom and look for evidence.

In the courtroom, evidence can be amassed to demonstrate the probability of His existence. Of course, if someone doesn't want to believe, unbelief never has enough evidence. However, if one has an open mind and is willing to go wherever the evidence leads, there is sufficient evidence to make belief in God a confident conclusion.

C. S. Lewis, the brilliant Christian scholar who taught at both Cambridge and Oxford, readily admitted his reluctance to accept the existence of God. Yet he kept an open mind in the investigation of the evidence and found himself being convinced in spite of himself. He wrote in his book *Surprised by Joy* that he was teaching at Magdalen College at the University of Oxford when he had an encounter with an atheist intellectual:

> Early in 1926 the hardest boiled of all the atheists I ever knew sat in my room on the other side of the fire and remarked that the evidence for the historicity of the Gospels was really surprisingly good. "Rum thing," he went on. "Rum thing. It almost looks as if it had really happened once." To understand the shattering

impact of it, you would need to know the man (who has certainly never since shown any interest in Christianity). If he, the cynic of cynics, the toughest of the toughs, were not—as I would still have put it—"safe," where could I turn? Was there then no escape?

You must picture me alone in that room at Magdalen, night after night, feeling, whenever my mind lifted even for a second from my work, the steady, unrelenting hand of Him whom I so earnestly desired not to meet. That which I greatly feared had at last come upon me. In the Trinity Term of 1929 I gave in, and admitted that God was God, and knelt and prayed: perhaps, that night, the most dejected and reluctant convert in all England. I did not then see what is now the most shining and obvious thing: the Divine humility which will accept a convert even on such terms. The Prodigal Son at least walked home on his own feet. But who can duly adore the Love which will open the high gates to a prodigal who is brought in kicking, struggling, resentful, and darting his eyes in every direction for a chance of escape?

If you look for God in the laboratory, you will not find Him. If you look for Him in the courtroom, the evidence is overwhelming.

I. REVIEW

Repetition is the key to mental ownership!
Fill in the blanks.

THE DOCTRINE OF THE BIBLE

1. R_____
2. I_____
3. I_____
4. I_____

II. THE FOUR MAJOR SUBDIVISIONS OF THE DOCTRINE OF GOD

The four major subdivisions of the doctrine of God are:

 1. Existence

 2. Attributes

 3. Sovereignty

 4. Trinity

(As you read the definitions of the doctrine subdivisions, notice the words in italics. Immediately following the definitions, they are repeated with blank spaces in place of the italicized words. Fill in the blank spaces.)

Symbol:	Subdivision:	Definition:
	1. Existence:	God *exists*.
	Existence:	God _____.

In a scientific culture, some are reluctant to believe in a being they cannot see, hear, smell, taste, or touch. However, God cannot be dealt with in the laboratory. He must be dealt with in the courtroom. It is impossible to generate *proof* of His existence, so we must look for *evidence* of His existence. While the Bible simply assumes that God *exists*, it also provides excellent evidence, so that believing in His existence is an intellectually reasonable thing to do.

Central Passage:

For since the creation of the world His invisible attributes, His eternal power and divine nature, have been clearly seen, being understood through what has been made. (Romans 1:20)

Symbol:	Subdivision:	Definition:

2. Attributes: The fundamental *characteristics* of God.

Attributes: The fundamental _____ of God.

God is a personal being, and as such has individual *characteristics* that distinguish Him from all other beings. These characteristics are called "attributes." Some of His attributes are shared by mankind, since God created man after His personal image. These are called "personal" attributes. He has other characteristics, however, which go beyond man and are true of Him alone. These are the attributes that define "deity" and are called "divine" attributes. We will look more closely at them later.

Central Passage:

Selected passages to be seen later

Symbol:	Subdivision:	Definition:

3. Sovereignty: God can do whatever He *wills*.

Sovereignty: God can do whatever He _____.

God is all-powerful and has the ability to do whatever He wills. This sovereignty is only exercised in harmony with His goodness, righteousness, and other attributes, and it extends to the entirety of creation for all time. In His sovereignty, He has determined everything that has happened and will happen, and yet has done so in such a way that man has true "volition," or choice. This is one of the mysteries, or "unexplainable" things, of Scripture.

Central Passage:

For I know that the LORD is great, and that our Lord is above all gods. Whatever the LORD pleases, He does, in heaven and in earth, in the seas and in all deeps. (Psalm 135:5, 6)

Symbol:	Subdivision:	Definition:
	4. Trinity:	God is *three* persons, yet *one*.
	Trinity:	God is _____ persons, yet _____.

Another mystery of the Scripture is the Trinity. The Bible says distinctly that there is only one true God (Deuteronomy 6:4). But it also says with equal clarity that there was a man, Jesus Christ, who claimed equality with God the Father, and there is someone called the Holy Spirit who is also equal with God the Father. How do you put that together? Historically, the concept has been termed the "Trinity." There is *one* God who exists in *three* persons. While it is impossible to give an illustration of the Trinity, the evidence remains and has been embraced as a fundamental teaching of Christianity from the beginning.

Central Passage:

Hear, O Israel! The Lord is our God, the Lord is one! (Deuteronomy 6:4)

The grace of the Lord Jesus Christ, and the love of God, and the fellowship of the Holy Spirit, be with you all. (2 Corinthians 13:14)

THE DOCTRINE OF GOD

(Write the titles of the four subdivisions on the lines below.)

Symbol:	Subdivision:	Definition:
	1. E_____	God *exists*.
	Central Passage: Romans 1:20	

Symbol:	Subdivision:	Definition:
	2. A_____	The fundamental *characteristics* of God.
	Central Passage: Selected passages. (See pages 204–205.)	

Symbol: **Subdivision:**   **Definition:**

3. S_____   God can do whatever He *wills*.
Central Passage: Psalm 135:5, 6

Symbol: **Subdivision:**   **Definition:**

4. T_____   God is *three* persons, yet *one*.
Central Passage: Deuteronomy 6:4; 2 Corinthians 13:14

THE DOCTRINE OF GOD

(Name the four subdivisions of the doctrine of God, and fill in the key words in the definitions.)

Symbol: **Subdivision:**   **Definition:**

1. _____   God _____.
Central Passage: Romans 1:20

Symbol: **Subdivision:**   **Definition:**

2. _____   The fundamental _____
of God.
Central Passage: Selected passages.
(See pages 204–205.)

Symbol: **Subdivision:**   **Definition:**

3. _____   God can do whatever He _____.
Central Passage: Psalm 135:5, 6

Symbol: **Subdivision:**   **Definition:**

4. _____   God is _____ persons, yet
_____.
Central Passage: Deuteronomy 6:4; 2 Corinthians 13:14

SELF-TEST

(Fill in the blanks.)

1. E_____   God _____.
2. A_____   The fundamental _____
   of God.
3. S_____   God can do whatever He
   _____.
4. T_____   God is _____ persons,
   yet _____.

III. FURTHER CONSIDERATION OF THE ATTRIBUTES OF GOD

The attributes of God require further consideration. While God has many attributes, or characteristics, we will focus on six primary attributes. Three are divine attributes, and three are personal attributes.

A. Divine Attributes

1. Omnipotence: God is *all-powerful.*
   Central Passage:
   I know that You can do all things, and that no purpose of Yours can be thwarted. (Job 42:2)

2. Omnipresence: God is *present* everywhere simultaneously.
   Central Passage:
   If I ascend to heaven, You are there; if I make my bed in Sheol, behold, Your are there. (Psalm 139:8)

3. Omniscience: God *knows* all things.

   Central Passage:

   Even before there is a word on my tongue, behold, O LORD,
   You know it all. (Psalm 139:4)

Review Divine Attributes

1. Omnipotence: God is _____-_____.
   (Job 42:2)

2. Omnipresence: God is _____ everywhere
   simultaneously. (Psalm 139:8)

3. Omniscience: God _____ all things.
   (Psalm 139:4)

B. Personal Attributes

1. Holiness: God is *without evil* and is only good.
   Central Passage: Isaiah 5:16

2. Love: God seeks the *best* for *others*.
   Central Passage: 1 John 4:8

3. Justice: God applies righteous *consequences* equally
   to everyone.
   Central Passage: Psalm 19:9

Review Personal Attributes

1. Holiness: God is _____ _____ and is only good.
   (Isaiah 5:16)

2. Love: God seeks the _____ for _____.
   (1 John 4:8)

3. Justice: God applies righteous _____ equally to
   everyone. (Psalm 19:9)

SELF-TEST

*What you can learn tomorrow is built
on what you learn today!*

A. Match the six attributes of God with their definitions by writing the correct letter in the blank.

Omnipotence   _____   A. God seeks the *best* for *others*.

Omnipresence   _____   B. God applies righteous *consequences* equally to everyone.

Omniscience   _____   C. God is *without evil* and is only good.

Holiness   _____   D. God is *present* everywhere simultaneously.

Love   _____   E. God *knows* all things.

Justice   _____   F. God is *all-powerful*.

B. Fill in the blanks.

God's three divine attributes are:

1. _____
2. _____
3. _____

God's three personal attributes are:

1. _____
2. _____
3. _____

It is worth repeating that there are many more characteristics of God than these. These six were chosen because they were among the most striking and well-known attributes.

TEN GREAT DOCTRINES OF THE BIBLE

(From memory, fill in the names of doctrines one and two. See the appendix for answers.)

2. _____

1. _____

CHAPTER 23

THE DOCTRINE OF CHRIST

Attitudes about Jesus are varied and often are strongly held. From denying that a person named Jesus of Nazareth ever existed to believing that He was God incarnate, people demonstrate their conviction about Him by ignoring Him or worshiping Him, or something in between.

A popular concept of Jesus is that, while He was not divine, He was a great moral teacher and leader. While He is no more God than you or I, He is a wonderful example to follow.

This is a difficult concept to hold consistently. The reason is expressed skillfully by C. S. Lewis, who wrote in his book *Mere Christianity*:

> That is the thing we must not say. A man who was merely a man and said the sort of things that Jesus said would not be a great moral teacher. He would either be a lunatic on the level of a man who says he is a poached egg—or else he would be the devil of hell. You must make your choice. Either this man was, and is, the son of God; or else a madman or something worse. You can shut Him up for a fool, you can spit at Him and kill Him as a demon; or you can fall at His feet and call Him Lord and God.

But let us not come with any patronizing nonsense about His being a great human teacher. He has not left that open to us. He did not intend to.

The position of the Bible is straightforward in presenting Jesus as divine, the Son of God, the second person of the Trinity. He is fully man and fully God. If He were not man, He could not have died for our sins, and if He were not God, His death would have accomplished nothing.

To understand the Bible's position on Jesus, it must be grasped that Jesus is presented as the Messiah, the Savior of the world who was prophesied throughout the Old Testament, who would come to die for the sins of the world and who would come again to establish righteousness in a new heaven and new earth.

I. REVIEW

Repetition is the key to mental ownership!
(Fill in the blanks.)

THE DOCTRINE OF THE BIBLE

1. R_____
2. I_____
3. I_____
4. I_____

THE DOCTRINE OF GOD

1. E_____
2. A_____
3. S_____
4. T_____

II. THE FOUR MAJOR SUBDIVISIONS OF THE DOCTRINE OF CHRIST

The four major subdivisions of the doctrine of Christ are:

 1. Deity

 2. Humanity

 3. Resurrection

 4. Return

(As you read the definitions of the doctrine subdivisions, notice the words in italics. Immediately following the definitions, they are repeated with blank spaces in place of the italicized words. Fill in the blanks.)

Symbol:	Subdivision:	Definition:
	1. Deity:	Jesus of Nazareth was *God* incarnate.
	Deity:	Jesus of Nazareth was _____ incarnate.

Though Jesus was man, He was also *God*. The second member of the Trinity existed before He was born as Jesus of Nazareth. Christ was active in the creation of the world and during the Old Testament. When the timing was right, the Christ, the second person of the Trinity, became incarnate as Jesus of Nazareth but did not forfeit His divinity at any time.

Central Passage:

In the beginning was the Word, and the Word was with God, and the Word was God. (John 1:1)

Symbol:	Subdivision:	Definition:

2. Humanity: Christ was a *man*, Jesus of Nazareth.

Humanity: Christ was a _____, Jesus of Nazareth.

Though Jesus was God, He was also a *man*. Christ took on the form of humanity, and although He did not sin He tasted all other human experiences, including hunger, fatigue, and sorrow, etc. He was supernaturally conceived, was born of a virgin, and lived an apparently normal early life as a carpenter's son in Nazareth of Galilee. As a man, He was crucified, died, and was buried.

Central Passage:

And the Word became flesh, and dwelt among us, and we saw His glory, glory as of the only begotten from the Father, full of grace and truth. (John 1:14)

Symbol:	Subdivision:	Definition:

3. Resurrection: After being killed, Jesus was *raised* to life again.

Resurrection: After being killed, Jesus was _____ to life again.

After being falsely accused and tried in a series of kangaroo courts, Jesus was subjected to the form of capital punishment reserved for non-Roman citizens. He was flogged, a savage punishment that killed 60 percent of its victims; then He was nailed to a wooden cross where He died. Afterward, He was wrapped in burial cloths and placed in a sealed tomb where He remained for three days. At the end of that time, a miraculous earthquake moved the stone from the mouth of the tomb to reveal that Jesus was *raised* from the dead, just as He had said He would be.

Central Passage:

Who was declared the Son of God with power by the resurrection from the dead, according to the Spirit of holiness, Jesus Christ our Lord. (Romans 1:4)

Symbol:	Subdivision:	Definition:
	4. Return:	Jesus will *return* at some point in the future.
	Return:	Jesus will _____ at some point in the future.

The picture of the Messiah in the Old Testament was an uncertain one. Some of the prophetic passages spoke of a humble-servant Messiah, while other passages spoke of a glorious and powerful king. So stark was the contrast between these two kinds of passages that some Old Testament scholars thought there would be two Messiahs. With the additional revelation in the New Testament, we now know how to reconcile these passages. Jesus came the first time as a humble servant and died for the sins of mankind. After He was resurrected, He ascended into heaven to sit at the right hand of God the Father. Some day in the future, and according to biblical prophecy it could be soon, Jesus will *return* to earth as a powerful and glorious king to institute righteousness on the earth.

Central Passage:

Looking for the blessed hope and the appearing of the glory of our great God and Savior, Christ Jesus. (Titus 2:13)

THE DOCTRINE OF CHRIST

(Write the titles of the four subdivisions on the lines below.)

Symbol:	Subdivision:	Definition:
	1. D_____	Jesus of Nazareth was *God* incarnate.
	Central Passage: John 1:1	

Symbol:	Subdivision:	Definition:
	2. H_____	Christ was a *man*, Jesus of Nazareth.
	Central Passage: John 1:14	

Symbol:	Subdivision:	Definition:
	3. R_____	After being killed, Jesus was *raised* to life again.
	Central Passage: Romans 1:4	

Symbol:	Subdivision:	Definition:
	4. R_____	Jesus will *return* at some point in the future.
	Central Passage: Titus 2:13	

THE DOCTRINE OF CHRIST

(Name the four subdivisions of the doctrine of Christ, and fill in the key words in the definitions.)

Symbol:	Subdivision:	Definition:
	1. D_____	Jesus of Nazareth was _____ incarnate.
	Central Passage: John 1:1	

Symbol:	Subdivision:	Definition:
	2. H_____	Christ was a _____, Jesus of Nazareth.
	Central Passage: John 1:14	

Symbol:	Subdivision:	Definition:
	3. R_____	After being killed, Jesus was _____ to life again.
	Central Passage: Romans 1:4	

Symbol:	Subdivision:	Definition:
	4. R_____	Jesus will _____ at some point in the future.
	Central Passage: Titus 2:13	

SELF-TEST

*What you can learn tomorrow is built
on what you learn today!*

(Fill in the blanks.)

1. D_____ Jesus of Nazareth was _____ incarnate.

2. H_____ Christ was a _____, Jesus of Nazareth.

3. R_____ After being killed, Jesus was _____ to life again.

4. R_____ Jesus will _____ at some point in the future.

TEN GREAT DOCTRINES OF THE BIBLE

(From memory, fill in the names of doctrines one through three.
See the appendix for answers.)

2. _____

3. _____

1. _____

CHAPTER 24

THE DOCTRINE OF
THE HOLY SPIRIT

The IRS has a "Conscience Fund" that receives anonymous contributions from people who have cheated the government out of money in the past and who want to make up for it to clear their conscience but don't want to risk criminal prosecution. The Conscience Fund received a check from a man who included the following note:

> I have not been able to sleep ever since I cheated you out of some money, so here is a check for $500. If I still can't sleep, I'll send you the rest.

In another example of human frailty, a salesman called on a successful contractor with a bid for the materials for a large job the contractor was about to begin. He was invited into the contractor's office, where they chatted for a moment before a secretary came and summoned the contractor into another office. Alone, the salesman noticed that there was a bid from a competitor's firm on the contractor's desk with all the numbers written clearly. The total amount of the bid was hidden, however, covered by a small orange juice can. Unable to contain his curiosity, the salesman picked up the orange juice can. When he did, thousands of BB's came pouring from the bottom of the can which had been cut out, flooded over the surface of the desk, and rained down on the floor. Without saying a word, the salesman turned, walked out of the office, and never returned.

We laugh at the first story and cringe at the second, because we see ourselves in both of them. We all have shortcomings and weakness. We all want to be more than we are. But we need help. Sometimes we need information. Sometimes we need assistance. Sometimes, we need to be challenged or confronted to change. This is a primary role of the Holy Spirit, to work with us in a mystical sort of way to become Christians and then to grow as Christians. He transforms us from what we were like in the past to what we should be like in the future. He is a friend, indeed, because He knows all about us and loves us anyway. He commits Himself to us to help us change, to be the sort of man or woman we long to be deep down in our souls.

I. REVIEW

Repetition is the key to mental ownership!
(Fill in the blanks.)

THE DOCTRINE OF THE BIBLE

1. R_____
2. I_____
3. I_____
4. I_____

THE DOCTRINE OF GOD

1. E_____
2. A_____
3. S_____
4. T_____

THE DOCTRINE OF CHRIST

1. D_____
2. H_____
3. R_____
4. R_____

II. THE FOUR MAJOR SUBDIVISIONS OF THE DOCTRINE OF THE HOLY SPIRIT:

The four major subdivisions of the doctrine of the Holy Spirit are:

 1. Personality

 2. Deity

 3. Salvation

 4. Gifts

(As you read the definitions of the doctrine subdivisions, notice the words in italics. Immediately following the definitions, they are repeated with blank spaces in place of the italicized words. Fill in the blank spaces.)

Symbol:	Subdivision:	Definition:
	1. Personality:	The Holy Spirit is a *personal* being, not an impersonal force.
	Personality:	The Holy Spirit is a _____ being, not an impersonal force.

The Holy Spirit is sometimes perceived as the religious equivalent of school spirit. This is not accurate. In the Bible, the Holy Spirit is treated as a person and given the attributes of *personality*, such as emotions, actions, intellect, and relationships.

Central Passage:

And do not grieve the Holy Spirit of God, by whom you were sealed for the day of redemption. (Ephesians 4:30)

Symbol:	Subdivision:	Definition:
	2. Deity:	The Holy Spirit is *divine*, the third person of the Trinity.
	Deity:	The Holy Spirit is _____, the third person of the Trinity.

Not only is the Holy Spirit a personal being, He is also *divine*. He possesses divine attributes, such as omnipresence and omnipotence. He performed miracles only God could do, such as participating in the creation of the world and the miraculous conception of Jesus. In addition, He is associated on an equal plane with the other members of the Trinity.

Central Passage:

The grace of the Lord Jesus Christ, and the love of God, and the fellowship of the Holy Spirit, be with you all. (2 Corinthians 13:14)

Symbol:	Subdivision:	Definition:
	3. Salvation:	The Holy Spirit is *instrumental* in personal salvation.
	Salvation:	The Holy Spirit is _____ in personal salvation.

The Holy Spirit plays the *instrumental* role in the personal salvation of individuals who become Christians. It is the Holy Spirit who enables us to see our sinfulness and realize that we should turn from sin. It is the Holy Spirit who helps us see that, in order to become Christians, we must believe in Jesus, ask Him to forgive us of our sins and give us eternal life, and commit our lives to living for Him.

Central Passage:

Selected passages to be seen later.

(Note: There are five primary areas of involvement by the Holy Spirit in personal salvation: conviction, regeneration, indwelling, baptism, and sealing. The first letters from each of these words spell "CRIBS." We will study the CRIBS concept in more detail later.)

Symbol:	Subdivision:	Definition:
	4. Gifts:	The Holy Spirit imparts *spiritual* abilities to Christians.
	Gifts:	The Holy Spirit imparts _____ abilities to Christians.

God wants to use each of us to minister to others. The Holy Spirit gives us a special *spiritual* "gift" to minister to others. It is something we enjoy doing and something at which we are effective. However, since God is working through us with this gift, the results must always be attributed to Him and not to ourselves. We must guard against two imbalances. We must not become discouraged if our results are meager, and we must not become inflated if our results are abundant. For in the true exercise of spiritual gifts, it is God who produces the results, whether meager or abundant.

Central Passage:

Now there are varieties of gifts, but the same Spirit. . . . But one and the same Spirit works all these things, distributing to each one individually just as He wills. (1 Corinthians 12:4, 11)

THE DOCTRINE OF THE HOLY SPIRIT

(Write the titles of the four subdivisions on the lines.)

Symbol: **Subdivision:**   **Definition:**

1. P_____   The Holy Spirit is a *personal* being,
                        not an impersonal force.

Central Passage: Ephesians 4:30

Symbol: **Subdivision:**   **Definition:**

2. D_____   The Holy Spirit is *divine*, the third
                        person of the Trinity.

Central Passage: 2 Corinthians 13:14

Symbol: **Subdivision:**   **Definition:**

3. S_____   The Holy Spirit is *instrumental* in
                        personal salvation.

Central Passage: Selected passages
                   (See pages 223–224.)

Symbol: **Subdivision:**   **Definition:**

4. G_____   The Holy Spirit imparts *spiritual*
                        abilities to Christians.

Central Passage: 1 Corinthians 12:4, 11

THE DOCTRINE OF THE HOLY SPIRIT

(Name the four subdivisions of the doctrine of the Holy Spirit and fill in the key words in the definitions.)

Symbol: **Subdivision:**   **Definition:**

1. _____   The Holy Spirit is a _____
                        being, not an impersonal force.

Central Passage: Ephesians 4:30

Symbol:	Subdivision:	Definition:
	2. _____	The Holy Spirit is _____, the third person of the Trinity.
	Central Passage:	2 Corinthians 13:14

Symbol:	Subdivision:	Definition:
	3. _____	The Holy Spirit is _____ in personal salvation.
	Central Passage:	Selected passages (See pages 223–224.)

Symbol:	Subdivision:	Definition:
	4. _____	The Holy Spirit imparts _____ abilities to Christians.
	Central Passage:	1 Corinthians 12:4, 11

SELF-TEST

*What you can learn tomorrow is built
on what you learn today!*

(Fill in the blanks.)

1. P_____   The Holy Spirit is a _____
   being, not an impersonal force.

2. D_____   The Holy Spirit is _____,
   the third person of the Trinity.

3. S_____   The Holy Spirit is _____
   in personal salvation.

4. G_____   The Holy Spirit imparts _____
   abilities to Christians.

III. FURTHER CONSIDERATION OF THE HOLY SPIRIT'S WORK IN SALVATION

The work of the Holy Spirit in personal salvation requires further consideration. There are five primary areas of involvement.

1. Conviction: Revealing a *need* to *change*.

   The Holy Spirit convinces a person of his or her *need* to *change* some thought, attitude, or action. This phenomenon is sometimes accompanied by an acute sense of guilt over wrongdoing.

   Central Passage:

   And He [the Holy Spirit], when He comes, will convict the world concerning sin, and righteousness, and judgment. (John 16:8)

2. Regeneration: Imparting a new spirit and *eternal life* with God.

   According to the Bible, everyone lives forever, either with God in heaven or separated from Him in hell. When a person becomes a Christian, the Holy Spirit imparts to him or her a new spirit and *eternal life* with God in heaven.

   Central Passage:

   He saved us, not on the basis of deeds which we have done in righteousness, but according to His mercy, by the washing of regeneration and renewing by the Holy Spirit. (Titus 3:5)

3. Indwelling: Living *within* a believer.

   The Holy Spirit mysteriously "takes up residence" *within* a person when the person becomes a believer, encouraging and strengthening him or her to live a proper lifestyle.

   Central Passage:

   You are not in the flesh but in the Spirit, if indeed the Spirit of God dwells in you. But if anyone does not have the Spirit of Christ, he does not belong to Him. (Romans 8:9)

4. Baptism:

Placing a believer, spiritually, in the body of Christ.

The "body of Christ" is a term given to the totality of all believers in Him. To *baptize* means to "place into." Technically, to be baptized into the body of Christ means to become a member of that spiritual organism.

Central Passage:

For by one Spirit we were all baptized into one body, whether Jews or Greeks, whether slaves or free, and we were all made to drink of one Spirit. (1 Corinthians 12:13)

5. Sealing:

Guaranteeing the believer's relationship to God.

The Holy Spirit becomes the *guarantee* of our spiritual inheritance, to be fully realized when we die. This means once a person has been regenerated, indwelt, and baptized into the body of Christ, his or her position is secure, "sealed with the Holy Spirit of promise" until the day of redemption. (Ephesians 1:13)

Central Passage:

In Him [Christ] you also trusted, after you heard the word of truth, the gospel of your salvation; in whom also, having believed, you were sealed with the Holy Spirit of promise. (Ephesians 1:13, 14)

SELF-TEST

*What you can learn tomorrow is built
on what you learn today!*

A. The five works of the Holy Spirit in personal salvation are:

1. C_____
2. R_____
3. I_____
4. B_____
5. S_____

B. Match the term with the definition by writing the correct letter in the blank.

Conviction   _____   A. Imparting a new spirit and
                              eternal life with God.

Regeneration _____   B. *Guaranteeing* the believer's
                              relationship with God.

Indwelling   _____   C. Revealing a *need* to *change*.

Baptism   _____   D. Living *within* a believer

Sealing   _____   E. *Placing* a believer, spiritually,
                              in the body of Christ.

TEN GREAT DOCTRINES OF THE BIBLE

(From memory, fill in the names of doctrines one through four. See the appendix for answers.)

2. _____

4. _____

3. _____

1. _____

CHAPTER 25

THE DOCTRINE
OF ANGELS

In his book entitled *Angels*, Billy Graham tells the story of Dr. S. W. Mitchell, a well-known Philadelphia neurologist, who was awakened from sleep one rainy night by a little girl, poorly dressed and very upset. She said her mother was very sick, and would he come right away. He followed the girl and found the mother desperately ill with pneumonia. After attending her and arranging for medical care, he complimented the sick woman on the intelligence and persistence of her little daughter. As *Reader's Digest* reported in the original story, the woman looked at Dr. Mitchell strangely and said, "My daughter died a month ago." She added, "Her shoes and coat are in the closet there." Puzzled, Dr. Mitchell went to the closet and opened the door. There hung the very coat worn by the little girl who had brought him to care for her mother. It was warm and dry and could not possibly have been out in the inclement weather.

Might the "little girl" have been an angel, sent to aid the stricken mother?

Mr. Graham also tells the story of John G. Paton, a missionary in the New Hebrides Islands. One evening, natives surrounded the missionary compound with the intent of burning down the compound and killing Mr. Paton and his wife. The missionaries prayed fervently all night and were surprised and relieved to witness the natives leaving the next morning.

A year later, the chief of the hostile tribe was converted to Christianity. He told the Patons that he and his tribe had fully intended to destroy the compound and kill the Patons that fateful night a year ago but had been stopped by the army of men surrounding the compound. "Who were all those men you had with you there?" the chief asked. "There were no men there; just my wife and I," replied Mr. Paton. The chief argued that they had seen many men standing guard—hundreds of big men in shining garments with drawn swords in their hands. They seemed to circle the mission station so that the natives were afraid to attack.

This story is consistent with an invisible army of angels seen in Scripture as well (2 Kings 6:15–17).

By contrast, angels sometimes show up in disguise, doing their work without anyone knowing they are angels. Many stories are told of extraordinary circumstances involving strangers who showed up at just the right time to "save the day," only to disappear and never be heard from again. To conclude that they might be angels is consistent with the passage in Hebrews that says, "Do not neglect to show hospitality to strangers, for by this some have entertained angels without knowing it" (13:2).

When the brilliant scholar Mortimer Adler undertook to edit *Great Books of the Western World* for the Encyclopedia Britannica Company, he included "Angels" as one of the great themes. Personally curious, Mr. Adler went on to write a book on angels, and in doing so, discovered that from before Aristotle's time to the present day, scholars and philosophers have taken angels seriously.

It is difficult to prove the existence and work of angels. They are not usually perceived by our five senses and are therefore not subject to scientific scrutiny. Nevertheless, they are found throughout the Bible, interwoven into many of the major events of Scripture.

I. REVIEW

Repetition is the key to mental ownership!
(Fill in the blanks.)

THE DOCTRINE OF THE BIBLE

1. R_____
2. I_____
3. I_____
4. I_____

THE DOCTRINE OF GOD

1. E_____
2. A_____
3. S_____
4. T_____

THE DOCTRINE OF CHRIST

1. D_____
2. H_____
3. R_____
4. R_____

THE DOCTRINE OF THE HOLY SPIRIT

1. P_____
2. D_____
3. S_____
4. G_____

II. THE FOUR MAJOR SUBDIVISIONS OF THE DOCTRINE OF ANGELS

The four major subdivisions of the doctrine of angels are:

 1. Angels

 2. Demons

 3. Satan

 4. Defenses

(As you read the definitions of the doctrine subdivisions, notice the words in italics. Immediately following the definitions, they are repeated with blank spaces in place of the italicized words. Fill in the blank spaces.)

Symbol:	Subdivision:	Definition:

1. Angels: Ministering *spirits* from God.

   Angels: Ministering _____ from God.

   The Bible teaches that God uses a numberless army of angels to help execute His will in heaven and earth, and that among their duties is ministering to Christians. Perhaps this is where the concept of guardian angels came from. They are personal beings, *spirits* that God created before Adam and Eve, and are not "ghosts" of people who have died.

   Central Passage:

   Are they [angels] not all ministering spirits, sent out to render service for the sake of those who will inherit salvation? (Hebrews 1:14)

Symbol: **Subdivision:**   **Definition:**

2. Demons: Angels who *fell*.

   Demons: Angels who _____.

The Bible teaches that a large number of the "righteous angels" rebelled against God and now form an evil army under the command of the devil, who uses them to further his will, which is counter to the will of God. This corruption is often referred to as the *"fall"* of these angels.

Central Passage:

And the angels who did not keep their proper domain, but left their own abode, He has reserved in everlasting chains under darkness for the judgment of the great day. (Jude 6 NKJV)

Symbol: **Subdivision:**   **Definition:**

3. Satan: The highest angel who *fell*.

   Satan: The highest angel who _____.

The Bible teaches that Satan was originally the highest angel, but because of pride he *fell*, rebelling against God and leading many lesser angels to rebel against Him also. In doing this he became evil and corrupt. He is a real entity who oversees the forces of darkness in the world and seeks to neutralize and overthrow the will of God.

Central Passage:

Be sober, be vigilant; because your adversary the devil walks about like a roaring lion, seeking whom he may devour. (1 Peter 5:8 NKJV)

Symbol: **Subdivision:**   **Definition:**

4. Defenses: Using God's *protection*.

   Defenses: Using God's _____.

In the Bible, Satan is called the deceiver and the destroyer. He deceives in order to destroy. A primary strategy is to make that which is wrong look right and that which is right look wrong.

The Bible teaches that *protection* from Satan is available to the Christian. These spiritual defenses will be dealt with in greater detail later.

Central Passage:

Selected passages to be seen later

THE DOCTRINE OF ANGELS

(Write the titles of the four subdivisions on the lines below.)

Symbol: **Subdivision:**   **Definition:**

1. A_____   Ministering *spirits* from God.
   Central Passage: Hebrews 1:14

Symbol: **Subdivision:**   **Definition:**

2. D_____   Angels who *fell*.
   Central Passage: Jude 6

Symbol: **Subdivision:**   **Definition:**

3. S_____   The highest angel who *fell*.
   Central Passage: 1 Peter 5:8

Symbol: **Subdivision:**   **Definition:**

4. D_____   Using God's *protection*.
   Central Passage: Selected passages (See page 233–234.)

THE DOCTRINE OF ANGELS

(Name the four subdivisions of the doctrine of angels and fill in the key words in the definitions.)

Symbol: **Subdivision:**   **Definition:**

1. _____   Ministering _____ from God.
   Central Passage: Hebrews 1:14

Symbol:	Subdivision:	Definition:
	2. _____	Angels who _____.
	Central Passage: Jude 6	

Symbol:	Subdivision:	Definition:
	3. _____	The highest angel who _____.
	Central Passage: 1 Peter 5:8	

Symbol:	Subdivision:	Definition:
	4. _____	Using God's _____.
	Central Passage: Selected passages (See page 234.)	

SELF-TEST

*What you can learn tomorrow is built
on what you learn today!*

(Fill in the blanks.)

1. A_____   Ministering _____ from God.
2. D_____   Angels who _____.
3. S_____   The highest angel who _____.
4. D_____   Using God's _____.

III. FURTHER CONSIDERATION OF THE BELIEVER'S DEFENSES

The believer's defenses against the efforts of Satan to deceive and destroy him or her require further consideration. There are three primary facets to the believer's defense system.

1. Alertness: The Christian must know Satan's intention and be *alert* to his advances.

    Central Passage:

    Be sober, be vigilant; because your adversary the devil walks about like a roaring lion, seeking whom he may devour. (1 Peter 5:8 NKJV)

2. Armor: The Christian has defenses that are metaphorically called *armor*, which protect him or her from Satan's devices.

    Central Passage:

    Therefore take up the whole armor of God, that you may be able to withstand in the evil day, and having done all, to stand. (Ephesians 6:13 NKJV)

3. Resistance: Once the Christian is aware of Satan's intentions and is using the "spiritual armor" discussed in Ephesians 6, he or she may resist any suspected satanic advances with confidence of victory.

    Central Passage:

    Therefore submit to God. Resist the devil and he will flee from you. (James 4:7 NKJV)

SELF-TEST

What you can learn tomorrow is built on what you learn today!

A. The believer's defenses are:

1. A_____
2. A_____
3. R_____

TEN GREAT DOCTRINES OF THE BIBLE

(From memory, fill in the names of doctrines one through five.
See the appendix for answers.)

CHAPTER 26

THE DOCTRINE OF MAN

In this chapter, we use the word *man* in its classical and biblical sense, as synonymous with "humanity" or "mankind." As we see in Genesis 1:27, this term includes both male and female.

If the full power of the human mind were manifested by an individual, the world would assume that person was a god. The power of the brain is beyond comprehension. Scientists estimate that the most brilliant among us use perhaps 10 percent of its capacity. Yet that might be wildly overstated when we ponder glimpses of its potential.

Mozart wrote his first full-length orchestral piece when he was only eight years old. Amazing as that is, it pales in comparison with other possibilities.

One of the most arresting speculations arises from an observation of people suffering from the "savant" syndrome. These people are disabled. Yet they possess astounding powers in very limited areas.

For example, there are twins from New York who can calculate the day of the week of any date you mention. If asked in which months and years of this century the twenty-first will fall on a Thursday, the brothers can give you the correct answer instantly.

Another savant can hear a long, intricate classical piano piece for the first time and immediately sit down at a piano without the music and play it back flawlessly.

A man from Edinburgh, Scotland, was legally blind and so severely impaired he could barely speak. Yet he drew pictures with crayons that betrayed the skill of a master and sold for fabulous prices around the world.

The minds of savants are like calculators or tape recorders or cameras—able to capture the specific details of pictures or songs or mathematical formulas and then use those details with exacting precision.

Perhaps these examples give us a glimpse of what God originally intended our whole mind to be capable of doing.

The indications from Scripture suggest that man's capacity before the Fall and his capacity once restored and glorified in heaven are unimaginable to us now. Someone once speculated that if we were to see our glorified selves walking down the street toward us, we would be tempted to fall at our feet and worship ourselves. Such is the future of humanity in Christ.

I. REVIEW

Repetition is the key to mental ownership!
(Fill in the blanks.)

THE DOCTRINE OF THE BIBLE

1. R_____
2. I_____
3. I_____
4. I_____

THE DOCTRINE OF GOD

1. E_____
2. A_____
3. S_____
4. T_____

THE DOCTRINE OF CHRIST

1. D_____
2. H_____
3. R_____
4. R_____

THE DOCTRINE OF THE HOLY SPIRIT

1. P_____
2. D_____
3. S_____
4. G_____

THE DOCTRINE OF ANGELS

1. A_____
2. D_____
3. S_____
4. D_____

II. THE FOUR MAJOR SUBDIVISIONS OF THE DOCTRINE OF MAN

The four major subdivisions of the doctrine of man are:

 1. Origin

 2. Nature

 3. Distinctiveness

 4. Destiny

(As you read the definitions of the doctrine subdivisions, notice the words in italics. Immediately following the definitions, they are repeated with blank spaces in place of the italicized words. Fill in the blank spaces.)

Symbol:	Subdivision:	Definition:

1. Origin: Man was *created* by God in His image.

   Origin: Man was _____ by God in His image.

Man's purpose is to "know God and enjoy Him forever." Man was *created* in perfect fellowship and harmony with God, in His image. This does not mean physical likeness, for God does not have a physical body. But it means in the psychological, emotional, and spiritual likeness of God.

Central Passage:

And God created man in His own image, in the image of God He created him; male and female He created them. (Genesis 1:27)

Symbol:	Subdivision:	Definition:

2. Nature: Man has a *spiritual* as well as a physical dimension.

   Nature: Man has a _____ as well as a physical dimension.

Man is *spiritual* as well as physical. Man's earthly physical body is destined to die. The moment he is born, the process is set in motion for him to die. His spirit, however, lives forever and transcends his physical limitations. After man dies, he receives a new body that lives forever.

Central Passage:

Now may the God of peace Himself sanctify you entirely; and may your spirit and soul and body be preserved complete, without blame at the coming of our Lord Jesus Christ. (1 Thessalonians 5:23)

Symbol:	Subdivision:	Definition:
	3. Distinctiveness:	Man has *capacities* that go beyond those of any animals and mark him as the pinnacle of God's creation.
	Distinctiveness:	Man has _____ that go beyond those of any animals and mark him as the pinnacle of God's creation.

Man possesses intellect, emotion, and will. With intellect he can know, reason, and think. With emotion he can feel, empathize, and experience. With will he can choose. These are all characteristics of God and, as such, are part of the "image of God" within man. In addition, man has the capacity for self-awareness, an awareness of God, an awareness of afterlife, and the ability to envision life in the future under different scenarios such as heaven and hell, etc. Man certainly has characteristics that overlap with the animals, but his capacities not only go beyond those of animals, he has *capacities* that no animals have.

Central Passage:

Then God said, "Let Us make man in Our image, according to Our likeness; and let them rule over the fish of the sea and over the birds of the sky and over the cattle and over all the earth, and over every creeping thing that creeps on the earth." (Genesis 1:26)

Symbol:	Subdivision:	Definition:
	4. Destiny:	Man will live *forever* in heaven or hell.
	Destiny:	Man will live _____ in heaven or hell.

Destiny in hell is portrayed as agonizing torment, though little is known of the specifics of that torment. Existence in heaven is pictured in greater detail, though we still wish for more details. The heavenly body is beautiful beyond imagination, exceedingly powerful, and not subject to time and space limitations. The citizen of heaven will rule in the celestial realm and will possess power, wisdom, and unbounded creativity. Greater attention will be given to man's destiny later in this chapter and in the chapter on the doctrine of future things.

Central Passage:

It is appointed for men to die once and after this comes judgment. (Hebrews 9:27)

THE DOCTRINE OF MAN

(Write the titles of the four subdivisions on the lines below.)

Symbol:	Subdivision:	Definition:
	1. O_____	Man was *created* by God in His image.
	Central Passage: Genesis 1:27	

Symbol:	Subdivision:	Definition:
	2. N_____	Man has a *spiritual* as well as a physical dimension.
	Central Passage: 1 Thessalonians 5:23	

Symbol:	Subdivision:	Definition:
	3. D_____	Man has *capacities* that go beyond those of any animals and mark him as the pinnacle of God's creation.
	Central Passage: Genesis 1:26	

Symbol:	Subdivision:	Definition:
	4. D_____	Man will live *forever* in heaven or hell.
	Central Passage: Hebrews 9:27	

THE DOCTRINE OF MAN

(Name the four subdivisions of the doctrine of man and fill in the key words in the definitions.)

Symbol:	Subdivision:	Definition:

1. _____ Man was _____ by God in His image.

Central Passage: Genesis 1:27

Symbol:	Subdivision:	Definition:

2. _____ Man has a _____ as well as a physical dimension.

Central Passage: 1 Thessalonians 5:23

Symbol:	Subdivision:	Definition:

3. _____ Man has _____ that go beyond those of any animals and mark him as the pinnacle of God's creation.

Central Passage: Genesis 1:26

Symbol:	Subdivision:	Definition:

4. _____ Man will live _____ in heaven or hell.

Central Passage: Hebrews 9:27

SELF-TEST

What you can learn tomorrow is built on what you learn today!

(Fill in the blanks.)

1. O_____ Man was _____ by God in His image.
2. N_____ Man has a _____ as well as a physical dimension.

3. D_____ Man has _____ that go beyond those of any animals and mark him as the pinnacle of God's creation.

4. D_____ Man will live _____ in heaven or hell.

TEN GREAT DOCTRINES OF THE BIBLE

(From memory, fill in the names of doctrines one through six. See the appendix for answers.)

2. _____

4. _____

3. _____

5. _____

1. _____

6. _____

CHAPTER 27

THE DOCTRINE OF SIN

I grew up in rural northern Indiana where pig farming is common. As a teenager, I used to have to work among the pigs, feeding them, tending to their physical and medical needs, and cleaning up after them. If you have never worked around farm animals, you probably cannot imagine how bad a pigpen in a barn stinks when pigs have been shut up in it all winter. It literally will bring tears to your eyes, take your breath away, and, in my case, cause you to long for a professional job.

But one thing I noticed. The pigs didn't mind it. I never saw a pig walk into a pen, sniff the air in disgust, and turn around and walk out because the place smelled so bad. It always seemed OK to the pig. Every pig I ever saw looked completely at home in a pigpen.

When it comes to sin, we're a little like the pigs. The smell of sin doesn't seem so bad to us. We don't even notice a lot of it. But to God, it smells like a thousand pigs were kept in His living room for the winter.

Man does not and cannot grasp the awfulness of sin to the degree God does. But for two reasons we must try to grasp as much as we can. First, sin is harmful to us; it is self-destructive. All sins are boomerangs; they come back to hurt us every time. Second, sin separates us from God, and if we hope to live a life in fellowship with Him, it means accepting the challenge of growing in righteousness.

I. REVIEW

Repetition is the key to mental ownership!
(Fill in the blanks.)

THE DOCTRINE OF THE BIBLE

1. R_____
2. I_____
3. I_____
4. I_____

THE DOCTRINE OF GOD

1. E_____
2. A_____
3. S_____
4. T_____

THE DOCTRINE OF CHRIST

1. D_____
2. H_____
3. R_____
4. R_____

THE DOCTRINE OF THE HOLY SPIRIT

1. P_____
2. D_____
3. S_____
4. G_____

THE DOCTRINE OF ANGELS

1. A_____
2. D_____

3. S_____
4. D_____

THE DOCTRINE OF MAN

1. O_____
2. N_____
3. D_____
4. D_____

II. THE FOUR MAJOR SUBDIVISIONS OF THE DOCTRINE OF SIN

The four major subdivisions of the doctrine of sin are:

 1. Nature

 2. Fall

 3. Corruption

 4. Rebellion

(As you read the definitions of the doctrine subdivisions, notice the words in italics. Immediately following the definitions, they are repeated with blank spaces in place of the italicized words. Fill in the blank spaces.)

Symbol:	Subdivision:	Definition:
	1. Nature:	Sin is any lack of conformity to the moral *perfection* of God.

Nature: Sin is any lack of conformity to the moral
               _____ of God.

All that is good, right, and pleasant comes from God. Anything
that does not come from God is the opposite. By definition,
it must be bad, wrong, and unpleasant. We are creatures who
sin. When we do, we bring bad, wrong, and unpleasant things
into our lives, we diminish the reputation of God, since we are
His children, and we decrease the interest the non-Christian
world might have in God because they do not see the difference
between being Christian and not being Christian.

Central Passage:

All unrighteousness is sin. (1 John 5:17)

Symbol:	Subdivision:	Definition:

2. Fall: The *separation* of Adam and Eve from God in
               the Garden of Eden because of original sin.

   Fall: The _____ of Adam and Eve from
               God in the Garden of Eden because of
               original sin.

All the pain, all the evil, all the suffering that is in the world,
that has ever been in the world, and that will ever be in the world
can be traced back to one event: when Adam and Eve disobeyed
God in the Garden. Because of the cataclysmically negative
effects of that event, it has been referred to as the Fall of man.

Central Passage:

When the woman saw that the tree was good for food, and
that it was a delight to the eyes, and that the tree was desirable
to make one wise, she took from its fruit and ate; and she
gave also to her husband with her, and he ate. (Genesis 3:6)

Symbol:	Subdivision:	Definition:

3. Corruption: Mankind as a whole was *corrupted* by the
                original Fall.

   Corruption: Mankind as a whole was _____ by
                the original Fall.

Sin entered mankind, and now all men are *corrupted* with sin. It is not that man is not capable of doing good (for certainly some people do wonderful things), or even that he is as bad as he could be (many people could be much worse than they are). It is just that he cannot keep from doing that which is bad, because his essential nature has been corrupted. David said, "in sin my mother conceived me" (Psalm 51:5). This does not mean that his mother sinned, but that all men are born sinners. We are not sinners because we sin. We sin because we are sinners.

Central Passage:

And you were dead in your trespasses and sins. . . . Among them we too all formerly lived in the lusts of our flesh, indulging the desires of the flesh and of the mind, and were by nature children of wrath. (Ephesians 2:1, 3)

Symbol:	**Subdivision:**	**Definition:**
⊘	4. Rebellion:	Because man's internal nature has been corrupted by sin, he cannot keep from committing *personal* sins.
	Rebellion:	Because man's internal nature has been corrupted by sin, he cannot keep from committing _____ sins.

Man's heart has been corrupted, and therefore he commits individual, *personal* sins. Some of these sins are sins of commission (things we ought not to do, but do) and some are sins of omission (things we ought to do but don't). They may be tangible acts, or they may be deficient attitudes, motives, or perspectives. When we compare ourselves with other people on external things, we might not do so badly. But when we compare ourselves with Jesus, who had no imperfections in act, thought, motive, word, or deed, we see that we fall short.

Central Passage:

For all have sinned and fall short of the glory of God. . . . For the wages of sin is death. (Romans 3:23; 6:23)

THE DOCTRINE OF SIN

(Write the titles of the four subdivisions on the lines below.)

Symbol: **Subdivision:**   **Definition:**

1. N_____   Sin is any lack of conformity to the
                    moral *perfection* of God.

Central Passage: 1 John 5:17

Symbol: **Subdivision:**   **Definition:**

2. F_____   The *separation* of Adam and Eve from
                    God in the Garden of Eden because of
                    original sin.

Central Passage: Genesis 3:6

Symbol: **Subdivision:**   **Definition:**

3. C_____   Mankind as a whole was *corrupted* by
                    the original Fall.

Central Passage: Ephesians 2:1, 3

Symbol: **Subdivision:**   **Definition:**

4. R_____   Because man's internal nature has been
                    corrupted by sin, he cannot keep from
                    committing *personal* sins.

Central Passage: Romans 3:23; 6:23

THE DOCTRINE OF SIN

(Name the four subdivisions of the doctrine of sin and fill in the key words in the definitions.)

Symbol: **Subdivision:**   **Definition:**

1. _____   Sin is any lack of conformity to the
                   moral _____ of God.

Central Passage: 1 John 5:17

Symbol:	Subdivision:	Definition:
	2. _____	The _____ of Adam and Eve from God in the Garden of Eden because of original sin.

Central Passage: Genesis 3:6

Symbol:	Subdivision:	Definition:
	3. _____	Mankind as a whole was _____ by the original Fall.

Central Passage: Ephesians 2:1, 3

Symbol:	Subdivision:	Definition:
	4. _____	Because man's internal nature has been corrupted by sin, he cannot keep from committing _____ sins.

Central Passage: Romans 3:23; 6:23

SELF-TEST

*What you can learn tomorrow is built
on what you learn today!*

(Fill in the blanks.)

1. N_____   Sin is any lack of conformity to the moral _____ of God.

2. F_____   The _____ of Adam and Eve from God in the Garden of Eden because of original sin.

3. C_____   Mankind as a whole was _____ by the original Fall.

4. R_____ Because man's internal nature has been corrupted by sin, he cannot keep from committing _____ sins.

TEN GREAT DOCTRINES OF THE BIBLE

(From memory, fill in the names of doctrines one through seven. See the appendix for answers.)

2. _____

4. _____

3. _____

5. _____

1. _____

6. _____

7. _____

CHAPTER 28

THE DOCTRINE OF SALVATION

During a British conference on comparative religions, experts from around the world debated what, if any, belief was unique to the Christian faith. They began eliminating possibilities. Incarnation? Other religions had different versions of gods appearing in human form. Resurrection? Again, other religions had accounts of return from death. The debate went on for some time until C.S. Lewis wandered into the room.

"What's the rumpus about?" he asked, and heard in reply that his colleagues were discussing Christianity's unique contribution among the world religions. Lewis responded, "Oh, that's easy. It's grace."

After some discussion, the conferees had to agree. The notion of God's love coming to us free of charge, no strings attached, seems to go against every instinct of humanity. The Buddhist eightfold path, the Hindu doctrine of karma, the Jewish covenant, the Muslim code of law—each of these offers a way to earn approval. Only Christianity dares to make God's love unconditional (*What's So Amazing about Grace?* 45).

In all other religions, we must do something to earn salvation. In Christianity, salvation is by grace through faith in Jesus.

Faith is crucial because it is the only thing we can do and still not do anything. Romans 6:23 says, "For the wages of sin is death, but the free gift of God is eternal life in Christ Jesus our Lord." No wonder the gospel is called the "good news."

I. REVIEW

Repetition is the key to mental ownership!
(Fill in the blanks.)

THE DOCTRINE OF THE BIBLE

1. R_____
2. I_____
3. I_____
4. I_____

THE DOCTRINE OF GOD

1. E_____
2. A_____
3. S_____
4. T_____

THE DOCTRINE OF CHRIST

1. D_____
2. H_____
3. R_____
4. R_____

THE DOCTRINE OF THE HOLY SPIRIT

1. P_____
2. D_____
3. S_____
4. G_____

THE DOCTRINE OF ANGELS

1. A_____
2. D_____
3. S_____
4. D_____

THE DOCTRINE OF MAN

1. O_____
2. N_____
3. D_____
4. D_____

THE DOCTRINE OF SIN

1. N_____
2. F_____
3. C_____
4. R_____

II. THE FOUR MAJOR SUBDIVISIONS OF THE DOCTRINE OF SALVATION

The four major subdivisions of the doctrine of salvation are:

1. Basis

2. Result

3. Cost

4. Timing

(As you read the definitions of the doctrine subdivisions, notice the words in italics. Immediately following the definitions, they are repeated with blank spaces in place of the italicized words. Fill in the blank spaces.)

Symbol:	Subdivision:	Definition:

1. Basis: Salvation is a *gift* God gives to those who believe.

Basis: Salvation is a _____ God gives to those who believe.

We cannot earn our salvation. We are imperfect, and we cannot make ourselves perfect. Yet God demands perfection. In His mercy, God offers, by grace through faith in Jesus, to forgive our sin and give us the *gift* of new life in Christ.

Central Passage:

For by grace you have been saved through faith; and that not of yourselves, it is the gift of God; not as a result of works, so that no one may boast. (Ephesians 2:8, 9)

Symbol:	Subdivision:	Definition:

2. Result: God extends *forgiveness* of sin and eternal life to those who accept Him.

Result: God extends _____ of sin and eternal life to those who accept Him.

God's solution to man's being cut off from Him is to offer him *forgiveness* of his sins and cause him to be born again to eternal life in Christ (1 Peter 1:3), giving him a new nature that is not flawed by sin, created in the very likeness of God, holy and righteous (Ephesians 4:24).

Central Passage:

If we confess our sins, He is faithful and righteousness to forgive us our sins and to cleanse us from all unrighteousness. (1 John 1:9)

Symbol:	Subdivision:	Definition:

3. Cost: The penalty of sin is paid for by the *substitutionary* death of Christ.

Cost: The penalty of sin is paid for by the _____ death of Christ.

Sin brings death. Since all have sinned, all have died, spiritually, and are separated from God (Romans 3:23; 6:23). Jesus was without sin, and He willingly died so that His death could count as a *substitution* for our own. If you believe in Jesus and receive Him as your personal Savior, God will then count His death for yours and give you eternal life.

Central Passage:

For Christ also died for sins once for all, the just for the unjust, so that He might bring us to God, having been put to death in the flesh, but made alive in the spirit. (1 Peter 3:18)

Symbol:	Subdivision:	Definition:
	4. Timing:	Our salvation is completed at the *death* of the *body*.
	Timing:	Our salvation is completed at the _____ of the _____.

Man is a spirit that has a body. Upon becoming a Christian, a person's spirit is born again and he is given eternal life (John 3:3, 16). However, his body, at that point, remains unchanged. It is corrupted by sin, is susceptible to disease and death, and is in bondage to sin (Romans 7:23). The brain, which is part of the physical body, is still corrupted with old programming that is counter to biblical truth. Because of this, the Christian experiences a continuous struggle between the born again inner man who wishes to serve God and the physical body, the outer man, that is pulled to sin (see Romans 7:15–20). This conflict continues until the *death* of the *body*, at which time the born again spirit of the Christian is transported immediately to heaven to receive a new body, untouched by sin. (Romans 8:23)

Central Passage:

And not only this, but also we ourselves, having the first fruits of the Spirit, even we ourselves groan within ourselves, waiting eagerly for our adoption as sons, the redemption of our body. (Romans 8:23)

THE DOCTRINE OF SALVATION

(Write the titles of the four subdivisions on the lines below.)

Symbol:	Subdivision:	Definition:

1. B_____   Salvation is a *gift* God gives to those who believe.

Central Passage: Ephesians 2:8, 9

Symbol:	Subdivision:	Definition:

2. R_____   God extends *forgiveness* of sin and eternal life to those who accept Him.

Central Passage: 1 John 1:9

Symbol:	Subdivision:	Definition:

3. C_____   The penalty of sin is paid for by the *substitutionary* death of Christ.

Central Passage: 1 Peter 3:18

Symbol:	Subdivision:	Definition:

4. T_____   Our salvation is completed at the *death* of the *body*.

Central Passage: Romans 8:23

THE DOCTRINE OF SALVATION

(Name the four subdivisions of the doctrine of salvation and fill in the key words in the definition.)

Symbol:	Subdivision:	Definition:

1. _____   Salvation is a _____ God gives to those who believe.

Central Passage: Ephesians 2:8, 9

Symbol:	Subdivision:	Definition:
	2. _____	God extends _____ of sin and eternal life to those who accept Him.
	Central Passage: 1 John 1:9	

Symbol:	Subdivision:	Definition:
	3. _____	The penalty of sin is paid for by the _____ death of Christ.
	Central Passage: 1 Peter 3:18	

Symbol:	Subdivision:	Definition:
	4. _____	Our salvation is completed at the _____ of the _____.
	Central Passage: Romans 8:23	

SELF-TEST

What you can learn tomorrow is built on what you learn today!

(Fill in the blanks.)

1. B_____ Salvation is a _____ God gives to those who believe.

2. R_____ God extends _____ of sin and eternal life to those who accept Him.

3. C_____ The penalty of sin is paid for by the _____ death of Christ.

4. T_____ Our salvation is completed at the _____ of the _____.

TEN GREAT DOCTRINES OF THE BIBLE

(From memory, fill in the names of doctrines one through eight. See the appendix for answers.)

2. _____

4. _____   3. _____

5. _____   1. _____

6. _____

7. _____   8. _____

CHAPTER 29

THE DOCTRINE OF THE CHURCH

It is no secret that the church has had its detractors over the years. Founding Father Thomas Paine once wrote, "All national institutions of churches . . . appear to me no other than human inventions, set up to terrify and enslave mankind, and monopolize power and profit."

Even modern church father John Wesley once said, "The Church recruited people who had been starched and ironed before they were washed."

Yet, Gerald Vann was most accurate when he said, "If you say that the history of the Church is a long succession of scandals, you are telling the truth, though if that is all you say, you are distorting the truth."

While the church has not always represented itself admirably, the problem has been in the execution, not the institution.

The church, also called in Scripture the "body of Christ," is to be the physical representation of Christ on earth now that He has returned to heaven. What Christ said, we are to say. What Christ did, we are to do. The message Christ proclaimed, we are to proclaim, and the character Christ manifested, we are to manifest. The world can no longer see Christ living on earth. He is removed physically, though

He lives in the hearts of His children. Because the world can no longer see Christ living on earth, it should be able to get a pretty good idea of Christ by looking at His church.

As C. S. Lewis once wrote, "The Church exists for nothing else but to draw men into Christ, to make them little Christs. If they are not doing that, all the cathedrals, clergy, missions, sermons, even the Bible itself, are simply a waste of time. God became Man for no other purpose."

The time has come for a clarification of the purpose of the church, and resurgence of respect for the church, to hold her with the same regard with which God holds her. The time has come to believe Jesus' promise in Matthew 16:18: "I will build My church." Then, we humbly ask Him, "What would you have me to do?"

I. REVIEW

Repetition is the key to mental ownership!
(Fill in the blanks.)

THE DOCTRINE OF THE BIBLE

1. R_____
2. I_____
3. I_____
4. I_____

THE DOCTRINE OF GOD

1. E_____
2. A_____
3. S_____
4. T_____

THE DOCTRINE OF CHRIST

1. D_____
2. H_____
3. R_____
4. R_____

THE DOCTRINE OF THE HOLY SPIRIT

1. P_____
2. D_____
3. S_____
4. G_____

THE DOCTRINE OF ANGELS

1. A_____
2. D_____
3. S_____
4. D_____

THE DOCTRINE OF MAN

1. O_____
2. N_____
3. D_____
4. D_____

THE DOCTRINE OF SIN

1. N_____
2. F_____
3. C_____
4. R_____

THE DOCTRINE OF SALVATION

1. B_____
2. R_____
3. C_____
4. T_____

II. THE FOUR MAJOR SUBDIVISIONS OF THE DOCTRINE OF THE CHURCH

The four major subdivisions of the doctrine of the church are:

 1. Universal

 2. Local

 3. Leadership

 4. Membership

(As you read the definitions of the doctrine subdivisions, notice the words in italics. Immediately following the definitions, they are repeated with blank spaces in place of the italicized words. Fill in the blank spaces.)

Symbol:	Subdivision:	Definition:
	1. Universal:	The universal church is the totality of all *believers* in Jesus.
	Universal:	The universal church is the totality of all _____ in Jesus.

The universal church, also called the body of Christ (Colossians 1:24), refers to all people in all parts of the world who have become Christians since the beginning of the church and who will become Christians before Christ returns. The church began on the day of Pentecost (Acts 2), and will culminate when Christ returns. Christ is the head of the church (Colossians 1:18), and the universal church is to be the representation of Christ on earth, collectively doing His will.

Central Passage:

And I say to you that you are Peter, and on this rock I will build My church, and the gates of Hades shall not prevail against it. (Matthew 16:18 NKJV)

Symbol:	Subdivision:	Definition:
	2. Local:	A local assembly of believers *organized* to carry out the responsibilities of the universal church.
	Local:	A local assembly of believers _____ to carry out the responsibilities of the universal church.

The church is not a building, but people. At any given time and place, Christians are to band together to carry out the responsibilities of the universal church. As such, they organize to govern themselves, select spiritual leaders, collect money for ministry, observe baptism and communion, exercise church discipline, engage in mutual edification and evangelism, and worship God.

Central Passage:

Paul, called as an apostle of Jesus Christ by the will of God, . . . to the church of God which is at Corinth. (1 Corinthians 1:1, 2)

Symbol:	Subdivision:	Definition:
	3. Leadership:	Those in the church worthy of being followed because of their *spiritual* maturity.
	Leadership:	Those in the church worthy of being followed because of their _____ maturity.

Leadership in the local church is invested in pastor-teachers, elders, and deacons and deaconesses. The Scripture appears to give freedom as to how this leadership is organized and functions, but it is quite specific about the *spiritual* qualifications. Only spiritually mature people are to be given high positions of spiritual leadership in the church.

Central Passage:

An overseer, then, must be above reproach, the husband of one wife, temperate, prudent, respectable, hospitable, able to teach, not addicted to wine or pugnacious, but gentle, peaceable, free from the love of money. He must be one who manages his own household well, keeping his children under control with all dignity . . . and not a new convert, . . . and he must have a good reputation with those outside the church. (1 Timothy 3:2–4, 6, 7)

Symbol:	Subdivision:	Definition:

4. Membership: *Belonging* to the universal church and a local church.

   Membership: _____ to the universal church and a local church.

When a person becomes a Christian, he or she immediately and automatically becomes a member of the universal church, the body of Christ. Throughout church history, local churches have had varying requirements for membership that range from very limited to very strict. This appears to be a point of freedom given local churches in the Scripture. An important point, however, is that everyone should be a part of a local church. God never intended for Christians to try to make it alone. Placing oneself under spiritual authority and in mutual ministry with others is essential to spiritual health.

Central Passage:

Let us consider how to stimulate one another to love and good deeds, not forsaking our own assembling together, as is the habit of some, but encouraging one another; and all the more, as you see the day drawing near. (Hebrews 10:24, 25)

THE DOCTRINE OF THE CHURCH

(Write the titles of the four subdivisions on the lines below.)

Symbol:	Subdivision:	Definition:
	1. U_____	The universal church is the totality of all *believers* in Jesus.
	Central Passage:	Matthew 16:18

Symbol:	Subdivision:	Definition:
	2. L_____	A local assembly of believers *organized* to carry out the responsibilities of the universal church.
	Central Passage:	1 Corinthians 1:1, 2

Symbol:	Subdivision:	Definition:
	3. L_____	Those in the church worthy of being followed because of their *spiritual* maturity.
	Central Passage:	1 Timothy 3:2–4, 6, 7

Symbol:	Subdivision:	Definition:
	4. M_____	*Belonging* to the universal church and a local church.
	Central Passage:	Hebrews 10:24, 25

THE DOCTRINE OF THE CHURCH

(Name the four subdivisions of the doctrine of the church and fill in the key words in the definitions.)

Symbol:	Subdivision:	Definition:
	1. _____	The universal church is the totality of all _____ in Jesus.
	Central Passage:	Matthew 16:18

Symbol:	Subdivision:	Definition:
2. _____	A local assembly of believers _____ to carry out the responsibilities of the universal church.

Central Passage: 1 Corinthians 1:1, 2

Symbol:	Subdivision:	Definition:
3. _____	Those in the church worthy of being followed because of their _____ maturity.

Central Passage: 1 Timothy 3:2–4, 6, 7

Symbol:	Subdivision:	Definition:
4. _____	_____ to the universal church and a local church.

Central Passage: Hebrews 10:24, 25

SELF-TEST

What you can learn tomorrow is built on what you learn today!

(Fill in the blanks.)

1. U_____   The universal church is the totality of all _____ in Jesus.

2. L_____   A local assembly of believers _____ to carry out the responsibilities of the universal church.

3. L_____   Those in the church worthy of being followed because of their _____ maturity.

4. M_____ _____ to the universal church

and a local church.

TEN GREAT DOCTRINES OF THE BIBLE

(From memory, fill in the names of doctrines one through nine.
See the appendix for answers.)

2. _____

4. _____   3. _____

5. _____   1. _____

6. _____   9. _____

7. _____   8. _____

CHAPTER 30

THE DOCTRINE OF FUTURE THINGS

The story of Little Lord Fauntleroy is an engaging and instructive one. The son of an English earl marries an American woman and is consequently disinherited. Some years later, he dies at sea, and his widow and son live humbly in New York City. The disinherited man's father, the Earl of Darringcourt, becomes aged and is concerned for the succession to his fortune and family line. His ten-year-old American grandson is his only legal heir, so he sends a representative to America to offer to have his grandson come to live on the fabulous estate as Lord Fauntleroy and eventually succeed him as Earl of Darringcourt.

When the earl's representative first comes to America with the proposal, a circumstance arises that is analogous to the life of a Christian. He describes what life will be like as Lord Fauntleroy. Wealth, power, honor, and glory are his. He is a royal heir. Yet he will have to wait until he gets to England to experience it. For now, he will have some limited benefits, but for the most part, until he crosses the Atlantic, the life of Lord Fauntleroy has to wait.

The Bible presents a picture of a future for Christians that is difficult to imagine. Power, glory, wealth, and honor are ours. But in large measure, we must wait until we get to heaven to experience it.

For now, the limitations of earth are very much with us. Until we cross the Atlantic, the life of Lord Fauntleroy will have to wait.

The information the Bible presents about future things is hazy. The prophetic information in the Bible is not given to satisfy our innate curiosity about the future, but to encourage us to live like royalty while we are still here on earth. It is given, not to impact our curiosity, but our lifestyle.

Therefore, while the information is incomplete as to details we might desire to know, it is adequate for us to take our present life seriously. We are royalty with a celestial inheritance, and while we are presently misplaced, we are nevertheless to live like who we have become.

I. REVIEW

Repetition is the key to mental ownership!
(Fill in the blanks.)

THE DOCTRINE OF THE BIBLE

1. R_____
2. I_____
3. I_____
4. I_____

THE DOCTRINE OF GOD

1. E_____
2. A_____
3. S_____
4. T_____

THE DOCTRINE OF CHRIST

1. D_____
2. H_____
3. R_____
4. R_____

THE DOCTRINE OF THE HOLY SPIRIT

1. P_____
2. D_____
3. S_____
4. G_____

THE DOCTRINE OF ANGELS

1. A_____
2. D_____
3. S_____
4. D_____

THE DOCTRINE OF MAN

1. O_____
2. N_____
3. D_____
4. D_____

THE DOCTRINE OF SIN

1. N_____
2. F_____
3. C_____
4. R_____

THE DOCTRINE OF SALVATION

1. B_____
2. R_____
3. C_____
4. T_____

THE DOCTRINE OF THE CHURCH

1. U_____
2. L_____
3. L_____
4. M_____

II. THE FOUR MAJOR SUBDIVISIONS OF THE DOCTRINE OF FUTURE THINGS

The four major subdivisions of the doctrine of future things are:

 1. Return

 2. Judgment

 3. Universe

 4. Eternity

(As you read the definitions of the doctrine subdivisions, notice the words in italics. Immediately following the definitions, they are repeated with blank spaces in place of the italicized words. Fill in the blank spaces.)

Symbol:	Subdivision:	Definition:

1. Return: Jesus will *return* to earth again.

Return: Jesus will _____ to earth again.

Jesus of Nazareth was crucified, buried, and resurrected about A.D. 30. He ascended into heaven, where He has remained for the last two thousand years. At some time in the future, and from prophetic information it could be at any time, He will *return* to earth. When He does, it will not be as a carpenter's son but as a Monarch's Son, in power and glory, revealing His true cosmic sovereignty. During His first visit to earth, He came as a servant with an emphasis on His humanity. During His second visit to earth He will come as a King, emphasizing His deity.

Central Passage:

For the Son of Man is going to come in the glory of His Father with His angels. (Matthew 16:27)

Symbol:	Subdivision:	Definition:

2. Judgment: God will *confirm* the eternal *destiny* of all individuals.

Judgment: God will _____ the eternal _____ of all individuals.

At two different times and places, God will conduct audiences with all humanity to *confirm* our eternal *destiny*. Those who believed in Jesus and received Him will then be confirmed to eternity in heaven with Him. Those who did not believe in Him and receive Him will be confirmed to eternal separation from Him in hell.

Central Passage:

For we must all appear before the judgment seat of Christ, so that each one may be recompensed for his deeds in the body, according to what he has done, whether good or bad. (2 Corinthians 5:10)

And if anyone's name was not found written in the book of life, he was thrown into the lake of fire. (Revelation 20:15)

Symbol:	Subdivision:	Definition:

 3. Universe: The old universe will be destroyed and *replaced* with a new one.

Universe: The old universe will be destroyed and _____ with a new one.

The present universe was corrupted with sin at the time of the "Fall" of man. While much of nature is beautiful, much of it is also destructive and uninhabitable. The universe will be destroyed with an apocalyptic cosmic fire and *replaced* with a new universe and a new earth that will have no harmful features. (See 2 Peter 3:12, 13; Revelation 21:4.)

Central Passage:

And I saw a new heaven and a new earth; for the first heaven and the first earth passed away, and there is no longer any sea. (Revelation 21:1)

Symbol:	Subdivision:	Definition:

4. Eternity: Christians will live with God *forever.*

Eternity: Christians will live with God _____.

Jesus will reign in absolute righteousness. Only goodness and beauty will exist. Believers will rule with Him *forever* as vice-regents. They will govern angelic beings and kingdoms in the new earth. They will be beings of beauty and power who will participate in glorious celestial ceremonies. Believers themselves will receive much personal glory by the grace and goodness of God, as well as spend generous time worshiping and praising God. Intellect, beauty, power, and talent will be virtually limitless as believers both serve Jesus the King and rule with Him in a world that glorifies God and brings great joy and individual satisfaction.

Central Passage:

In My Father's house are many dwelling places; if it were not so, I would have told you; for I go to prepare a place for you.

If I go and prepare a place for you, I will come again, and receive you to Myself, that where I am, there you may be also. (John 14:2, 3)

And they [Christians] will reign forever and ever. (Revelation 22:5)

THE DOCTRINE OF FUTURE THINGS
(Write the titles of the four subdivisions on the lines below.)

Symbol:	Subdivision:	Definition:
	1. R_____	Jesus will *return* to earth again.
	Central Passage: Matthew 16:27	

Symbol:	Subdivision:	Definition:
	2. J_____	God will *confirm* the eternal *destiny* of all individuals.
	Central Passage: 2 Corinthians 5:10; Revelation 20:15	

Symbol:	Subdivision:	Definition:
	3. U_____	The old universe will be destroyed and *replaced* with a new one.
	Central Passage: Revelation 21:1	

Symbol:	Subdivision:	Definition:
	4. E_____	Christians will live with God *forever*.
	Central Passage: John 14:2, 3; Revelation 22:5	

THE DOCTRINE OF FUTURE THINGS
(Name the four subdivisions of the doctrine of future things and fill in the key words in the definitions.)

Symbol: **Subdivision:**   **Definition:**

1. _____   Jesus will _____ to earth again.

Central Passage: Matthew 16:27

Symbol: **Subdivision:**   **Definition:**

2. _____   God will _____ the eternal _____ of all individuals.

Central Passage: 2 Corinthians 5:10; Revelation 20:15

Symbol: **Subdivision:**   **Definition:**

3. _____   The old universe will be destroyed and _____ with a new one.

Central Passage: Revelation 21:1

Symbol: **Subdivision:**   **Definition:**

4. _____   Christians will live with God _____.

Central Passage: John 14:2, 3; Revelation 22:5

SELF-TEST

What you can learn tomorrow is built on what you learn today!

(Fill in the blanks.)

1. R_____   Jesus will _____ to earth again.

2. J_____   God will _____ the eternal _____ of all individuals.

3. U_____ The old universe will be destroyed and
_____ with a new one.

4. E_____ Christians will live with God
_____.

TEN GREAT DOCTRINES OF THE BIBLE

(From memory, fill in the names of all the doctrines. See the appendix for answers.)

2. _____

4. _____   3. _____

5. _____   1. _____   10. _____

6. _____   9. _____

7. _____   8. _____

Fill in the names of the doctrines and their subdivisions on the lines below:

1. B _____
     R _____
     I _____
     I _____
     I _____

2. G_____
     E _____
     A _____
     S _____
     T _____

3. C_____
     D _____
     H _____
     R _____
     R _____

4. H_____ S_____
     P _____
     D _____
     S _____
     G _____

5. A_____
     A _____
     D _____
     S _____
     D _____

6. M _____
   O _____
   N _____
   D _____
   D _____

7. S _____
   N _____
   F _____
   C _____
   R _____

8. S _____
   B _____
   R _____
   C _____
   T _____

9. C _____
   U _____
   L _____
   L _____
   M _____

10. F _____ T _____
    R _____
    J _____
    U _____
    E _____

Congratulations! You have just completed an overview of the ten major doctrines of the Bible. There is still much more about Bible doctrines to be learned. This is not the most you need to know; it is the least. It is not the end of your learning, but the beginning . . . and a good beginning!

In a sense, you have learned a very broad outline, and much of the Bible is dedicated to filling in the details. Nevertheless, you now have a structure for acquiring an advanced knowledge of the doctrines of the Bible.

NANOSUMMARY OF
THE BIBLE

Understanding the Bible
in 3,000 Words

We started by saying that the Bible is an enormous book, very complicated and difficult to understand. So, to gain a better understanding, we took a view from 35,000 feet (getting the big picture of the history and doctrines, leaving behind many details, but capturing the overview), like moving from the individual pieces of a puzzle lying randomly on the table to looking at the picture on the top of the puzzle box.

But to complete our overview of the Bible, we want to go even higher, to get a satellite view from two hundred miles up. From there, we can see even fewer details but have an even better picture of the "whole."

From that altitude, we want to look at three things that will complete our understanding of the overview:

The Story of the Bible in 1,000 words (the people, places, and events of the Bible)

The Teachings of the Bible in 1,000 words (the truth we are to believe)

The Main Message of the Bible in 1,000 words (the offer we are to receive)

THE STORY OF THE BIBLE IN 1,000 WORDS

The People, Places, and Events of the Bible

The Old Testament begins when God created Adam and Eve in a perfect paradise. They later sinned and were driven out of the Garden of Eden, forced to live "by the sweat of [their] face" in an imperfect world (Genesis 3:19). As their offspring multiplied, sin also multiplied. Eventually, humanity became so sinful that, as judgment, God destroyed the earth with a worldwide flood, preserving only Noah and his immediate family on the ark to repopulate the earth.

Sin kept its hold over humanity, however, and once again people forgot God. As the years passed, God revealed Himself to Abraham (two thousand years before Christ), promising him a nation, many descendants, and a blessing that would ultimately extend to everyone on the earth. Abraham believed God and became the father of the Hebrew people. Abraham had a son, Isaac, and Isaac had a son, Jacob. The promises God made to Abraham were passed down through Isaac and Jacob. Jacob had twelve sons, and the promises were passed to all twelve sons, who became the fathers of the twelve tribes of Israel.

Jacob and his family of about seventy people were living in the land of Canaan when a famine hit. They were forced to migrate to Egypt to get food. In time, they became so numerous that they were perceived as a threat by the Egyptian people, and the Egyptians enslaved the Hebrew people. After nearly four hundred years in Egypt, God raised up Moses to lead them out of captivity. With many astounding miracles, including the crossing of the Red Sea, they escaped Egypt and went to Mount Sinai, where they received the Ten Commandments. Shortly after, they rebelled against God again, refusing to enter the Promised Land because they feared giants living in the land, and as a judgment, wandered in the wilderness for the next forty years. Then Moses died, and under the leadership of Joshua, they entered the Promised Land and conquered it.

Israel lived in the Promised Land in a loose governmental system ruled by judges for the next four hundred years. Samson and Samuel are among the most well-known judges. Then Israel insisted on establishing a monarchy (approximately one thousand years before Christ), and the Hebrews were ruled by kings for the next four hundred years. Saul, David, and Solomon were the first three kings, who ruled over a united monarchy for 120 years (forty years each). When Solomon died, the nation divided over the issue of taxation. There was now a Northern Kingdom, which kept the name Israel because a majority (ten) of the tribes were loyal to the north, and a Southern Kingdom, which was called Judah, because Judah was the larger of the two southern tribes.

Because of the accumulating sin of Israel, Assyria, a nation to the northeast, came and conquered Israel and scattered many of the people throughout that part of the world. About one hundred fifty years later, because of the accumulating sin of Judah, Babylonia came and conquered Judah, destroyed Jerusalem, and took many of the people into captivity in Babylonia.

About seventy years later, Persia defeated Babylonia, who had previously defeated Assyria. Thus Persia now ruled from the eastern shores of the Mediterranean Sea to the borders of India. The king of Persia allowed the Israelites living in captivity in Babylonia to return to Jerusalem to rebuild it. Fifty thousand people returned (approximately five hundred years before Christ), rebuilt the city, rebuilt the temple, and restored ceremonial worship of God. They continued to live that way for the next four hundred years. During that time, Persia fell to Greece, which in turn fell to Rome. Rome was ruling that part of the world when Jesus was born.

The ministry of Jesus was preceded by the ministry of His cousin, John the Baptist, who warned the Jews to get ready for the coming of the Messiah. Jesus was born in Bethlehem, near Jerusalem, in fulfillment of Old Testament prophecy. Then Jesus and His parents, Mary and Joseph, moved back to their hometown in Nazareth, in the northern part of the country, just west of the Sea of Galilee. There Jesus lived an apparently normal childhood until the age of thirty, when teachers, by Jewish custom, began their ministry. Jesus began His ministry in Judea; it was marked by both authoritative teaching and remarkable miracles.

Because of mounting opposition to His ministry on the part of the Jewish religious leaders, Jesus went north to the area around the Sea of Galilee, making Capernaum on the north shore His home base. Much of His three-year ministry was conducted in the area around Capernaum, though many events did not actually take place in Capernaum. Eventually, He went to Jerusalem and, because of the jealousy of the religious leaders, was soon crucified. Three days later He rose from the dead, and He showed Himself to His disciples several times over the next forty days. Then, with His disciples gathered around Him on the Mount of Olives, just outside Jerusalem, He visibly ascended into heaven.

He had commissioned His disciples to take the new message of salvation through Christ to Jerusalem, Judea, and Samaria (the surrounding regions), and to the uttermost parts of the earth. The church was established in Jerusalem, and the first Christians were Jews. The church there was overseen by Jesus' apostles. The spread of the gospel to the surrounding area and uttermost parts of the earth was largely undertaken by the apostle Paul, who conducted missionary journeys into areas of Asia Minor and Greece. Finally, Paul was arrested and taken to Rome, where he was eventually executed for his faith. There were enough disciples, however, not only in Jerusalem, but also in Asia Minor, Greece, and Rome, that the message not only lived on, but it grew until it became the dominant world religion.

THE TEACHINGS OF THE BIBLE IN 1,000 WORDS

The Truth We Are to Believe

When we add all the authors of the Bible and all the books of the Bible together, and boil them down to their irreducible minimum, we learn fundamental truth about *ten major subjects*. This summary is certainly not all one should know about revealed truth, but it is presented as an introduction, a *getting wet of the feet*, in the pursuit of greater and more in-depth knowledge.

1. **The Bible:** We learn that the Bible was revealed by God to man. That is, God made known to mankind, through supernatural means, including visions, dreams, direct conversation, divine inspiration, and so forth, what He wanted mankind to know (Hebrews 3:7). Some of this revelation was recorded in the Bible. That information was inspired, meaning that God saw to it that when men wrote down His revelation, they did so without error (2 Peter 1:21). However, people do not naturally grasp the deeper spiritual truths of Scripture. Therefore, the Holy Spirit enables sincere and earnest Christians to gradually understand and embrace the truth of the Bible, illumining their minds to understand the deeper things God has for them (1 Corinthians 2:12). Christians must be diligent students of Scripture, however, if they are to benefit from the Holy Spirit's illumining ministry, studying with an attitude of faith and obedience (2 Timothy 2:15).

2. **God:** In Scripture, we learn that God exists, as seen through nature and through our conscience (Romans 1:20). In addition, we learn His characteristics, what He is like. His traits are many, but they include that He is all-powerful (Job 42:2), present everywhere simultaneously (Psalm 139:8), and all-knowing (Psalm 139:4). We learn also that He is holy (Isaiah 5:16), loving (1 John 4:8), and just (Psalm 19:9). God is sovereign and can do whatever He wills (Psalm 135:5, 6); and He exists in the Trinity, meaning that there is only one God, but that He exists as three co-equal and co-eternal Persons, the same in substance, but distinct in subsistence (Deuteronomy 6:4; 2 Corinthians 13:14).

3. **Christ:** Jesus of Nazareth is God incarnate, the second member of the Trinity (John 1:1). He is fully human (John 1:14), and yet at the same time fully divine, the only God-man ever to exist. He lived a sinless life, was crucified, and rose again from the dead (Romans 1:4). He is now in heaven but will return to earth someday to fulfill the plan of God (Titus 2:13).

4. **Holy Spirit:** The Holy Spirit, the third member of the Trinity (2 Corinthians 13:14), is also God, a personal being, not an impersonal religious force like "school spirit" (Ephesians 4:30). The Holy Spirit plays an instrumental role in each person's salvation, including conviction: revealing to us a need to repent (John 16:8); regeneration: imparting a new spirit and eternal life (Titus 3:5); indwelling: living within us once we are true Christians (Romans 8:9); baptism: placing a believer into the body of Christ (1 Corinthians 12:13); and sealing: guaranteeing the believer's relationship to God (Ephesians 1:13, 14). God wants each of us to serve Him and minister to others, so the Holy Spirit gives each of us special gifts to do so (1 Corinthians 12:4, 11).

5. **Angels:** Angels are spirit beings who serve God and do His will (Hebrews 1:14). Demons are once-righteous angels who fell, rebelling against God and following Satan (Jude 6). Satan is the highest once-righteous angel who fell, becoming evil and corrupt. He is a real person who oversees demons and seeks to neutralize and overthrow the will of God (1 Peter 5:8). God has given us supernatural defenses to protect us from Satan's attempts to discourage, defeat, and even destroy us. These defenses are called the armor of God (Ephesians 6:13–17).

6. **Man:** In Genesis, the term *man* includes both male and female (1:27). Humans were created by God as the pinnacle of His creation. We were created in the spiritual, intellectual, emotional,

and moral image of God (1:27). Our purpose is to glorify God and enjoy Him forever. We humans have a spiritual, as well as physical, dimension (1 Thessalonians 5:23), and our spirits live forever, either in heaven or in hell (Hebrews 9:27). Man is distinct in God's creation, having capacities higher than those of the animals (Genesis 1:26).

7. **Sin:** Sin is the lack of conformity to the moral perfection of God. All humans have been contaminated by sin (1 John 5:17). Adam and Eve, the first humans, were the first to sin. Their sin brought into the world all the pain, evil, and suffering that has been passed down to all other humans, and is so bad that it was called the "Fall" of humanity (Genesis 3:6). We are not sinners because we sin, rather we sin because we are sinners (Ephesians 2:1, 3). Because our internal nature has been corrupted, we cannot keep from sinning (Romans 3:23; 6:23), a fact that brings spiritual death to each one of us.

8. **Salvation:** Salvation is a gift God gives to those who believe (Ephesians 2:8, 9). We are separated from God because of our sin, and when we believe in Jesus and receive Him as our Lord and Savior, God forgives our sin and gives us eternal life (1 John 1:9). The penalty for our sin was paid for by Jesus when He died on the cross for our sin, which is called the substitutionary death of Christ (1 Peter 3:18). Our spiritual salvation begins when we receive Christ, but our ultimate salvation is complete when we die, or when Jesus returns, whichever comes first (Romans 8:23).

9. **Church:** The universal church is the totality of all believers in Jesus, from His first coming to His second coming, and is to be the representation of Christ on earth, collectively doing His will (Matthew 16:18). A local church is a local assembly of believers who organize to carry out the ideals of the universal

church (1 Corinthians 1:1, 2). A local church is to be led by pastor-teachers, elders, and deacons. Only spiritually mature people are to be given positions of spiritual leadership (1 Timothy 3:2–4, 6, 7). When a person becomes a Christian, he or she instantly becomes a member of the universal church, and should also become committed to a local church, placing himself or herself under the spiritual authority of qualified leadership and becoming involved in mutual ministry to other believers (Hebrews 10:24–25).

10. **Future Things:** As certain future events begin to unfold, Jesus will return to earth as King to establish righteousness (Matthew 16:27). At two different times and places, God will judge all humanity to confirm their eternal destiny, either in heaven or hell (2 Corinthians 5:10; Revelation 20:15). Then, the old universe will be destroyed (2 Peter 3:7, 10) and made new (Revelation 21:1), and Christians will live with God in glory, joy, and love forever (Revelation 22:5).

THE MAIN MESSAGE OF THE BIBLE IN 1,000 WORDS

The Offer We Are to Receive

It has been said that the message of the Bible is so simple the smallest child can understand it, and yet so deep that the most profound scholar cannot plumb its depths. On its simplest level, the Bible tells us that God created us in His image and loves us with a love so great we cannot comprehend it. For reasons hidden in the mystery of God's will, humanity sinned against Him. This sin separated all mankind from God and destined us for an eternity in hell. Yet, because God so loved each one of us, He sent His Son, Jesus, to die in our place. If Jesus were not a human, He could not have died for our sins, and if He were not God, it wouldn't have mattered if He had. Because He was both human and God, the Father was willing to place our sin on Jesus and impart Jesus' righteousness to us. He does this when we believe in Jesus as the risen Son of God, and receive Him, or accept Him, as our God. This we must do by a simple act of faith. When, in faith, we acknowledge to God that we believe in Jesus and accept Him as our personal Lord and Savior, being willing to turn from our own life to follow Him, God forgives our sin—past, present and future—and gives us eternal life. From that moment, we are destined for heaven as a child of God. God wants us to live for Him while still on earth, so our lives must be committed to following God as best we know how. We discern His will for our lives by reading Scripture and doing what we find there, as best we can. In addition, we pray and integrate our lives with other committed Christians who can also help us live the life to which we are now called. Jesus said the greatest Commandment is to love the Lord our God with all our heart, soul, and mind, and that the second is to love our neighbor as ourselves (Matthew 22:37–40). This is our task, in its broadest sense, while on earth. When we die, we go to heaven.

If you have never become a Christian, and you are now prepared to respond to God in this way, tell Him you have decided to trust Jesus for your salvation and follow Him as Lord the best way you know how. If you would like some guidance, read the following Scriptures, and pray accordingly.

1. Believe that God created you and loves you, and He wants you to have a meaningful life on earth and eternal life with Him in heaven (John 3:16; 10:10; Ephesians 1:3–8).

2. Tell God that you know you have sinned and are therefore separated from Him, destined for an eternity in hell, and that you want to be saved from your sin and its consequences (Acts 16:30, 31; Romans 3:23; 6:23).

3. Believe that Jesus is the only way your sins can be forgiven and be made right with God (John 14:6; Romans 5:8).

4. Accept Jesus as the Lord of your life, giving yourself to Him to trust and obey, primarily by reading Scripture, praying, and becoming involved with other sincere Christians in a local church. Trust that you are truly made right with God through your act of faith in Jesus (John 1:12; Ephesians 2:8, 9; Revelation 3:20).

If you are ready to give your life to Jesus, you might pray something like the following:

Father in heaven, I believe in You, and I trust that You love me and want me to have a meaningful life here on earth and eternal life in heaven. I acknowledge that I have sinned against You. I am prepared to turn from my sin as best I can. Please forgive my sin. I want to be saved from my sin and its terrible consequences. I believe that only through Jesus can my sins be forgiven. I believe in Him and invite Him to come into my life and be my Savior and Lord. I will live for Him as best I can, trying my best to discern His will for my life through reading Scripture, prayer, and joining a church of sincere Christians who will help me. I know that I will repeatedly fail, but I invite You to come into my life and make me into the kind of person You want me to be, and take me to heaven when I die. Amen.

If you prayed this prayer, meaning it sincerely, then you are now a Christian. Your sins are forgiven. The Bible says that the Holy Spirit comes into your life to help you become what God wants you to be. It is an imperfect process. You may sometimes feel that you are taking one step forward and two steps back. But God will be faithful and will help you. Never give up, no matter what. Join a good church of sincere Christians who believe and follow the Bible. That will be the key to your success. You will flounder otherwise. Get a Bible and begin reading it. Don't worry about what you don't understand. There will likely be much. Just try to follow what you do understand. The Holy Spirit will gradually enable you to understand more and more.

Also, pray to God. Tell Him your deepest thoughts. Ask Him to guide you, to help you discern His will for your life, and to bless your life as you live for Him. Learn more about prayer by reading the Bible and by joining with other Christians for prayer.

There are many good preachers on television and the radio, but be sure to compare everything they say with Scripture. There are also some who will lead you astray if you are not careful. There are good books, also. Ask the Lord to guide you to the help you need to grow in Him. You might get *The New Christian's Handbook*, another book I have written, to give you an overview of your new life in Christ and how to begin growing.

HOW TO
MASTER THE BIBLE SO
WELL THAT THE BIBLE
MASTERS YOU

Now that you have finished the thirty chapters overviewing the story and doctrines of the Bible, and now that you have read the very tight nanosummaries of the story of the Bible, the teachings of the Bible, and the main message of the Bible, you have the necessary foundation to begin to master the Bible so well that the Bible masters you.

There is a very close connection between God and His Word. Jesus Himself is called *the Word of God* (John 1:1, 14; Revelation 19:13). To know God, you must know His Word; to honor God, you must honor His Word; to be in touch with God, you must be in touch with His Word. Mighty promises are given to those who master the Bible so well that the Bible masters them.

We are promised spiritual stability, fruitfulness, and true prosperity as we meditate on His Word day and night (Psalm 1:1–3).

When the words of Jesus abide in us, our desires will be given to us, according to God's will (John 15:7).

Meditating on God's Word leads to prosperity and success in our endeavors (Joshua 1:8).

We will have more wisdom than our enemies, more insight than our teachers, and more understanding than the aged (Psalm 119:97–100).

We will have greater power over sin (Psalm 119:11).

We will have comfort in affliction (Psalm 119:50).

By drawing near to God, we have His promise that He will draw near to us (James 4:8).

These astonishing observations, these magnificent claims, these profound promises—they help us to realize how important the Bible is, and what remarkable potential we bring to our lives when we become serious students of Scripture. That's why it's so important that we commit ourselves to mastering the Bible so well that the Bible masters us.

There are four steps to mastering the Bible so well that the Bible masters you:

1. Read the Bible
2. Study the Bible
3. Memorize the Bible
4. Meditate on the Bible

Seems simple. Obvious, even, for those who have been Christians for a while. Yet very few people take all four steps. Many take one step. Some take two steps. A few take three steps. Very few take all four steps. As a result, very few people ever experience the full life transformation, the fellowship with God, the spiritual stability and strength, the power in ministry, the joy in worship, and the spiritual prosperity that the Bible promises to those who master it so well that it masters them.

STEP #1: READ THE BIBLE FOR BREADTH OF KNOWLEDGE.

To begin a mastery of the Bible, you must read the Bible. This may seem self-evident to some, but to others who have never developed the habit, it is groundbreaking. Some Christians do not read the Bible, or they only read snippets that are attached to daily devotionals. This will not get you where you want to go. You must begin to read the Bible widely.

It is only by covering a lot of territory in Scripture that you gain a breadth of knowledge. If you never read the Old Testament, you will never have a general knowledge of it. If you only read the Gospels, or the Epistles, you will never have a basic grasp of the other sections of the Bible. As a result, your life will be untouched by important truth, plus your ability to connect the dots from various different Scripture passages—a critical component of a mature Christian experience—will be limited.

The New Testament tells us that many stories in the Old Testament were "written for our instruction, upon whom the ends of the ages have come" (1 Corinthians 10:11). If we never read those Old Testament stories, we will never gain the insight, the power, or the freedom that become ours when we do.

The good news is that there is a simple way to read for breadth of knowledge. If you read the Bible for five minutes a day, you will read the Bible over thirty hours a year! (5 minutes × 365 days = 1,825 minutes divided by 60 minutes per hour = 30.4 hours!)

Think of it!! Thirty hours a year! Perhaps no other discipline will provide a breadth of Bible knowledge more easily. If you want to master the Word so well that the Word masters you, begin by reading it.

Very early in my Christian experience, I was challenged to read the Bible at least five minutes a day. I took that challenge, and have not missed my daily time in God's Word in over forty years. As a result, I have read the Bible for a couple thousand hours! And it was all done at the manageable pace of five minutes a day. There is no easier way I could have gained and maintained the breadth of knowledge of Scripture than by taking this simple step. I urge you to take this first step, too.

Pick a readable translation. To begin with, pick a translation that is easy for you to read. Many Christians have a New International Version of the Bible, which is a fairly readable translation. I study out of the New American Standard Bible, which is a good study Bible because the translation is very literal. However, for those times of just reading for the story and flow, and breadth of knowledge, I have found that more conversational translations sometimes allow the Bible to come alive in a way that the NASB does not. I experimented for years with more conversational Bibles and, frankly, was disappointed with them for two reasons. First, they often interpret unclear passages for you to make it more readable, and I didn't always agree with the translators' interpretation. Second, in their attempt to be conversational, they often dumb down the language so that it is unsatisfying to read.

However, I have found *The New Living Translation* to be an effective reading Bible. This version began as a paraphrase that author and publisher Ken Taylor wrote to help his young children understand the Bible better. In a paraphrase, you start with an English Bible and reword it to make it easier to understand. But in 1995, Taylor commissioned a team of translation experts to go back to the original Hebrew and Greek manuscripts and change whatever needed to be changed in order to bring the version up to the level of a translation. In my opinion, they did a commendable job.

All Bible versions have strengths and weaknesses. More literal translations have the strength of being closer to the original languages but the weakness of sometimes being more difficult to understand. More conversational translations are often easier to understand, but sometimes that clarity comes at the expense of accuracy, especially when a difficult passage may have two possible meanings in the original language.

For those reasons, I prefer having both a more literal translation for studying and a more conversational translation for reading. This way, I can compare both translations to gain a fuller understanding.

Pick a time to read. I read before I go to sleep. By experimentation, I learned that I could always carve out five minutes before I go to sleep. But when I tried to read in the morning, sometimes I would get too busy and forget, and I would end up having to read in the evening, so I just switched to reading in the evening.

I found that I can always stay up an extra five minutes to read. No matter how late it is, another five minutes is not going to make or break my evening's rest. There have been times I have been so tired I had to read standing up so I wouldn't fall asleep, but I did it. I have been accused of being legalistic. I'm not. I'm being realistic and disciplined. I've learned that if I give myself an excuse one day, I am likely to give myself an excuse another day and another day. So, I have just not given myself an excuse. And more than two thousand hours of reading the Bible later, with a breadth of knowledge of Scripture I could never have gained or maintained any other way, I am glad I haven't.

Others find that they must read first thing in the morning. It really doesn't matter when you read. The bottom line is: read when it is best for you.

Read for understanding. This was a recommendation given to me by the man who led me to the Lord. He said, "When you read, don't get bogged down by anything you don't understand. Just skip over it, and read for the things you do understand . . . and underline everything that seems especially important." This counsel was extremely valuable to me, and it set me on a course of Bible-knowledge acquisition I'm not sure I would have taken any other way. Without that advice, whenever I would come to something in the text I didn't understand, I would grind to a halt, or be forced to stop reading and start studying, both of which destroyed the original intent.

Read with a plan: Many people are motivated by the goal of reading through the Bible in a year. I think it is something that everyone might want to do at least once, just to know that one has read the entire Bible. However, it is not an easy task, and many who start the project do not complete it. You might set a goal of reading through the Bible without committing to having to do it in a year. Just read five minutes a day, and let it take however long it takes to get through the entire Bible. Other reading plans can be found online.

If the Bible is new to you, I recommend what my mentor recommended to me when I first became a Christian. Read the Gospel of John six times in a row, not worrying about what you don't understand but underlining everything that seems especially important. Then you might read the rest of the Gospels and then the New Testament. After that, you might read the first seventeen books of the Old Testament, known as the historical books. Or, there are eleven primary historical books that you might start with: Genesis, Exodus, Numbers, Joshua, Judges, 1 Samuel, 2 Samuel, 1 Kings, 2 Kings, Ezra, and Nehemiah. Those are the eleven books that tell the story of the Old Testament. The other Old Testament books give additional information, but do not advance the Old Testament story significantly. Then, reading Psalms and Proverbs is always a profitable experience.

On the other hand, if you are a more seasoned Christian and are generally familiar with the Bible, read what is interesting to you in your current circumstances . . . but be open to stretching yourself into other territory from time to time, remembering the importance of reading for breadth of knowledge.

STEP #2: STUDY THE BIBLE FOR DEPTH OF KNOWLEDGE.

Few of us can gain a depth of knowledge without sitting under skilled teachers. So, for most people, they must sit under effective preaching from the Bible and be involved in a Bible study taught by an effective teacher. For maximum benefit, Bible study must have assignments that get you studying and interacting with the Bible on your own. To gain a depth of knowledge, you cannot be passive. You must become active in the process of deepening your knowledge. Crawl before you walk, and walk before you run, but this should be your goal. That is the only way you will progress to a depth of knowledge.

If this is new to you, begin by attending a church that is committed to teaching the Bible, not only from the pulpit during sermons, but also in small groups or Sunday school classes. You might also find helpful information in Christian bookstores or online. More seasoned Christians might be able to give you helpful suggestions as well. If you are an avid reader, there is a wealth of knowledge available to you as well through good books available online or at Christian bookstores. On the resources page, I have included a short list of a few excellent ministries offering Bible studies online

STEP #3: MEMORIZE TO MASTER THE BIBLE.

As we transition from knowing about the Bible, through reading and studying, to knowing the Bible, through memorization, we begin to master the Bible. Until then, our knowledge of Scripture often lies dormant in our memory bank during the ups and downs of life, and may not impact our immediate thoughts and emotions.

The key is to memorize the Scripture deeply . . . so deeply that you can recite it without any struggle, so deeply you can recite it as easily as you can the Pledge of Allegiance, so deeply that someone could wake you at midnight and say, "Quick, what is Romans 12:1–2?" and you could rattle it off without hesitation.

I used to think that it was better to have a lot of verses memorized, but in my effort to have as many verses as possible memorized, I had them memorized shallowly. I might have to struggle to get started, or get partway through a passage and have to paraphrase the rest. Now, I realize it is much better to have fewer verses memorized very deeply—that is where the power comes from. Rather than memorize a mile wide and an inch deep, it is better to memorize an inch wide and a mile deep. That is a key difference, because until we memorize verses deeply and spend time meditating on them, the truth of the passages does not seep deeply into our subconscious to influence our thoughts, attitudes, actions, and emotions.

When we memorize Scripture this deeply, it will often then jump into our minds as our first reaction to life's circumstances, helping guide our decisions and influence our emotions. Even Jesus, when He was tempted by the devil in Matthew 4, quoted Scripture in response to the temptation. When we know Scripture well enough to quote it immediately in response to life's challenges, the Bible begins to take on a power that it did not previously have in our life.

Memorize whatever passages seem especially important to you in whatever season of spiritual life you find yourself at the moment. As you read the Bible, underline verses that jump out at you. Then, spend time memorizing the ones most significant to you.

Just as there are superfoods that pack extraordinary nutritional wallop, so there are super-verses that pack extraordinary spiritual wallop. A key is to develop your list of super-verses, start with the most important ones, memorize them so deeply you can recite them without struggle, and then add the next ones.

The key, however, is to review your super-verses regularly. I review mine almost daily. When you add a new verse or passage, keep reviewing the old ones. If you have them memorized deeply, it doesn't take long. It is amazing how many passages you can review at the speed of an auctioneer.

Memorize one verse so that you can say it without hesitation. Then, memorize another, but link it to the first. Then memorize a third one, but link it to the first two, and so on. Keep doing it the rest of your life. Pretty soon, your command of Scripture will be a mile wide and a mile deep.

As a practical suggestion, don't bite off more than you can chew. If you memorize slowly but faithfully, it will eventually pay big dividends. I am not a great memorizer, but I have worked on it at a manageable pace for years now. And when you stay with something that long, the results are amazing. Just as reading the Bible five minutes a day soon begins to accumulate impressive results, so does memorizing verses at a manageable pace. As we keep up the practice, adding verses that are important to us without dropping off the old ones, we find that we will eventually have many, many verses memorized very deeply. That is the ultimate goal.

Be a spiritual tortoise, not a spiritual hare.

STEP #4: MEDITATE FOR THE BIBLE TO MASTER YOU.

The dictionary defines meditation as "the act of thinking deeply or carefully about something." Biblical meditation might add the idea of frequently: "the act of thinking deeply, carefully, and frequently about Scripture." To meditate on Scripture simply means to think about it over and over, repeatedly reciting it from memory in an attempt to gain new insight from it, along with additional application to one's life. Also, the repetition drives it more deeply into our hearts and subconscious mind.

Many people know passages of Scripture, but have not spent enough time meditating on them enough for the truth of the passages to penetrate deeply into their mind and heart.

In the book *Change Your Heart, Change Your Life*, Gary Smalley makes a compelling case for meditating on Scripture. He states that what we think about all day long, over long periods, eventually seeps into our heart as controlling beliefs. When we learn the right thoughts and mentally chew on them over and over, day after day, they lodge in our hearts as beliefs, and these beliefs become the controlling influences of our lives. If we do not think about Scripture enough, the truth of Scripture may be in our heads as knowledge but not in our hearts as deep, controlling beliefs.

What we think about all day long determines our controlling beliefs, so even if we know a lot of verses, if we don't spend time thinking about them, they will not become controlling beliefs in our lives.

Smalley challenges us to meditate, think about, ponder, and recite Scripture until the Scripture becomes a *path* in our minds and hearts . . . then ponder it some more until the Scripture becomes a *road* in our minds and hearts . . . then ponder it some more until it becomes a *four-lane freeway*. Then, and only then, will the Scripture migrate from information in our heads to deep, controlling beliefs in our hearts. Only then will the Bible begin to fully transform our emotions and empower our living. Only then will the Holy Spirit have the freedom in our lives to govern our thoughts, attitudes, and actions.

The point is that a verse a day doesn't keep the devil away. Rather, it takes washing the mind with the Word of God through frequent meditation over time. I encourage you to consider getting *Change Your Heart, Change Your Life* for additional help in pursuing this goal.

Scientist George Washington Carver found hundreds of uses for the peanut. The number of uses was so astonishingly high that people wanted to know how in the world he came up with so many. When asked, he replied, "If you love something enough, it will reveal its secrets to you." If that is true about peanuts, how much more is it true of Scripture? When thinking about the Bible, beyond the natural process involved, there is also a supernatural process. The Holy Spirit will reveal deeper truth to us as we spend time mentally reviewing Scripture (Psalm 119:97–100).

Through my experience in teaching this material, I have learned that most Christians are busy—so busy that they have difficulty disciplining themselves to implement the four-step process of mastering the Bible so well that the Bible masters them. If that is the case for you, I offer two responses. First, I encourage you to start, even on a modified and very small level. Start by reading the Bible five minutes a day. Choose one verse to memorize, and begin meditating on it. Also, make sure you regularly attend a Bible-teaching church where you can get good instruction in the Bible.

Once you get started, it is easy to expand your efforts. *The key is just to start!* That way, it will help prepare you for the next major issue that rocks your boat on the sea of life. You will be way ahead of the game in dealing with it.

Second, I hope you will start immediately, but *if you do not*, then be sure to remember this book, and put it some place where you can find it easily. You may find you will desperately need it in the future, and then you will have the motivation to begin. My emotional stress was perhaps not as great as Smalley's, but it was severe. It was so severe that it was negatively affecting me physically as well as emotionally and spiritually. The results of this level of stress can be very significant. This information could easily be your lifeline to God's grace.

If you commit yourself to this four-step process, you will begin to master the Bible so well that the Bible begins to master you. And as the Bible begins to master you, you will enjoy the inner peace, love, and joy that is the fruit of the Holy Spirit. In addition, you will experience a peace and power in life and ministry that the Holy Spirit gives to those who meditate on and practice His Word.

CONCLUSION

Spelunkers explore caves while wearing miner's helmets with small electric lights attached. Far back into the caves, the darkness is so complete that without lights, few explorers would ever return. Responsible cavers take helmet lights, handheld flashlights, and a fistful of spare batteries.

The electric lights on the helmets are surprisingly weak. The weaker the bulb, the longer the battery will last. The fact is, back in that utter blackness, you don't need a lot of light. Just a hint of light is enough to allow you to find your way out of the cave. But without the light, there would be no way to escape from some of the more complex caves.

When you cannot see at all, you are a victim of your surroundings. You stumble into unseen dangers. You unknowingly pass by ways of escape. You are imprisoned by the blindness, doomed to a fate beyond your control.

But . . . just light one lamp, and deliverance is on the way.

This gives new meaning to the scriptures, "Your Word is a lamp to my feet and a light to my path" and "The unfolding of Your words gives light" (Psalm 119:105, 130). The metaphor is clear. If we do not know the Word of God, or if we have not mastered the Word sufficiently that it penetrates our hearts and minds, and controls our beliefs, emotions, and behavior, we are groping through the darkness of life without a light. We stumble into unseen dangers, we unknowingly pass by avenues of escape. We wander in circles, doomed to a fate beyond our control.

But, just add God's truth to our lives, and suddenly we can see. It keeps us from stepping into danger or taking the wrong path. It is the light we need to find our way in this dark world, and walk in peace and power with Him.

I urge you: Do not try to make it through the darkness without a light! Take the four steps to mastering the Bible so well that the Bible masters you.

May God's grace be sufficient for you as you faithfully follow the light of His Word. Remember God's mighty promises to those who do.

TEACHING PLAN

INTRODUCTION

The book *30 Days to Understanding the Bible* is an excellent tool for people who want to learn more about the Bible and its life-transforming message. The book features such learning helps as maps, charts, tables, review exercises, and self-tests to encourage reader interaction with the material in order to increase learning and comprehension.

Group study of *30 Days* adds another dimension to the learning process. In a group, students can interact with the teacher as well as one another to deepen their insights into the nature and purpose of the Bible. The following teaching suggestions are designed to help you lead an effective group study of this important book.

Your students will be expected to read the book on their own. But they will attend the group study to process what they are learning, discuss their ideas with others, clarify the insights and facts to which they are being exposed, and perhaps even celebrate with one another the blessings that come with greater understanding of God's Word.

PREVIEW OF THE STUDY

The first thirty chapters of *30 Days to Understanding the Bible* will be covered in the following thirteen sessions:

Session 1: Structure of the Bible, Old Testament Geography, and Historical Books (Chs. 1–3)

Session 2: The Old Testament Story, Creation–Conquest (Chs. 4–7)

Session 3: The Old Testament Story, Judges–Silence (Chs. 8–12)

Session 4: Poetical and Prophetical Books (Chs. 13 and 14)

Session 5: New Testament Geography and Structure (Ch. 15)

Session 6: Gospel/Church Eras (Chs. 16 and 17)

Session 7: Missions Era/Epistles (Chs. 18 and 19)

Session 8: Foundations of Christian Belief (Chs. 20 and 21)

Session 9: God and His Son (Chs. 22 and 23)

Session 10: The Holy Spirit and Angels (Chs. 24 and 25)

Session 11: Man and Sin (Chs. 26 and 27)

Session 12: Salvation and the Church (Chs. 28 and 29)

Session 13: The Doctrine of Future Things (Ch. 30)

REPRODUCIBLE IMAGES FOR TEACHING

Visit Biblein30Days.com to download and print images that can be used in electronic presentations. Picked up from various places throughout this book, these images will be used in various sessions throughout this study. For your convenience, here's a complete list of these images. (Details on how to use them appear in the individual session plans below.)

- Old Testament Books/New Testament Books
- The Three Kinds of Books in the Old Testament
- The Three Kinds of Books in the New Testament
- Work Map: Locations of the Old Testament
- Map: State of Texas/Land of the Bible
- Overview of Old Testament History
- Arc of Bible History
- Bodies of Water in the Gospels
- The Geography of Acts
- Overview of New Testament History

- Timeline of the New Testament
- Map of Galilee, Samaria, and Judea
- Map of the New Testament World
- Ten Great Doctrines of the Bible
- Four Major Subdivisions of the Doctrine of the Bible
- Four Major Subdivisions of the Doctrine of God
- Four Major Subdivisions of the Doctrine of Christ
- Four Major Subdivisions of the Doctrine of the Holy Spirit
- Four Major Subdivisions of the Doctrine of Angels
- Four Major Subdivisions of the Doctrine of Man
- Four Major Subdivisions of the Doctrine of Sin
- Four Major Subdivisions of the Doctrine of Salvation
- Four Major Subdivisions of the Doctrine of the Church
- Four Major Subdivisions of the Doctrine of Future Things
- Review of Ten Great Doctrines and Their Subdivisions

GENERAL PREPARATION FOR THE STUDY

In order to lead students in this study of the Bible, you must be well prepared yourself. Here are some practical steps you can take to make sure you are ready before the time for Session 1 rolls around.

1. Read this book thoroughly at least once. Take time to complete the written exercises in the book. This will give you a good idea of the challenges and rewards your students will face in the study of the material.

2. Look over the teaching plans for all thirteen sessions. Note especially those sessions that suggest that you give advance assignments to students. Make a note of the students whom you will ask to do these extra tasks. Begin now to enlist students in advance for these assignments.

3. Pull together a selection of reference books that might be helpful to students who agree to do these extra assignments. Bible dictionaries, Bible handbooks, and books that overview the entire Bible should be especially helpful.

4. Prepare the room by arranging the chairs in circular fashion in order to generate dialogue and discussion among the students. Collect equipment and learning aids you will need— computer, television, chalkboard, or dry erase board, pencils or pens, felt-tip pens, and so forth.

5. Pray that the Lord will bless your teaching and that the students will be open and receptive to truths and insights presented during this study.

6. Remember, these lesson outlines are guides, not straitjackets. Feel free to amend them so they meet your needs. You may have to add or subtract material based on your students' previous knowledge or the amount of time you have. You may want to cover the material in six sessions or sixteen rather than thirteen. The procedures offered here assume a class session of forty-five minutes to one hour.

NOTE: Before the first class, have the students read Chapters 1–3, but they should not fill in the blanks in their books.

SESSION 1: STRUCTURE OF THE BIBLE, OLD TESTAMENT GEOGRAPHY, AND HISTORICAL BOOKS

Overview: This session covers the material in Chapters 1–3.

Before the Session

1. Prepare the following items from the website for display during this session:

- Old Testament/New Testament Books
- The Three Kinds of Books in the Old Testament
- The Three Kinds of Books in the New Testament
- Work Map: Locations of the Old Testament
- Map: State of Texas/Land of the Bible
- Overview of Old Testament History

2. Review Chapters 1–3 to call to mind the content to be covered in this session. Be sure to complete all the self-tests, writing the answers to the questions in your book.

3. Read carefully Section 4 of this book, "NanoSummary of the Bible," while looking at the "Geography of the Old Testament" map to be sure you have the big picture of the story in your mind.

4. Prepare a poster with the titles of all thirteen sessions of this study (see "Preview of the Study" above). Place this poster in a prominent place in the room. Leave the poster up throughout the study as a visible reminder to the students of the progress they are making. You might even place a check mark on each session as it is completed, and remind them at the beginning of each session of the lessons they have already completed.

During the Session

1. Open with prayer that this will be a profitable and encouraging study for everyone.

2. As an icebreaker, have the students break into pairs (assuming they do not know each other), introduce themselves to one another and chat for two or three minutes. Then ask them to introduce their partners to the rest of the group, telling their name and other information such as family, employment, hobbies, and so on.

3. Direct the students' attention to the wall poster with an outline of all thirteen sessions of the study, commenting on the scope of this challenging learning opportunity. Remind students that they will be expected to complete the reading for each session in their books before they come to class, but they will not fill in the blanks. This will be done in class after a review of the material. If they want to take the quiz at home when they read the chapter, have them write the answers on another sheet of paper.

4. Display the "Old Testament Books/New Testament Books" chart. Review the information, then have them close their books and ask them how many books are in the Old Testament, in the New Testament, and the whole Bible.

   Finally, have them write the answers in their books.

   NOTE: This pattern of orally drilling the students until they seem to know the answers, then having them fill in the blanks in their books, will be used frequently throughout the book.

5. Display the "The Three Kinds of Books in the Old Testament" chart, followed by "The Three Kinds of Books in the New Testament." Review the information on these charts, then drill the students until they can give you the responses readily. Then, have them complete the self-tests on pages 14–15. Remind them that they will learn more about these books and the categories of literature to which they belong in later sessions of this study.

6. Have one or more persons read aloud "NanoSummary of the Bible." On the map of the Old Testament, draw the arrows for each number in the story that show the movement of the story.

7. Display the "State of Texas/Land of the Bible" map. Explain that the entire territory known as the "Old Testament World" is approximately the same size as the state of Texas. Most

students are surprised to learn that the Old Testament world was no larger than this. Ask, "How does this compare with what you had previously thought about the size of the Old Testament world?"

8. Display the "Work Map: Locations of the Old Testament." Point out the locations A through G and 1–8 on this map, commenting briefly on the significance of each. Then point at each of these places again, asking the students to provide the correct name. Next, have the students do the same for their partners, and the partners for the students. Finally, ask them to complete the self-test.

9. Display the "Overview of Old Testament History," explaining that this chart is a summary of all the material covered in Chapter 3 in their books. More than two thousand years of biblical history are represented by this chart.

   Cover the chart so that none of the information shows. Then ask students to search Chapter 3 in their books and find the following information. As they locate and call out the information, uncover it:

   • The nine eras of Old Testament history
   • The major figure or biblical personality of each era
   • The primary geographic location of the events in these nine different eras
   • The storylines that summarize these nine eras, their personalities, and their locations

10. If time permits, divide the students into teams of two. Ask them to work together to complete the remaining self-tests in Chapters 1–3. If time does not permit, you can tell them the answers to complete all the remaining self-tests.

11. Close with prayer.

Looking Ahead to the Next Session

Remind the students that the next session will cover Chapters 4–7. They should read the material, but not fill in the blanks in their books. This will be done in class.

SESSION 2: THE OLD TESTAMENT STORY (CREATION–CONQUEST)

Overview: This session covers the material in Chapters 4–7.

Before the Session

1. Prepare the following items from the back of this book or the website for display during this session:
    *   Overview of Old Testament History
    *   Arc of Bible History
2. Gather materials needed to create a "map" on the floor, so that as you review the Old Testament story, Creation–Conquest, you can point/walk to the place on the floor map where the event occurred. Use the Old Testament Work Map as your guide. The floor map only needs to approximate the accuracy of a real map, especially since you can display the real map as you lay out the floor map. You will need:
    *   Cord/string/rope long enough to use as the coastline for the Mediterranean Sea
    *   Shorter cord/string/rope for the Jordan, Tigris, and Euphrates Rivers
    *   Small paperback book (or anything else) to represent the Sea of Galilee
    *   Two larger books (or anything else) to represent the Dead Sea

- Styrofoam/plastic cups on which you can, with a felt-tip marker, write the names of cities, countries, etc.

Make the map as large as feasible for your room. Then, as you tell the story, you can walk or point to the appropriate place on the floor map.

3. Prepare a 15- to 30-minute (depending on how long your session is) presentation of the story of the Old Testament, Creation–Conquest. Follow the story in the book. Be sure to highlight the information called for in the self-test material. It is desirable for you to supplement the book material with your own knowledge and to be able to answer questions. If you need help preparing, consult a Bible handbook, Bible atlas, and other material.

4. Read Chapters 4–7 and complete the self-tests and learning exercises. Remember, a good teacher should always be at least a step or two ahead of his or her students!

During the Session

1. Open with prayer for God's guidance and blessing during this session.

2. As a review for students, display the "Overview of Old Testament History," which you used last session. Lead them to identify the nine eras of Old Testament history.

3. Display the "Arc of Bible History," pointing out that the first four eras of Old Testament history (Creation–Conquest) are represented by the first four icons on the chart (the next five represent the last five eras in Old Testament history, and the final three icons represent New Testament history). Point to each icon, and ask the students to name these four eras. Ask the students to quiz each other in teams of two until they readily identify the era by pointing to the icon. They can use their books for this review.

4. Talk through the history of Creation–Conquest, walking through the map as you do. After you have gone through it in-depth once, go through it quickly a time or two as review. After you have finished with the events in a given era, point to the icon on the "Arc of Bible History" to reinforce the era with the events.

5. If time permits, have the partners help each other as they fill in all the self-test material. If time does not permit, talk them through the answers yourself.

6. Close with a prayer of thanksgiving for the people of Old Testament times who obeyed God and passed His message on to succeeding generations, and who helped us understand how to live by faith.

Looking Ahead to the Next Session

Remind the students to read Chapters 8–12 before the next session.

SESSION 3: THE OLD TESTAMENT STORY (JUDGES–SILENCE)

Overview: This session covers the material in Chapters 8–12.

Before the Session

Make the same preparations for this session (Judges–Silence, Chapters 8–12) as you did for the last session.

During the Session

Use exactly the same procedures for this session as you did for the last session, but relate the information on Judges–Silence, found in Chapters 8–12.

Looking Ahead to the Next Session

Remind the students to read Chapters 13 and 14 before the next session.

SESSION 4: POETICAL AND PROPHETICAL BOOKS

Overview: This session covers the material in Chapters 13 and 14.

Before the Session

1. Prepare the following items from the website for display during this session:
   - The Three Kinds of Books in the Old Testament
   - Work Map: Locations of the Old Testament
2. Enlist a student in your class to do research on the poetical books of the Old Testament and to be prepared to present a five-minute report on this topic during Session 4. (If this does not fit your circumstances, prepare the report yourself.)
3. Enlist another student to do research on the prophetical books of the Old Testament and to be prepared to present a five-minute report on this topic during Session 4 (or do it yourself).
4. Review Chapters 13 and 14 to call to mind the content to be covered in Session 4. Be sure to complete the self-tests on pages 117 and 124–125, writing the answers to these questions in your book.
5. Enlist a student to read a short psalm from the Book of Psalms and to lead the class in prayer at the beginning of the session, if appropriate. If your class is geared to seekers or young/new Christians, be cautious of embarrassing them.

During the Session

1. Call on the student whom you have enlisted to read a short psalm and lead the class in prayer.

2. Remind the students that this psalm read at the beginning of the class is from the Book of Psalms—one of the great poetic books of the Old Testament. Then state that you will be studying the poetical and prophetical books of the Old Testament during this session.

3. Display "The Three Kinds of Books in the Old Testament" chart to show that poetical books make up one of the major categories of Old Testament literature.

4. Call on the student whom you have enlisted to give the report on the poetical books of the Old Testament. Ask the other students to open their books to pages 115–117 while this report is being presented and to compare the student report with this printed information. They might jot down in the margins of their books on these pages any important information covered by the student report.

5. After the student report, drill the students on the self-test. Then have them review the material with their partner. Finally, let the students complete the self-test on page 117.

6. Display "The Three Kinds of Books in the Old Testament" chart again. Ask which of these books are known as the *Major Prophets* and which are called the *Minor Prophets*. What do these two terms mean—*Major Prophets* and *Minor Prophets*?

7. Call on the student whom you have enlisted to give a report on the prophetical books of the Old Testament. Then ask the class to turn to the information on "Structure of the Prophetical Books" (pp. 122–123). Point out that the prophetical books were addressed to many different regions of the Old Testament world under many different situations and conditions.

8. Display the "Work Map: Locations of the Old Testament." Ask students to locate on this map the different nations and regions to which the prophetical books of the Old Testament were addressed.

9. Drill the students on the self-test for the prophetical books. Then have them review with their partners. Finally, have them complete the self-test on pages 124–125.

10. Ask a student to lead the closing prayer, if appropriate, expressing special thanks for the poetic and prophetic books of the Old Testament. If your students are unaccustomed to praying in public, close with prayer yourself.

Looking Ahead to the Next Session

Remind the class to read Chapter 15 of their books before the next class meeting, Session 5.

SESSION 5: NEW TESTAMENT GEOGRAPHY AND STRUCTURE

Overview: This session covers the material in Chapter 15.

Before the Session

1. Prepare the following items from the website for display during this session:
   - Bodies of Water in the Gospels
   - The Geography of Acts
   - Overview of New Testament History
   - Arc of Bible History

2. Review Chapter 15 to call to mind the content to be covered in this session. Be sure to complete the self-test on page 136, writing the answers in the blanks in your book.

3. Pray for the Holy Spirit's guidance as you prepare to lead the class in this important session on an introduction to the New Testament.

During the Session

1. Begin with a prayer of thanks to God for the two grand divisions of the Bible—the Old Testament and the New Testament. Ask for God's insight and guidance in this introductory study on the New Testament.

2. Call attention to the poster with titles of all thirteen sessions of this study of the Bible. Remind the students that you have now completed all sessions on the Old Testament and that this session marks the beginning of your studies of the New Testament. Use the following questions to generate interest and discussion about the New Testament and its relationship to the Old Testament.

   • What's your favorite section of the Bible—the Old Testament or the New Testament? Why?

   • What's the major difference between the Old Testament and the New Testament?

   • Which is more important—the Old Testament or the New Testament?

   • Which is easier to understand—the Old Testament or the New Testament?

3. Display the "Bodies of Water in the Gospels," asking students to identify these bodies of water in the New Testament world and to write these names in their books (p. 131).

4. Ask the students to open their books to pages 134–135 while you display "The Geography of Acts." Mention each of these sites and its significance, pointing out its location on the transparency. Then divide the class into teams of two and let them work together on learning these names and their locations, completing the blank map on page 137 of their books.

5. Display the "Overview of New Testament History." Then flash the "Overview of Old Testament History" briefly, followed by the "Overview of New Testament History." Note that Old Testament history features nine different eras covering about two thousand years, while New Testament history has only three different eras covering about a hundred years. Reinforce this truth by displaying the "Arc of Bible History," which shows all twelve eras of biblical history together.

6. Ask the students to turn to page 137 in their books. Then lead them to complete the exercises on page 138 and 140–141 and to write the answers in their books. Take time to answer questions or provide information as needed to broaden their understanding about the geography and structure of the New Testament.

7. Close with prayer.

Looking Ahead to the Next Session

Remind the class to read Chapters 16 and 17 of their books before the next class, Session 6.

SESSION 6: GOSPEL/CHURCH ERAS

Overview: This session covers the material in Chapters 16 and 17.

Before the Session

1. Prepare the map of Galilee, Samaria, and Judea from the website and have it ready to display during this session.

2. Review Chapters 16 and 17 to call to mind the content to be covered in this session. Be sure to complete the self-tests, writing the answers to these questions in your book.

3. Gather materials needed for a floor map of the New Testament area.

4. Write the following outline on the chalkboard or a large sheet of poster paper, leaving adequate space after each point for writing in major events from the life of Jesus:

MAJOR EVENTS IN JESUS' LIFE

1. Early Life: Childhood to Baptism
2. Early Ministry: Initial Acceptance
3. Later Ministry: Growing Rejection
4. Death and Resurrection: Final Rejection

Note that this outline comes from pages 145–147 of the book.

During the Session

1. Lead in a prayer of thanksgiving for the life and ministry of Jesus and His saving power, and ask for His blessings on the session.
2. Remind the students that today's study will focus on the life and ministry of Jesus and the beginning of the church. Point out that Jesus' ministry lasted only about three years, and it was conducted in an area only about thirty miles wide by ninety miles long.
3. Display the map of Galilee, Samaria, and Judea, pointing out the region's relatively small size. Ask the students to identify in the life of Jesus the significance of each of these five places on the map:
   - Bethlehem
   - Egypt
   - Nazareth
   - Capernaum
   - Jerusalem

4. Using the same materials you used for the Old Testament, lay out a map of the New Testament area on the floor of the room. Direct the students' attention to the outline, "Major Events in Jesus' Life," which you have posted in the room. Ask them to help you fill in this outline by recalling major events in His life and ministry under each point on the outline. Write these events on the outline as they are recalled by the class. As they are identified, trace the geographical movement on the floor map. Here are a few major events, just in case you don't get any help from your students. (Be sure you know where all these events took place.):

   i. Early Life

      Birth in Bethlehem

      Flight into Egypt

      Presentation as an infant in the temple

      Discussion with learned scholars in the temple

   ii. Early Ministry: Acceptance

      Temptations in the wilderness

      Miracles of healing

      Sermon on the Mount

      Calling of His disciples

   iii. Later Ministry: Rejection

      Clash with Pharisees and Sadducees

      Withdrawal with His disciples

      Teaching His disciples about His forthcoming death

      Peter's confession at Caesarea–Philippi

   iv. Death and Resurrection

      Triumphal entry into Jerusalem

      Last Supper with His disciples

      Agonizing prayer in the Garden of Gethsemane

      Crucifixion

Resurrection

Post-resurrection appearances

5. Ask the students to turn to page 147 in their books and to review with their partner before they complete the self-test and other exercises.

6. Display the "Map of the Holy Land" again and show on this map how the church spread from Jerusalem to Judea to Samaria after Jesus' ascension, in accordance with the promise and prediction of Jesus. Write "Judea" and "Samaria" on the map. Explain that this stage of the growth of the church is described in chapters 1–12 of the Book of Acts.

7. Close with a prayer of thanks for Jesus, the gospel, and the church.

Looking Ahead to the Next Session

Remind the class to read the text and complete the exercises in Chapters 18 and 19 of their books before the next meeting, Session 7.

SESSION 7: MISSIONS ERA/EPISTLES

Overview: This session covers the material in Chapters 18 and 19.

Before the Session

1. Prepare the following items from the back of this book or the website for display during this session:
   - Timeline of the New Testament
   - Map of the New Testament World

2. Enlist two students to research and prepare two different five-minute reports on the apostle Paul for presentation during Session 7. One report should focus on "The Life and Missionary Travels of Paul," while the other should cover "The Epistles and

Theological Contribution of Paul." If you have no volunteers, prepare them yourself.

3. Review Chapters 18 and 19 to call to mind the content to be covered in this session. Be sure to complete the self-tests.

During the Session

1. Begin the class with prayer, asking the Holy Spirit to direct the class during the session as you focus on the exciting years of the expansion of the early church.

2. Display the "Map of the New Testament World." Ask the students to open their books to pages 163–164. Explain that the person who took the lead in planting churches throughout the New Testament world during the first Christian century was the apostle Paul. Pages 163–164 in their books gives an outline of the missionary travels of this great "apostle to the Gentiles."

3. Introduce the student whom you have enlisted to give a report on "The Life and Missionary Travels of Paul." Ask the other students to take notes during this presentation, comparing the facts presented with the outline of Paul's travels on pages 163–164 in their books. After this presentation, generate additional discussion on Paul with questions such as these:

   • Why do you think Paul became the great "apostle to the Gentiles"? How was he uniquely qualified for his role as the first great missionary of Christianity?

   • How did Paul support himself during his missionary travels?

   • Who were some of the key helpers and companions who assisted Paul in his work?

4. After this discussion, ask students to turn to page 164 in their books and review with their partners before they complete the self-test on the major events in Paul's life.

5. Display the "Timeline of the New Testament." Ask the students to turn to page 172 in their books. Ask them to identify the twenty-year period during which the epistles of Paul were written by comparing these epistles with the timeline. Point out that Paul was more than a great missionary in early Christianity; he was also a great theologian and letter writer who wrote thirteen of the twenty-seven books of the New Testament.

6. Ask the students to open their books to pages 173–175, which discuss Paul's epistles to churches and individuals. Then introduce the student whom you have enlisted to present a report on "The Epistles and Theological Contribution of Paul." Ask them to fill in the blanks in their books regarding Paul's epistles as they listen to the presentation on this subject.

7. Refer the students to the information about the General Epistles on page 176 of their books. Lead a discussion of these books, helping them to fill in the blanks in their books with the missing information about these epistles.

8. Call on a student, if appropriate, to close with a prayer of thanksgiving for the apostle Paul and his contribution to God's kingdom.

SESSION 8: FOUNDATIONS OF CHRISTIAN BELIEF

Overview: This session covers the material in Chapters 20 and 21.

Before the Session

1. Prepare the following items from the back of this book or the website for display during this session:
   - Ten Great Doctrines of the Bible
   - Four Major Subdivisions of the Doctrine of the Bible

2. Review Chapters 20 and 21 in the book to call to mind the content to be covered in this session. Be sure to complete the self-tests on pages 189 and 196–197, writing the answers to these questions in your book.

3. Locate and read the Bible passages that relate to the four major subdivisions of the Bible: Hebrews 3:7; 2 Peter 1:21; 1 Corinthians 2:12; and 2 Timothy 2:15. Read these passages in several translations and be prepared to discuss them with the students.

4. List the ten great doctrines of the Bible on the chalkboard or white board.

During the Session

1. Open with prayer that this will be a profitable and rewarding learning experience for all students.

2. Display the "Ten Great Doctrines of the Bible." Explain that the final six sessions of the study will focus on these ten major doctrines.

3. Direct the students' attention to the ten major doctrines you have listed on the chalkboard or dry erase board. Ask them to match these words with the appropriate logos on the "Ten Great Doctrines" chart. Write these words in the appropriate spaces as they are matched correctly by the students.

4. After all the logos and words have been matched correctly, generate discussion on these doctrines by asking questions such as these:

   - Of these ten doctrines, which is most important, in your opinion?
   - Why do you think the Bible is listed as the first of these ten doctrines?
   - Why are God, Christ, and the Holy Spirit grouped together?

5. Display the "Four Major Subdivisions of the Doctrine of the Bible." Explain that these are important words about the Bible—revelation, inspiration, illumination, and interpretation—which every Christian needs to understand.

6. Call on one student to read aloud Hebrews 3:7, a second to read 2 Peter 1:21, a third to read 1 Corinthians 2:12, and a fourth to read 2 Timothy 3:15. Ask the other students to follow in their Bibles as these are being read. Then ask them to match these Bible verses with the "Four Major Subdivisions of the Doctrine of the Bible."

7. Have the students turn to pages 195–197 in their books and complete the review and self-test exercises on the Bible.

8. Close with a prayer of thanksgiving for these ten great doctrines of the Christian faith, especially the Bible and its influence in the lives of believers.

Looking Ahead to the Next Session

Remind the class to read the text and complete the learning exercises in Chapters 22 and 23 of their books before the next class session, Session 9.

SESSION 9: GOD AND HIS SON

Overview: This session covers the material in Chapters 22 and 23.

Before the Session

1. Prepare the following items from the website for display during this session:
   - Ten Great Doctrines of the Bible
   - Four Major Subdivisions of the Doctrine of God
   - Four Major Subdivisions of the Doctrine of Christ

2. Review Chapters 22 and 23 to call to mind the content to be covered in this session. Be sure to complete the self-tests on pages 206 and 214, writing the answers to these questions in your book.

3. Ask a student in advance to do some research on the doctrine of God and to be prepared to bring a five-minute report on the subject during the session. A good one-volume Bible dictionary should have an article on this subject. Ask him or her to concentrate specifically on the names and attributes of God in this report.

During the Session

1. Call on a student to lead in prayer for the Holy Spirit's guidance during this session.

2. Refer the students to the poster with the outline of this thirteen-session study, reminding them that you will be studying about God and His Son Jesus during this session.

3. Display the "Ten Great Doctrines of the Bible," leading the students to review and recall these ten major doctrines. Point to the triangle at the top and remind them that they will be studying about two persons of the Trinity during this session—God and His Son.

4. Display the "Four Major Subdivisions of the Doctrine of God." Lecture briefly on the "existence," "sovereignty," and "Trinity" points of this chart. Then introduce the student whom you enlisted in advance to present a brief report on the names and attributes of God. After the report, help the students to clarify their thinking by asking questions like these and leading them in a general discussion:

- What do we mean by the "attributes" of God?
- What do we mean when we say that God is "sovereign"?
- How do we know that God exists?

5. Break the students into several small groups. Have half the small groups work on the "divine attributes" section in their books (pages 204–205), while the other groups work on the "personal attributes" section (page 205). Ask them to look up all the Scriptures mentioned and discuss these in their small groups, writing in the answers in their books.

6. Display the "Four Major Subdivisions of the Doctrine of Christ." Break the class into four smaller groups. Group 1 should search their Bibles for evidence of the deity of Christ; while group 2 should search for evidence of His humanity; group 3, His resurrection; and group 4, His return. If time permits, have each group give a brief report on its findings to the rest of the class.

7. Working individually, the students should complete the self-tests in their books on God (page 206) and Christ (page 214).

8. Close with prayer that truths that you have discovered about God and Christ will provide guidance and direction for daily living for every member of the class.

Looking Ahead to the Next Session

1. Remind the class to read the text and complete the learning exercises in Chapters 24 and 25 of their books before the next class session.

2. Ask the students during the time before the next session to be on the lookout for "angel evidence"—articles in newspapers and magazines about angels, books on angels in bookstores, testimonies from people who claim to have experienced encounters with angels, etc. The class will discuss this "angel evidence" in Session 10.

SESSION 10: THE HOLY SPIRIT AND ANGELS

Overview: This session covers the material in Chapters 24 and 25.

Before the Session

1. Prepare the following items from the website for display during this session:
    - Ten Great Doctrines of the Bible
    - Four Major Subdivisions of the Doctrine of the Holy Spirit
    - Four Major Subdivisions of the Doctrine of Angels
2. Review Chapters 24 and 25 to call to mind the content to be covered in this session. Be sure to complete the self-tests on pages 225 and 233–234, writing the answers to these questions in your book.

During the Session

1. Begin with a prayer of thanks for the truths and insights you are learning about the great doctrines of the Christian faith.
2. To make sure the students are reading the material and completing the exercises in their books, call for the answers to the self-tests on pages 225 and 233–234. Remind the class that they should be completing the exercises *before* the class sessions.
3. Display the "Ten Great Doctrines of the Bible" and lead the class to identify the three great truths that you have already studied—the Bible, God, and His Son. Remind them that you will be studying the third person of the Trinity—the Holy Spirit—as well as the doctrine of angels during this session.
4. Display the "Four Major Subdivisions of the Doctrine of the Holy Spirit." Lecture briefly on the meaning of "personality" and "deity." Then ask the students to search their books for the meaning of the CRIBS acrostic, which represents "salvation." When the students find this information and call it out, write this acrostic on the chalkboard:

C-onviction

R-egeneration

I-ndwelling

B-aptism

S-ealing

5. Ask a student to read aloud 1 Corinthians 12:4, 11, one of the classic passages in the New Testament about spiritual gifts given to believers by the Holy Spirit. Ask what spiritual gifts are necessary for the proper functioning of a church.

6. Display the "Four Major Subdivisions of the Doctrine of Angels." Lead the class in a general discussion of the "angel evidence" in our contemporary culture, drawing from their observations of this phenomenon during the past week. Ask why there is a fascination with angels in our society. Do some people have a false view of who angels are and what they do? Ask them to find the biblical definition of angels in their books (p. 230 beside the angel icon).

7. Refer the students to the logos of demons and Satan on the transparency. Ask, Why are *demons* and *Satan* included in this discussion of *angels*? Then ask them to find the three passages of Scripture in their books that represent the protection or defense available to Christians in their fight against Satan. As these passages are discovered (pp. 233–234), write them on the chalkboard:

   - 1 Peter 5:8
   - Ephesians 6:13
   - James 4:7

8. Ask a student to close with prayer, thanking God for His provision of the Holy Spirit and angels for the guidance and protection of believers.

Looking Ahead to the Next Session

Remind the class to read the text and complete the learning exercises in Chapters 26 and 27 of their books before the next class session.

SESSION 11: MAN AND SIN

Overview: This session covers the material in Chapters 26 and 27.

Before the Session

1. Prepare the following items from the website for display during this session:
   - Ten Great Doctrines of the Bible
   - Four Major Subdivisions of the Doctrine of Man
   - Four Major Subdivisions of the Doctrine of Sin
2. Review Chapters 26 and 27 to call to mind the content to be covered in this session. Be sure to complete the self-tests on pages 242–243 and 250–251, writing the answers to these questions in your book.

During the Session

1. Begin with a prayer for God's guidance during this session.
2. Display the "Four Major Subdivisions of the Doctrine of Man." Lecture briefly on the high points of this doctrine, drawing from the material on pages 239–241 of the book.
3. Point out that the doctrine of man is related closely to another major doctrine of the Christian faith—man's sin. Display the "Four Major Subdivisions of the Doctrine of Sin." Lecture briefly on this doctrine, drawing from the material on pages 246–248 of the book.
4. Display the "Ten Great Doctrines of the Bible."

5. Divide the class into several smaller groups, with three or four people in each group. Inform them that they will work together as small groups during the remainder of this session. They will search the Bible together to find evidence of the sinful nature of man and how God deals with sin. They will also work together to review all the great doctrines they have studied so far, completing the review exercise on pages 245–246 of their books. In their groups, they should discuss everything they have studied so far, clarifying their thoughts with one another and turning to previous sections of their books to find needed information. Make yourself available to all groups as a resource person to help them in this review process.

6. After the small groups have concluded their work, lead the class in a general discussion of the doctrines of man and sin, supplementing their ideas, as needed, with additional information. Answer their questions about any doctrine they have studied up to this point.

7. Call on a member of the class to lead in a prayer of thanks for this student-to-student sharing session.

Looking Ahead to the Next Session

Remind the class to read the text and complete the learning exercises in Chapters 28 and 29 of their books before the next class session.

SESSION 12: SALVATION AND THE CHURCH

Overview: This session covers the material in Chapters 28 and 29.

Before the Session

1. Prepare the following items from the website for display during this session:

- Four Major Subdivisions of the Doctrine of Salvation
- Four Major Subdivisions of the Doctrine of the Church

2. Review Chapters 28 and 29 to call to mind the content to be covered in this session. Be sure to complete the self-tests on pages 258 and 267–268, writing the answers to these questions in your book.

3. Make copies of the following fill-in-the-blanks exercise for distribution to students during this session. (You will find these statements on pages 261–263, and 263–265 of the book.)

IMPORTANT FACTS ABOUT THE CHURCH

1. The church is not a building, but _____.
2. The church began on the _____.
3. Augustine said: "_____."
4. The universal church is also called the _____.
5. Every believer should be a part of a _____.
6. Only _____ are to be given high positions of spiritual leadership in the church.
7. The universal church is to be the _____ _____, collectively doing His will.

During the Session

1. Remind the students that the doctrine of sin, which you discussed during Session 11, leads logically to the doctrine of salvation. God's provision of salvation is necessary because of our sin.

2. Display the "Four Major Subdivisions of the Doctrine of Salvation." Ask for some authentic truths about salvation. Guide the class to highlight the truths about salvation discussed on pages 255–256 of their books.

3. Display the "Four Major Subdivisions of the Doctrine of the Church." Distribute the fill-in-the-blanks exercise, "Important Facts about the Church." Give the students about five to ten minutes to find the answers to these questions in their books, then lead a general discussion of these truths and insights about the church.

Looking Ahead to the Next Session

Remind the class to read the text and complete the learning exercises in Chapter 30 of their books before the next class session. Ask them to be sure to complete the review of all ten major doctrines on pages 278–279, since you will spend some time in Session 13 reviewing what you have learned.

SESSION 13: THE DOCTRINE OF FUTURE THINGS

Overview: This session covers the material in Chapter 30.

Before the Session

1. Prepare the following items from the website for display during this session:
    - Ten Great Doctrines of the Bible
    - Four Major Subdivisions of the Doctrine of Future Things
    - Review of Ten Great Doctrines and Their Subdivisions
2. Review Chapter 30 to call to mind the content to be covered in this session. Be sure to complete the self-test on pages 276–277, writing the answers to these questions in your book.
3. Enlist four students in advance to give brief reports on the four major subdivisions of the doctrine of future things: (1) return, (2) judgment, (3) universe, and (4) eternity.

During the Session

1. Call on a student to lead in prayer.

2. Display the "Four Major Subdivisions of the Doctrine of Future Things." Then introduce the four students who have agreed to bring brief reports on these four subdivisions. Follow up with a general discussion of the central Scriptures that support these points and the meaning of these truths for Christian believers.

3. Display the "Ten Great Doctrines of the Bible" and lead the students to name these ten doctrines by matching them with the appropriate logos.

4. Ask the students to open their books to the more detailed review of these major doctrines on pages 269–280 of their books. Display the "Review of Ten Great Doctrines and Their Subdivisions." With their books closed (if possible) and the review in place, lead them to complete each subpoint by naming it out loud as you point to each line on the chart.

5. Lead the class in a general discussion of truths they remember about each doctrine. List these on the chalkboard as they are called out.

6. Close with a prayer of thanksgiving for these ten great doctrines of the Bible and their meaning in the lives of believers.

BONUS CHAPTERS

CHAPTER 31

A COMPARISON OF THE FOUR GOSPELS

M any years ago, during a lull in the action near a war zone in Vietnam, a friend of mine started reading his Army-issued New Testament for the first time. He knew nothing about it, so when he read Matthew, an account of the life of Christ, it was what he expected. When he finished, he started Mark and was surprised that it, too, was an account of the life of Christ. So, when he started Luke and John, he saw the pattern: the New Testament is a succession of different accounts of the life of Christ.

Imagine his surprise when he came to the book of Acts. His feet went into midair! It was not an account of the life of Christ! Nor were any of the remaining books of the New Testament.

Many questions flooded his mind, but one of them was, "If not all books of the New Testament are accounts of the life of Christ, then why are there four?"

Well, the greater the person, the more books are written about them after they die. For instance, you'd find a great many books written about Thomas Jefferson, Abraham Lincoln, and Winston Churchill. The reason is that different authors have different perspectives and different pieces of information about them.

That, in essence, is why there are four Gospels in the New Testament. These four men all either knew Jesus or had learned a great deal about Him from others who did. They all had different perspectives on His life. They were writing for different audiences. Matthew was a Jew and a tax collector. Mark was a young follower of Jesus. Luke was a Gentile and a physician. John was Jesus' closest friend on earth. They each had a different perspective on the life of Jesus. And by having books written by more than one author with more than one perspective, we have a more complete picture of Jesus.

The New Testament opens with the four books called Gospels, because they present the "good news" (the literal meaning of *gospel*) that God has come to die for mankind so that mankind can live with God. The four Gospels are targeted at different audiences, and each emphasizes a distinctive aspect of Jesus' identity and mission. Together these complementary accounts provide a rich and clear picture of Jesus. Matthew, Mark, and Luke are called the Synoptic (literally, "seen together") Gospels because, in contrast to John, they view Christ's life from much the same viewpoint and share many common details. John is different from the Synoptic Gospels and stands alone as a unique picture of the life of Christ.

1. MATTHEW

a. Overview

Matthew is the Gospel best suited to serve as the bridge between the Old Testament and the New. Matthew presents Jesus as Israel's promised Messianic King. It was written by a Jew to convince a Jewish audience that Jesus was the Messiah, and thus it has a strong Jewish flavor. The book begins with a genealogy that goes back to Abraham, the father of all Jews, to show Jesus' legal right to the throne of David. Matthew makes a special effort to demonstrate that all the significant events in the life of Jesus—His birth, birthplace, home, ministry, and death—directly fulfilled Old Testament prophecy, and he quotes from the Old Testament more than any other Gospel writer.

b. Authorship

Matthew, also known as Levi (Mark 2:14; Luke 5:27), was a publican, a Jewish tax collector who collected taxes for the occupying Roman government, but who became one of Jesus' twelve disciples.

c. Occasion and Purpose

Matthew wanted to convince unbelieving Jews that Jesus is the Messiah.

Summary: The Gospel of Matthew was written by a Jew to an audience of Jews to convince them that Jesus was the Messiah, the *King* of the Jews.

Review

The Gospel of Matthew was written by a Jew to an audience of Jews to convince them that Jesus was the Messiah, the _____ of the Jews.

2. MARK

a. Overview

Mark's Gospel presents Jesus as the Servant who came "to serve, and to give His life a ransom for many" (10:45). This shortest of the Gospels is direct and to the point, emphasizing action rather than detailed teaching. The word *immediately* is found again and again throughout the book.

b. Authorship

Mark was a Jewish Christian who was not one of Jesus' twelve disciples. He may have become a Christian under the influence of Peter (note 1 Peter 5:13, where Peter referred to him as "my son").

c. Occasion and Purpose

The Gospel of Mark was likely written in Rome, primarily for Gentile Roman Christians.

Mark presents Jesus as One who came "to serve, and to give His life as a ransom for many" (10:45).

Summary: Mark wrote to Gentile Roman Christians, presenting Jesus as a perfect *Servant*.

Review

Mark wrote to Gentile Roman Christians, presenting Jesus as a perfect _____.

3. LUKE

a. Overview

Luke wrote his Gospel for Gentiles, and he presents Jesus as the perfect "Son of Man" who came "to seek and to save that which was lost" (19:10). Luke emphasizes the perfect humanity of Jesus, which would be of particular interest to his intended audience.

b. Authorship

Luke was a physician (Colossians 4:14) and fellow missionary with the apostle Paul.

c. Occasion and Purpose

Luke's Gospel is dedicated to "most excellent Theophilus" (1:3), a name meaning "dear to God" or "friend of God." The title "most excellent" or "most noble" indicates high social standing (compare with Acts 23:26; 24:3; and 26:25, where it is used to describe government officials).

Luke's purpose was to present Jesus as the Son of Man who has brought the salvation of God's kingdom to all who follow Him.

Summary: Luke wrote to a Gentile audience to convince them that Jesus was the perfect Son of *Man*.

Review

Luke wrote to a Gentile audience to convince them that Jesus was the perfect Son of _____.

4. JOHN

a. Overview

John wrote to convince a universal audience that Jesus is the Son of God so that they might have eternal life through belief in Him (20:30–31). To this end, John built his Gospel around seven miraculous signs that Jesus did. In addition to the seven signs, John recorded seven great sayings of Christ that begin with the words "I am."

b. Authorship

John and his brother James were sons of Zebedee; Jesus nicknamed them "Sons of Thunder" (Mark 3:17). John was a Galilean fisherman before becoming one of Jesus' twelve disciples.

c. Occasion and Purpose

This Gospel clearly states its purpose: "These [miraculous signs] are written that you may believe that Jesus is the Messiah, the Son of God, and that by believing you may have life in his name" (20:31 NIV). John picked certain signs to prove that Jesus was worthy of faith. He wrote not so much to present new information as to confront his readers with the necessity of making a choice so that they might gain eternal life.

Summary: John wrote to a universal audience to convince them that Jesus was the Son of *God*.

Review

John wrote to a universal audience to convince them that Jesus was the Son of _____.

REVIEW

Repetition is the key to mental ownership!

1. Overview:

    A. The four Gospels record the life of Jesus, each from a different *perspective*.

    B. Three Gospels are called synoptic (literally, "seen together") because they present the life of Christ from basically the same *historical* point of view. They are Matthew, Mark, and Luke.

    C. John presents the life of Christ from a *thematic* viewpoint, highlighting seven miracles and seven "I am" sayings of Christ.

2. Gospels:

    A. Matthew was a Jew, writing to an audience of Jews to convince them that Jesus was the Messiah, the *King* of the Jews.

    B. Mark wrote to Gentile Roman Christians, presenting Jesus as a perfect *Servant*.

    C. Luke wrote to a Gentile audience to convince them that Jesus was the perfect Son of *Man*.

    D. John wrote to a universal audience to convince them that Jesus was the Son of *God*.

SELF-TEST

*What you can learn tomorrow is built
on what you learn today!*

1. Overview:

A. The four Gospels record the life of Jesus, each from a
   different _____.

B. Three Gospels are called synoptic (literally, "seen
   together") because they present the life of Christ from
   basically the same _____ point of view. They
   are Matthew, Mark, and Luke.

C. John presents the life of Christ from a _____
   viewpoint, highlighting seven miracles and seven "I am"
   sayings of Christ.

2. Gospels:

A. Matthew was a Jew, writing to an audience of Jews
   to convince them that Jesus was the Messiah, the
   _____ of the Jews.

B. Mark wrote to Gentile Roman Christians, presenting
   Jesus as a perfect _____.

C. Luke wrote to a Gentile audience to convince them that
   Jesus was the perfect Son of _____.

D. John wrote to a universal audience to convince them that
   Jesus was the Son of _____.

CHAPTER 32

THE PARABLES
OF JESUS

We all love a good story, so we all love a good storyteller. A person who can tell a good story will never lack an audience. All comedians are, essentially, just good storytellers. The most popular speakers are often good storytellers. President John Kennedy was a great storyteller. His humor, candor, and ability to poke fun at himself was a winsome characteristic that endeared him to the American public.

During World War II, Kennedy held a commission in the U.S. Navy and served in the Pacific. In August of 1943, in Blackout Strait in the Solomon Islands, a Japanese destroyer rammed his ship. Kennedy, with some others, reached a nearby island but found it was held by the Japanese. He and another officer then swam to another island, where they persuaded the inhabitants to send a message to other U.S. forces, who rescued them. After his election as president, Kennedy's comment on his reputation as a hero was, "It was involuntary. They sank my boat."

Jesus was a great storyteller. Not in the same way that Kennedy was. Kennedy's stories were often funny. And while Jesus' stories sometimes contained humorous elements, they were primarily told to impart spiritual information and wisdom. His stories were called *parables*. Approximately one-third of Jesus Christ's teaching as recorded in the Gospels is in this distinctive literary form. Indeed, Jesus used parables so often that Matthew wrote, "he did not say anything to them without using a parable" (13:34 NIV). What are parables? Why did Jesus employ them so frequently? How are parables to be interpreted? What are some of the key truths Christ sought to communicate through this form? These are the questions we will answer in this chapter.

1. THE NATURE OF PARABLES

A parable is a saying or story that drives home a point by illustrating it with a familiar situation from everyday life.

The form of the parable Jesus used most frequently to teach His hearers was the story. The story-parable teaches truth by telling a story as an illustration or example of a larger truth. Jesus introduced His parables with words such as, "There was a man who had two sons" (Luke 15:11 NIV) and, "In a certain town there was a judge" (Luke 18:2 NIV).

Summary: A parable is a story intended to communicate a spiritual truth, illustrating it with a familiar situation from everyday life.

Review

A parable is a story intended to communicate a _____ truth, illustrating it with a familiar situation from everyday life.

2. THE PURPOSE OF PARABLES

Why did Jesus use parables so often?

First, to reveal truth to believers. Parables can communicate truth more vividly and more powerfully than ordinary dialogue. For example, Christ could have simply told His disciples to be persistent in prayer. Instead, He told them the story of a widow whose continuous pleading for help finally persuaded an unjust judge to grant her requests so that she would stop bothering him (Luke 18:1–8). The lesson: If an unjust and uncaring judge will respond to relentless pleas, how much more will our loving heavenly Father answer persistent prayer? The parable made the answer more vivid, more memorable, and more likely to be learned and followed.

The second purpose of parables is to hide truth from those who have already hardened their hearts against it. Christ taught a mixed audience, some of whom had accepted Him, while others had already decided to reject Him. He wanted to teach believers but not increase the responsibility (and guilt) of those who had already rejected Him (see Luke 12:47–48). Rejection of spiritual truth hardens the heart and makes one less and less able to understand and respond in faith.

Summary: Jesus taught in parables to *reveal* truth to believers and to *conceal* truth from unbelievers.

Review

Jesus taught in parables to _____ truth to believers and to _____ truth from unbelievers.

3. THE INTERPRETATION OF PARABLES

Each parable was told to communicate one central idea; extraneous details that are not part of the main point may not be significant. For example, the parable of the persistent widow (Luke 18:1–8) focuses not on the character of the judge but on the persistence of the widow as an illustration of how we should persist in prayer. If we give too much weight to the judge's character, we might (falsely) conclude that God is an unrighteous and uncaring person who will only answer our prayers if we wear Him down with relentless requests.

Summary: Parables must be interpreted in light of the *main point* they are making.

Review

Parables must be interpreted in light of the _____
_____ they are making.

4. THE HISTORICAL SETTING OF PARABLES

You cannot understand the parable of the sower unless you understand the process of sowing seeds. You cannot understand the parable about putting new wine into old wineskins unless you understand the process of winemaking in Jesus' day. We need to understand the details from the perspective of Christ's original hearers. Tools such as a biblical encyclopedia or Bible commentary can help you understand the culture, customs, and daily life of those to whom Christ was communicating.

Summary: Parables must be interpreted in light of the *historical* setting in which they occur.

Review

Parables must be interpreted in light of the _____ setting in which they occur.

REVIEW

Repetition is the key to mental ownership!

1. A parable is a story intended to communicate a *spiritual* truth, illustrating it with a familiar situation from everyday life.
2. Jesus taught in parables to *reveal* truth to believers and to *conceal* truth from unbelievers.
3. Parables must be interpreted in light of the *main point* they are making.

4. Parables must be interpreted in light of the *historical* setting in which they occur.

SELF-TEST

*What you can learn tomorrow is built
on what you learn today!*

1. A parable is a story intended to communicate a
   _____ truth, illustrating it with a familiar situation
   from everyday life.
2. Jesus taught in parables to _____ truth to believers
   and to _____ truth from unbelievers.
3. Parables must be interpreted in light of the _____
   _____ they are making.
4. Parables must be interpreted in light of the _____
   setting in which they occur.

CHAPTER 33

MIRACLES IN THE BIBLE

Though God cannot be restricted by any framework, it is important to understand the nature of miracles and what they reveal to us about the God who does them. In this chapter we will look at miracles in the Bible to gain a clearer understanding and a greater appreciation of them.

1. THE POSSIBILITY AND NATURE OF MIRACLES

Miracles are events that run contrary to what we know of nature, but which are *possible* if God exists. Different words are used in the Bible to refer to miracles, highlighting different aspects of their nature. For example, the word *wonder* reveals that such events are amazing, while the term *power* implies the need for more than human capability. The word *sign* indicates that they are given for a purpose.

Some people think that miracles such as those described in the Bible are impossible. But one can only deny the possibility of miracles if one denies the existence of God. The very definition of God includes His ability to do miracles. What good is a God who cannot do miracles? He'd just be one of us.

Summary: Miracles are events that run contrary to what we know of nature but which are *possible* if God exists.

Review

Miracles are events that run contrary to what we know of nature, but which are _____ if God exists.

2. THE PURPOSE OF BIBLICAL MIRACLES

Miracles in the Bible often served to validate the authority of a divine message as well as a divine messenger. For example, in Hebrews 2:2–4, we read that signs and wonders and various miracles were given to validate the message of the gospel.

In addition, in Exodus 4:5 God instructed Moses to perform miracles "that they may believe that the LORD, the God of their fathers, . . . has appeared to you." Likewise, miracles supported the claims of Jesus and demonstrated, as they did for Moses (Deuteronomy 18:15), that He was the promised Prophet. Nicodemus recognized that Jesus was a teacher from God because of the miraculous signs He was performing (John 3:2).

Summary: Miracles *validate* the authority of a divine message as well as a divine messenger.

Review

Miracles _____ the authority of a divine message as well as a divine messenger.

3. THE PERIODS OF BIBLICAL MIRACLES

Most (but not all) biblical miracles revolve around the giving of new revelation in three periods of biblical history: the two-generation eras of Moses and Joshua, Elijah and Elisha, and Jesus and the apostles. Of course, there are miracles found at other times in the Bible, but comparatively fewer miracles are recorded during the intervening centuries. Let's look at each of these periods.

a. Moses and Joshua (1441–1370 B.C.)

During the life of Moses and Joshua, many stupendous miracles were performed, but they always were for the purpose of bolstering the faith of the people to believe in God and to trust Him in their everyday lives through obedience.

b. Elijah and Elisha (870–785 B.C.)

Worship of the false god Baal had become a serious threat to Israel's existence as a nation under God. It seems incredible, but even the Israelites were worshiping the false god. Therefore, God raised up Elijah and Elisha as prophets to promote revival and call the people to repentance. Miracles were used to prove that these men came from God, and that God was superior to Baal. One noteworthy example is found in 1 Kings 18:20–40, where there was a great contest, if you will, between God and Baal. God won through a demonstration of His power.

c. Jesus and the apostles (c. 30–70 A.D.)

Proof was needed to demonstrate that Jesus was both God and man. John tells us that Jesus did many miraculous signs John did not record, but that the signs he did include were "written that you may believe that Jesus is the Christ, the Son of God; and that believing you may have life in His name" (John 20:31). The miracles of Jesus also reveal to us the heart of God. Seven times the Gospel writers connected Jesus' compassion with the working of a miracle (Matthew 14:14; 15:32; 20:34; Mark 1:41; 5:19; Luke 7:13–14).

Although God can perform a miracle whenever He chooses, Paul wrote that one reason for the apostles' miracles was to prove their authority (2 Corinthians 12:12) as they taught the new message of God made flesh.

Summary: Miracles occurred primarily in *three* concentrated times in history, although God can perform a miracle whenever He chooses.

Review

Miracles occurred primarily in _____ concentrated times in history, although God can perform a miracle whenever He chooses.

REVIEW

Repetition is the key to mental ownership!

1. Miracles are events that run contrary to what we know of nature but which are *possible* if God exists.
2. Miracles *validate* the authority of a divine message as well as a divine messenger.
3. Miracles occurred primarily in *three* concentrated times in history, although God can perform a miracle whenever He chooses.

SELF-TEST

What you can learn tomorrow is built on what you learn today!

1. Miracles are events that run contrary to what we know of nature but which are _____ if God exists.
2. Miracles _____ the authority of a divine message as well as a divine messenger.
3. Miracles occurred primarily in _____ concentrated times in history, although God can perform a miracle whenever He chooses.

CHAPTER 34

MESSIANIC PROPHECIES

I t is a pretty amazing thing when someone can tell the future. Every year, grocery store tabloids are full of New Year predictions, yet none of the predictions come true on any credible level. But in the Old Testament, if a prophet predicted something that didn't come true, he was to be stoned to death.

If grocery store tabloid writers got stoned to death for their missed predictions, the pages would be blank each January.

God places His credibility on the line by declaring events ahead of time, giving us reason to believe in Him.

1. THE IMPORTANCE OF MESSIANIC PROPHECY

God's true divinity is demonstrated by His practice of predicting events before they happen (see, for example, Isaiah 48:3, 5). God placed more than three hundred references to the Messiah in the Old Testament, and they were fulfilled by Jesus Christ in order to help the Jews recognize their Messiah when He came.

Despite this help, Christ's disciples and contemporaries did not immediately grasp how He fulfilled all of the prophecies. It was only after the resurrection that they were able to understand (Luke 24:44–45).

Once the disciples thoroughly understood these things, Christ's fulfillment of the Old Testament Messianic prophecies became central to their presentation of the gospel. Paul wrote to the Corinthians that the gospel was "that Christ died for our sins *according to the Scriptures,* that he was buried, that he was raised on the third day *according to the Scriptures*" (1 Corinthians 15:3–4 NIV, emphasis added).

Summary: The ability to predict events before they occur demonstrates God's *power.*

Review

The ability to predict events before they occur demonstrates God's

_____.

2. KEY MESSIANIC PROPHECIES FULFILLED BY JESUS

Sixty-one major prophecies in the Old Testament were fulfilled by Jesus. Some of the key prophecies include:

	Prophesied	**Fulfilled**
From the Tribe of Judah	Genesis 49:10: The scepter shall not depart from Judah, nor the ruler's staff from between his feet, until Shiloh comes, and to him shall be the obedience of the peoples.	Luke 3:33: The son of Amminadab, the son of Admin, the son of Ram, the son of Hezron, the son of Perez, the son of Judah.
Heir to the Throne of David	Isaiah 9:7: There will be no end to the increase of His government or of peace, on the throne of David and over his kingdom, to establish it and to uphold it with justice and righteousness from then on and forevermore. The zeal of the LORD of hosts will accomplish this.	Luke 1:32, 33: He will be great, and will be called the Son of the Most High; and the Lord God will give Him the throne of His father David, and He will reign over the house of Jacob forever, and His kingdom will have no end.

Born in Bethlehem	Micah 5:2: But as for you, Bethlehem Ephrathah, too little to be among the clans of Judah, from you One will go forth for Me to be ruler in Israel. His goings forth are from long ago, from the days of eternity.	Luke 2:4–5, 7: And Joseph also went up from Galilee, from the city of Nazareth, to Judea, to the city of David, which is called Bethlehem, because he was of the house and family of David, in order to register, along with Mary, who was engaged to him, and was with child. . . . And she gave birth to her firstborn son; and she wrapped Him in cloths, and laid Him in a manger, because there was no room for them in the inn.
Would Die for Our Sins	Isaiah 53:5-6: But he was pierced for our transgressions, he was crushed for our iniquities; the chastening for our well-being fell upon Him, and by his scourging we are healed. All of us like sheep have gone astray, each of us has turned to his own way; but the LORD has caused the inequity of us all to fall on Him.	Luke 23:33: When they came to the place called The Skull, there they crucified Him and the criminals, one on the right and the other on the left.
Would Be Resurrected	Psalm 16:10: For You will not abandon my soul to Sheol; nor will You allow Your Holy One to undergo decay.	Matthew 28:6: He is not here, for He has risen, just as He said. Come, see the place where He was lying.

Summary: Sixty-one major prophecies in the Old Testament were *fulfilled* by Christ.

Review

Sixty-one major prophecies in the Old Testament were _____ by Christ.

3. THE PURPOSE OF PROPHECY

The purpose of prophecy is not to satisfy our curiosity but to purify our lives. Prophecy is always given to get us to live properly. In chapter 3 of his second letter, the apostle Peter, after announcing some rather stunning prophecies about the end of the world, then said, "Since all these things are to be destroyed in this way, what sort of people ought you to be in holy conduct and godliness" (2 Peter 3:11). His purpose in telling them about things in the future was to purify their lives now.

Summary: The purpose of prophecy is not to satisfy our curiosity but to *purify* our lives.

Review

The purpose of prophecy is not to satisfy our curiosity but to _____ our lives.

REVIEW

Repetition is the key to mental ownership!

1. The ability to predict events before they occur demonstrates God's *power*.
2. Sixty-one major prophecies in the Old Testament were *fulfilled* by Christ.
3. The purpose of prophecy is not to satisfy our curiosity but to *purify* our lives.

SELF-TEST

*What you can learn tomorrow is built
on what you learn today!*

1. The ability to predict events before they occur demonstrates God's _____.
2. Sixty-one major prophecies in the Old Testament were _____ by Christ.
3. The purpose of prophecy is not to satisfy our curiosity but to _____ our lives.

CHAPTER 35

PASSOVER AND THE LORD'S SUPPER

In her marvelous little book, *Tramp for the Lord*, Corrie ten Boom wrote of the time she was speaking to a group of young people about Jesus. Afterward the students joined her for coffee:

> One said to me, "I would love to ask Jesus to come into my heart, but I cannot. I am a Jew."
>
> I said, "You cannot ask Jesus into your heart because you are a Jew? Then you do not understand that with the Jew (Jesus) in your heart, you are a double Jew."
>
> He said, "Oh, then it is possible?"
>
> "On the divine side, He was God's Son. On the human side He was Jew. When you accept Him you do not become a Gentile. You become even more Jewish than before. You will be a completed Jew."
>
> With great joy the boy received the Lord Jesus as his Savior (p. 186).

The link between Judaism and Christianity is much stronger than many people realize. Christianity is merely Judaism taken to its logical conclusion. "Judaism and Christianity are as inseparable as seed and flower, or tree and fruit. Nowhere can the relationship between the two be observed more clearly than in the Passover of the Jews and the Last Supper as ordained by our Lord, when He and His twelve disciples sat around the Passover table" (*The Gospel in the Feasts of Israel*, 1). Paul emphasized this crucial connection when he identified Christ as the true Passover Lamb by writing to the Corinthians that "Christ, our Passover lamb, has been sacrificed" (1 Corinthians 5:7 NIV).

1. THE OLD TESTAMENT SIGNIFICANCE OF THE PASSOVER

The Passover commemorates God's deliverance of Israel from slavery in Egypt. The last of the ten plagues by which God judged Egypt was the death of each firstborn son (Exodus 11:5). Exodus 12:13 explains the name of the festival: God would "pass over" the Hebrew houses that applied a sacrificial lamb's blood to the sides and top of their door frames without taking the life of the firstborn.

The Passover in Jesus' day had a twofold significance. First, it looked back in commemoration of Israel's deliverance from slavery in Egypt (Exodus 12:14, 17). Second, it looked forward to the coming of the Lamb of God, the final Passover Lamb, who would take away the sin of the world.

The Passover represented a new birth, or new beginning, for the nation of Israel. By faith (placing the blood on their doorposts), they were delivered from slavery in Egypt. The Passover prepared them to enter into a new covenant with God at Sinai, which would establish them as a kingdom of priests and a holy nation (Exodus 19:6).

The Israelites were to observe the Passover each year until the coming of the Messiah.

Summary: The Old Testament significance of the Passover is that it looked back on Israel's deliverance from slavery in Egypt and looked forward to ultimate spiritual deliverance through the *Messiah*.

Review

The Old Testament significance of the Passover is that it looked back on Israel's deliverance from slavery in Egypt and looked forward to ultimate spiritual deliverance through the _____

2. THE PASSOVER AND THE LORD'S SUPPER

"The Lord's Supper" is a ceremonial meal designed to commemorate and communicate spiritual truth picturing the death of Christ to provide atonement for our sin. When Jesus observed the final Passover with His disciples the night before he was betrayed, He also established the first Lord's Supper (also sometimes called "Communion" and "Eucharist"). The Passover looked back to Israel's deliverance from physical slavery in Egypt through the faithful sacrifice of a lamb, while the Lord's Supper looks back to Christians' deliverance from spiritual slavery to sin by faith in the sacrifice of Jesus, the Lamb of God.

Summary: Jesus observed the Passover with His disciples the night before His death, not only in faithfulness as a Jew, but also in *prophetic* symbolism of His own forthcoming crucifixion.

Review

Jesus observed the Passover with His disciples the night before His death, not only in faithfulness as a Jew, but also in _____ symbolism of His own forthcoming crucifixion.

REVIEW

Repetition is the key to mental ownership!

1. The Old Testament significance of the Passover is that it looked back on Israel's deliverance from slavery in Egypt

and looked forward to ultimate spiritual deliverance through the *Messiah*.

2. Jesus observed the Passover with His disciples the night before His death, not only in faithfulness as a Jew, but also in *prophetic* symbolism of His own forthcoming crucifixion.

SELF-TEST

*What you can learn tomorrow is built
on what you learn today!*

1. The Old Testament significance of the Passover is that it looked back on Israel's deliverance from slavery in Egypt and looked forward to ultimate spiritual deliverance through the _____.

2. Jesus observed the Passover with His disciples the night before His death, not only in faithfulness as a Jew, but also in _____ symbolism of His own forthcoming crucifixion.

CHAPTER 36

THE RESURRECTION
OF JESUS CHRIST

The resurrection of Jesus is the pivotal event in the history of the world, to say nothing of being the main event of redemption. Paul went so far as to assert that the Christian faith and the salvation it promises stand or fall with the resurrection: "And if Christ has not been raised, your faith is futile; you are still in your sins. Then those also who have fallen asleep in Christ are lost. If only for this life we have hope in Christ, we are of all people most to be pitied" (1 Corinthians 15:17-19 NIV). If Christ was raised from the dead, then everything He said can be trusted. If He didn't, nothing He said can be trusted. It's true: everything stands or falls on the resurrection.

There are three common attempts to explain away the resurrection.

1. THE THEFT THEORY

The earliest attempt to explain away Christ's resurrection involved the assertion that His body was stolen. This theory is not believable. The disciples could not have stolen the body because the grave was being guarded by Roman soldiers (Matthew 26:62–66). Of course, the Jews would not have stolen the body because they did not want any rumors about a potential resurrection to get started; and if they did, the Jews would simply have produced the body to prove the resurrection did not happen.

Summary: The Theft Theory states that the *disciples* stole the body of Jesus from the tomb after He died. It is not believable because there were Roman soldiers *guarding* the body.

Review

The Theft Theory states that the _____ stole the body of Jesus from the tomb after He died. It is not believable because there were Roman soldiers _____ the body.

2. THE SWOON THEORY

This theory asserts that Christ did not really die on the cross. Rather, Christ appeared to be dead but had only swooned, sinking into a death-like coma from exhaustion, pain, and loss of blood, not only from the crucifixion but also from the brutal beating he took before the crucifixion. He revived when laid in the cool tomb. After leaving the tomb He appeared to His disciples, who mistakenly concluded He had risen from the dead.

This theory is not credible. The magnitude of the wounds Jesus suffered, both from the beating and the crucifixion, makes it incredible that anyone would *survive*, let alone be capable of normal activity so soon after the injuries. Anyone has ever sprained an ankle and taken weeks to be able to walk knows that it is absurd to suggest someone could have had nails driven through his feet and be able to walk any time soon . . . let alone all the other injuries. It is simply unbelievable. Not only that—Jesus was pierced by a Roman soldier's spear and confirmed dead on the scene (John 19:33–34).

Summary: The Swoon Theory states that Jesus did not die on the cross, but merely went into a death-like *coma* from which He revived after being laid in the cool tomb. That theory is not credible because the severity of the wounds Jesus experienced makes it incredible that anyone would *survive*, let alone be capable of normal activity that soon after the injuries.

Review

The Swoon Theory states that Jesus did not die on the cross, but merely went into a death-like _____ from which He revived after being laid in the cool tomb. That theory is not credible because the severity of the wounds Jesus experienced makes it incredible that anyone would _____, let alone be capable of normal activity that soon after the injuries.

3. THE WRONG TOMB THEORY

This theory states that the disciples went to the wrong tomb, an empty one, and mistakenly concluded that Jesus had risen from the dead. This theory is not believable because when rumors of the resurrection began to circulate, the Jews would simply have located the right tomb and produced the body. The Pharisees themselves said that if the rumor spread that Jesus had risen from the dead, they would be worse off than before, and they would have done whatever necessary to keep that from happening.

Summary: The Wrong Tomb Theory states that the disciples of Jesus went to the wrong tomb, an empty one, and *mistakenly* concluded that Jesus had risen from the dead. This theory is not believable because when rumors of the resurrection began to circulate, the Jews would have *located* the right tomb and produced the body.

Review

The Wrong Tomb Theory states that the disciples of Jesus went to the wrong tomb, an empty one, and _____ concluded that

Jesus had risen from the dead. This theory is not believable because when rumors of the resurrection began to circulate, the Jews would have _____ the right tomb and produced the body.

4. THE RESURRECTION AS HISTORY

If you apply the same tests to the resurrection as you would to any other historical event, and do so without an anti-supernatural presupposition, you come away concluding that the resurrection of Jesus actually happened. Every test of history validates it.

In his autobiography. *Surprised by Joy,* C. S. Lewis recounts a powerful story about the evidence for the resurrection. Shortly before Lewis's unwilling conversion from atheism to Christianity:

> The hardest boiled of all the atheists I ever knew sat in my room on the other side of the fire and remarked that the evidence for the historicity of the Gospels was really surprisingly good. "Rum thing," he went on. "All that stuff of Frazer's about the Dying God. Rum thing. It almost looks as if it had really happened once." To understand the shattering impact of it, you would need to know the man (who has certainly never since shown any interest in Christianity). If he, the cynic of cynics, the toughest of the toughs were not—as I would still have put it—"safe," where could I turn? Was there then no escape? (pp. 223–224)

If the resurrection did not occur, how can one account for the historical record that suggests He did? How would one account for the fact that more than five hundred people saw him after the resurrection? (1 Corinthians 15:6). How does one account for the transformation of Jesus' discouraged and defeated band of followers into dynamic, joyful people willing to suffer and die to preach a risen Savior? Twelve men would not live difficult lives and succumb to painful deaths for something they knew was not true!

To repeat, if you apply the same tests to the resurrection as you would to any other historical event, and do so without an anti-supernatural presupposition, you come away concluding that the resurrection of Jesus actually happened. Only those who do not want to believe it come to another conclusion, and must twist the arm of historical research to do so.

Summary: The Resurrection-as-History position states that Jesus *rose* from the dead, as He said He would.

Review

The Resurrection-as-History position states that Jesus _____ from the dead, as He said He would.

REVIEW

Repetition is the key to mental ownership!

1. The Theft Theory states that the *disciples* stole the body of Jesus from the tomb after He died. It is not believable because there were Roman soldiers *guarding* the body.
2. The Swoon Theory states that Jesus did not die on the cross, but merely went into a death-like *coma* from which He revived after being laid in the cool tomb. That theory is not credible because the severity of the wounds Jesus experienced makes it incredible that anyone would *survive*, let alone be capable of normal activity that soon after the injuries.
3. The Wrong Tomb Theory states that the disciples of Jesus went to the wrong tomb, an empty one, and *mistakenly* concluded that Jesus had risen from the dead. This theory is not believable

because when rumors of the resurrection began to circulate, the Jews would have *located* the right tomb and produced the body.

4. The Resurrection-as-History position states that Jesus *rose* from the dead, as He said He would.

SELF-TEST

*What you can learn tomorrow is built
on what you learn today!*

1. The Theft Theory states that the _____ stole the body of Jesus from the tomb after He died. It is not believable because there were Roman soldiers _____ the body.

2. The Swoon Theory states that Jesus did not die on the cross, but merely went into a death-like _____ from which He revived after being laid in the cool tomb. That theory is not credible because the severity of the wounds Jesus experienced makes it incredible that anyone would _____, let alone be capable of normal activity that soon after the injuries.

3. The Wrong Tomb Theory states that the disciples of Jesus went to the wrong tomb, an empty one, and _____ concluded that Jesus had risen from the dead. This theory is not believable because when rumors of the resurrection began to circulate, the Jews would have _____ the right tomb and produced the body.

4. The Resurrection as History position states that Jesus _____ from the dead, as He said He would.

CHAPTER 37

DISTINCTIVENESS OF CHRISTIANITY

Many people believe that all religions are fundamentally the same. They are simply different ways to the same god. Life is like climbing a mountain. As long as one reaches the top, it is argued, why does it matter what path one takes to get there?

Thus we are left with a fundamental question: Are all (or even some) of the world's religions essentially the same? Or is Christianity distinctive in crucial ways from other religions? We will first examine several areas of commonality among different religions, then consider how they differ. We will close with suggested principles for proclaiming the truth in a pluralistic world.

1. SIMILARITIES OF CHRISTIANITY WITH OTHER RELIGIONS

There are three areas of similarity among religions. First, they address transcendent human need, recognizing that something is wrong and that we need something to help or save us.

Second, all religions are sincere. People choose the religion they follow because they believe it is the answer to human need.

Third, all religions teach essentially a moral code. There is a remarkable similarity between the principles of behavior taught by the major world religions.

Summary: Christianity has *similarities* with other religions that must be recognized.

Review

Christianity has _____ with other religions that must be recognized.

2. DIFFERENCES BETWEEN CHRISTIANITY AND OTHER RELIGIONS

A Christian perspective on reality differs in many specific ways from perspectives held by Hindus, Buddhists, New Age thought, etc. The common denominator among most religions is that salvation depends upon the follower's good works. In contrast, the Bible teaches that salvation is a result of God's grace and that good works are the natural response to God's love (compare with Ephesians 2:8–10).

Second, the various religions differ greatly in their conception of God. The Bible reveals God to be a sovereign Creator-God who is one and yet exists in three Persons, God the Father, God the Son (Jesus Christ), and God the Holy Spirit.

In contrast, the Buddha never claimed deity and professed agnosticism as to whether God even existed. Even if God does exist, according to the Buddha, He could not help an individual achieve enlightenment.

Hindus are pantheists—that is, they believe everything is "God"; God and the universe are identical.

Islam and Judaism proclaim views of God that are much closer to the Christian conception. Both religions acknowledge God as personal and as separate from His creation. Yet they both reject Christ. Christianity is unique in that Jesus Christ claimed to be God.

Summary: Christianity has *differences* from other religions that make it distinctive.

Review

Christianity has _____ from other religions that make it distinctive.

3. CHRIST AS THE ONLY WAY TO GOD

The Bible asserts that Jesus Christ is the only way to God. Jesus, unlike other great religious teachers, made belief in His divine identity the focal point of His teaching. For example, Jesus proclaimed:

> No one knows the Father except the Son and those to whom the Son chooses to reveal him (Matthew 11:27 NIV).
> Whoever believes in him is not condemned, but whoever does not believe stands condemned already because they have not believed in the name of God's one and only Son (John 3:18 NIV).
> The work of God is this: to believe in the one he has sent (John 6:29 NIV).
> If you do not believe that I am [the one I claim to be], you will indeed die in your sins (John 8:24 NIV).
> I am the way and the truth and the life. No one comes to the Father except through me (John 14:6 NIV).

The clear, unequivocal teaching of the apostles was that "Salvation is found in no one else, for there is no other name under heaven given to mankind by which we *must be saved*" (Acts 4:12 NIV, emphasis added).

The Bible presents a unique perspective on reality as well as God's unique provision for our reconciliation through the substitutionary death of Jesus Christ.

Summary: Christianity's primary distinction is that *Christ* is the only way to God.

Review

Christianity's primary distinction is that _____ is the only way to God.

REVIEW

Repetition is the key to mental ownership!

1. Christianity has *similarities* with other religions that must be recognized.
2. Christianity has *differences* from other religions that make it distinctive.
3. Christianity's primary distinction is that *Christ* is the only way to God.

SELF-TEST

*What you can learn tomorrow is built
on what you learn today!*

1. Christianity has _____ with other religions that must be recognized.
2. Christianity has _____ from other religions that make it distinctive.
3. Christianity's primary distinction is that _____ is the only way to God.

CHAPTER 38

DIFFERENT LITERARY FORMS IN THE BIBLE

You cannot read history and poetry the same way. History is very factual. Poetry is very symbolic and figurative. If you take everything literally in poetry, you destroy the art. If you take everything figuratively in history you lose the facts.

So, in education, the kind of literature you are studying determines how you treat it. In poetry you look for art, symbolism, hidden meaning, and so forth. In history, biology, and physics, you look for facts and accuracy.

The same principle is true of the Bible. When trying to understand a particular biblical book or passage, the reader must understand what kind of literature he or she is reading. This characterization of literature is called its "literary form."

1. THE DIDACTIC FORM (EXPOSITION)

Didactic or expository literature teaches truth in a relatively direct manner. The argument or explanation usually moves from point to point in a logical, highly organized fashion. Because the author employs comparatively few figures of speech, the meaning of a didactic passage is often easy to understand. The more difficult challenge becomes obediently applying the truth to one's own life.

The meaning often lies close to the surface in didactic literature. For this reason most didactic books are very good starting points for people who are just beginning to study the Bible. However, the truths taught in the didactic literature are profound enough to warrant detailed analysis even by experienced Bible students.

Biblical examples of didactic literature include: Paul's letters; Hebrews; James; 1 and 2 Peter; 1, 2, and 3 John; and Jude.

Summary: Didactic literature *teaches* truth in a relatively direct manner.

Review

Didactic literature _____ truth in a relatively direct manner.

2. THE NARRATIVE FORM

Narrative literature emphasizes stories. One reason for the Bible's enduring popularity is its abundance of compelling stories. For instance, the Bible's first book (Genesis) tells such stories as God's creation of the world, the Flood, the Tower of Babel, how God began His plan to bless all nations through the family of Abraham, and how He worked in the lives of Abraham, Isaac, Jacob, and Joseph. Exodus picks up the story of this family, which has now become the Jewish nation, by telling how Moses led it out of captivity in Egypt. The book of Joshua tells how Joshua led the next generation of Israelites out of the wilderness and back into the Promised Land. The narrative books include all the books from Genesis through Esther, the four Gospels, and Acts.

How are we to understand the narrative sections of the Bible? What truths are the stories intended to convey? In what ways are these truths significant today?

Begin with a close reading of the text, focusing on the narrative flow and the plot. Determine how the story progresses. Who are the characters, and how are they presented? Study the effect of the setting (geographical, temporal, or social) on the plot. An awareness of the prevailing social customs will greatly enhance your understanding of many of the biblical stories.

Summary: Narrative literature tells a *story*.

Review

Narrative literature tells a _____.

3. THE POETIC FORM

Poetry appeals to our emotions and our imagination. The tremendous appeal of the Book of Psalms grows out of the depth and variety of the emotions the psalms convey. The books of the Bible that are mainly poetic are Job, Psalms, Proverbs, Ecclesiastes, and the Song of Solomon.

Hebrew poetry varies in important ways from English poetry. First, many of the psalms were composed to be sung rather than read. So, even though we do not have the music to which they were sung, it is even more important than for poetry in general that you listen to how they sound. Second, Hebrew poetry tends to rhyme thoughts and ideas, not the sound of words, as is common in much English poetry.

Be alert to the frequent use of figurative language. For instance, Hebrew poets frequently made their point by using *hyperbole*, a literary device that uses extreme or exaggerated language for emphasis.

Fourth, when possible, identify the historical background of the poetry. Knowing that David wrote Psalm 51 after being confronted regarding his sin with Bathsheba helps us understand the depth of David's spiritual agony and repentance.

Summary: Poetic literature must be *interpreted* in light of key principles.

Review

Poetic literature must be _____ in light of key principles.

4. THE PROVERB

This distinctive literary form concisely states a moral truth, frequently reducing life to black-and-white categories. As does poetry, proverbs often use parallelism to make their point. Metaphors and similes are two other frequently employed literary devices. Although individual proverbs do appear in other books of the Bible, the book known as Proverbs is the only place where proverbs are the major literary form.

Summary: Proverbial literature concisely states a moral truth in *story* form.

Review

Proverbial literature concisely states a moral truth in _____ form.

5. THE PROPHETIC AND APOCALYPTIC FORMS

Much of the Bible is prophetic. Although we often think of prophecy as a prediction of the future, this is only part of the biblical conception of prophecy. Prophecy is not just the *foretelling* of the future; it is also the *forthtelling* of God's message (whether encouragement, admonition, or warning) to the people. Sometimes God would have the prophet make a prediction of what would happen in the near future so that the event's occurrence would validate the rest of the prophet's message.

The Old Testament books from Isaiah to Malachi are prophetic. The New Testament book of Revelation is the primary example of a special category of prophetic literature known as *apocalyptic*. Apocalyptic literature focuses on the cataclysmic events having to do with the end of the world and God's ultimate triumph over evil. Apocalyptic literature makes especially heavy use of symbolism and vivid imagery. Large sections of apocalyptic material occur in the books of Daniel, Zechariah, and Revelation; other books have smaller amounts.

Interpretation of prophetic literature can be particularly challenging. Most Christians must rely heavily on skilled teachers to master the effective interpretation of prophetic literature in the Bible.

Summary: Prophetic literature proclaims the Word of God and sometimes tells the *future*, often in highly figurative and symbolic language.

Review

Prophetic literature proclaims the Word of God and sometimes tells the _____, often in highly figurative and symbolic language.

REVIEW

Repetition is the key to mental ownership!

1. Didactic literature *teaches* truth in a relatively direct manner.
2. Narrative literature tells a *story*.
3. Poetic literature must be *interpreted* in light of key principles.
4. Proverbial literature concisely states a moral truth in *story* form.
5. Prophetic literature proclaims the Word of God and sometimes tells the *future*, often in highly figurative and symbolic language.

SELF-TEST

*What you can learn tomorrow is built
on what you learn today!*

1. Didactic literature _____ truth in a relatively direct manner.
2. Narrative literature tells a _____.
3. Poetic literature must be _____ in light of key principles.
4. Proverbial literature concisely states a moral truth in _____ form.
5. Prophetic literature proclaims the Word of God and sometimes tells the _____, often in highly figurative and symbolic language.

APPENDIX

STORY OF THE BIBLE

Era	Figure	Location	Storyline Summary
Creation	*Adam*	*Eden*	Adam is created by God, but he *sins* and *destroys* God's original *plan* for man.
Patriarch	*Abraham*	*Canaan*	Abraham is *chosen* by God to "father" a *people* to *represent* God to the world.
Exodus	*Moses*	*Egypt*	Through Moses God *delivers* the Hebrew people from *slavery* in Egypt and then gives them the *Law*.
Conquest	*Joshua*	*Canaan*	Joshua leads the *conquest* of the *Promised Land*.
Judges	*Samson*	*Canaan*	Samson and others were chosen as *judges* to govern the people for *four hundred* rebellious years.
Kingdom	*David*	*Israel*	David, the greatest king in the new *monarchy*, is followed by a succession of mostly *unrighteous* kings, and God eventually *judges* Israel for her sin, sending her into exile.
Exile	*Daniel*	*Babylon*	Daniel gives *leadership* and encourages *faithfulness* among the *exiles* for the next seventy years.

Era	Figure	Location	Storyline Summary
Return	*Ezra*	*Jerusalem*	Ezra *leads* the people back from *exile* to rebuild *Jerusalem*.
Silence	*Pharisees*	*Jerusalem*	Pharisees and others entomb the Israelites in *legalism* for the next *four hundred* years.
Gospels	*Jesus*	*Galilee, Samaria, and Judea*	Jesus comes in fulfillment of the Old Testament *prophecies* of a savior and offers *salvation* and the true kingdom of God. While some accept Him, most *reject* Him, and He is crucified, buried, and resurrected.
Church	*Peter*	*Jerusalem*	Peter, shortly after the *Ascension* of Jesus, is used by God to *establish* the *church*, God's next major plan for man.
Mission	*Paul*	*Roman Empire*	Paul *expands* the church into the *Roman* Empire during the next two *decades*.

ARC OF BIBLE HISTORY

1. Creation	5. Judges	9. Silence
2. Patriarch	6. Kingdom	10. Gospels
3. Exodus	7. Exile	11. Church
4. Conquest	8. Return	12. Mission

TEN GREAT DOCTRINES OF THE BIBLE

2. ____God____

4. ____Holy Spirit____

3. ____Christ____

5. ____Angels____

1. ____The Bible____

10. ____Future Things____

6. ____Man____

9. ____Church____

7. ____Sin____

8. ____Salvation____